ACTIVITY AND UNDERSTANDING

Structure of Action and Orientated Linguistics

ACTIVITY AND UNDERSTANDING

Structure of Action and Orientated Linguistics

V. S. Fain & L. I. Rubanov
Institute for Information Transmission Problems
Russian Academy of Sciences
Moscow, Russia.

World Scientific
Singapore • New Jersey • London • Hong Kong

Published by

World Scientific Publishing Co. Pte. Ltd.

P O Box 128, Farrer Road, Singapore 9128

USA office: Suite 1B, 1060 Main Street, River Edge, NJ 07661

UK office: 57 Shelton Street, Covent Garden, London WC2H 9HE

Library of Congress Cataloging-in-Publication Data

Faǐn, V. S.
Activity and understanding : structure of action and orientated linguistics / V. S. Faǐn, L. I. Rubanov.
p. cm.
Includes bibliographical references and index.
ISBN 9810218370
1. Natural language processing (Computer science) I. Rubanov, L. I. (Lev Izrailevich) II. Title.
QA76.9.N38F35 1995
006.3'5--dc20 95-11497
CIP

This book is printed on acid-free paper.

Printed in Singapore by Uto-Print

Contents

Introduction

A subject's activity is termed *routine* if the subject needs nothing more than available methods to perform it. For example, a person is sure to do well without developing a new method of going upstairs when entering an unfamiliar house. By contrast, an activity can be named *heuristic* if one has to invent a new method or approach every time he acts. Luckily, really heuristic situations occur rather rarely; in most cases people can manage with routine activity. The great extent and role (and success!) of reflexive and instinctive activity in everyday life, the prevalence of long-termed and large-scale production in the present-day industry, the decisive role of knowledge and skills in professional activities illustrate this observation.

The aforesaid explains our special interest in routine activity. Our study of this kind of activity revealed an important and interesting fact: this activity suggests a standard and stable structure of any separate action (operation) as well as of the interconnection scheme of such actions. The construction principle of this structure remains the same for all kinds of the subject's routine activity in any field. This principle, termed Indirect Action Principle, follows from the so called OPT recursion theorem stated and proved in the book.

The further ideas of the book are connected with the following fact. The seemingly indivisible substance, called "subject", actually executes two different functions: he projects an action concerning the "object" and puts that project into life. Moreover, in many cases those who perform these functions are embodied in separate "sub-subjects". It should be emphasized that whenever the subject disintegrates into "sub-subjects", there starts a *dialogue* between them. If one of the "sub-subjects" is a computer, we should speak about a man-to-computer dialogue.

The search for the best means to support this sort of dialogues tops the agenda in computer science. Nowadays the most acknowledged way to have such a dialogue is a menu: one of the parties to the dialogue makes a passive choice among options offered by the other party. Some recently created software systems and shells implement the menu principle in an extremely smart and clear manner: the operating system of Macintosh computers as well as the Microsoft Windows shell should be specially noticed.

Nevertheless, something is still wrong, since the user remains dissatisfied with the way things stand. On analyzing this we discover that the cause is not how the menu principle is implemented but the passive nature of this very principle.

In fact, we want the computer to be our competent and quick-witted assistant, just like a man-assistant. But what would we say if the assistant whom we were going to set a task did not allow us to say a word but started to enumerate everything he knew or was able to do? Nobody knows whether we would succeed in recognizing something useful in his speech, and, even if we did, how quickly he would reach that option. This is why this kind of dialogue seems extremely unnatural and inconvenient.

In all likelihood, it would be more natural and convenient if we had an opportunity of setting the computer a direct task. Of course, there are some means of addressing the computer directly; these means appeared even earlier than menu systems. But they do not satisfy the mass users either, because they demand knowledge of programming languages and command formats as well as the accuracy of task text formulating.

The conclusion is obvious: the computer should understand users' tasks in the usual *free natural language* form. At the same time, natural language (NL) is an informal object in its normal man-to-man use. This fact is clearly reflected by the existing linguistics that basically leans upon human intuition and, in particular, lacks any formal definitions for its fundamental notions such as "sense", "understanding", "meaning" and so on. This essentially contradicts the formal cybernetic nature of the computer and computer software, resulting in the lack of any satisfactory NL understanding computer systems.

If our consideration concerned dialogues "in general" in any kind of activity, we could not expect another result either. However, in this book we keep the focus on routine activity. As we have already mentioned, the structures of both separate actions and their sequences become therefore standard and independent of the field of activity.

It would be rather strange if such stationarity of the activity structure imposed no strong restrictions upon the texts of NL dialogues between the "sub-subjects". These restrictions actually exist, though the "sub-subjects" themselves do not notice them. Furthermore, the theorems on the absolute non-uniexpressiveness of NL addresses and on the necessary uniexpressiveness of addresses in a non-stationary environment, stated and proved in the book, show that the restrictions are very considerable. Thus, on the one hand, NL in the man-to-computer dialogue remains quite free in the human party's opinion. On the other hand, its properties dramatically differ from those of "the entire NL". It becomes expedient to consider the language of the man-to-computer business dialogue as a new, alternative language. In the book we refer to this new language as "address language".

Then we are supposed to put forward some special linguistics to study this language, whose peculiar properties can impart new capabilities to this linguistics and make it a more formal theory than conventional linguistics. The linguistics of the address language will be called "orientated linguistics". The very structure of text processing and understanding in orientated linguistics radically differs from that in conventional one. We shall demonstrate what powerful advantages orientated linguistics brings to computer understanding of free NL dialogue addresses.

Besides the theoretical results, the book presents some ideas for implementing orientated linguistics in practice. Among them there is the inductive conception of the object domain expansion in an orientated NL understanding system. Its essence is the following: since routine activity is similarly structured in different fields, there is a certain similarity of the NL address structures. This implies a standard interpretation mechanism with a specific object domain represented as a set of parameters. Such a parametric organization of the understanding function provides an easy *readjustment* from one object domain to another by means of simple changes in the parameter complex. The book proposes a convenient method of parametrization for an orientated text processing system; this method exploits a modified version of the augmented transition networks (the so called ATNR — Augmented Transition Network with Returns).

Like in different object domains, there is a certain invariance in different languages, which allows an orientated system to switch easily from one national language to another. The mechanism of switching between languages looks like that of switching between object domains, and this was proved in practice. Furthermore, the system can automatically catch the moment of a dialogue going from one object domain to another and from one national language to another. In so doing it uses the so called *pre-recognition* which may be considered as another trait of orientated linguistics. It is worth mentioning that in conventional linguistics such a switch means a complete redevelopment of the system.

Another practical problem is to combine an orientated NL understanding system with other "business" software in use, i.e. to provide data and control interchange between independently developed software products (the NL understanding and "business" blocks). We propose a special "embedment" method to solve this problem. The method leads to free and easy natural language communication with existing software without any modification of the latter.

Thus, we developed orientated linguistics theoretically, tested it experimentally and embodied its ideas in a few facile and cheap systems. All the same, we can not expect these systems to become popular enough. In fact, there is an inner incongruity which nullifies all the effect. On the one hand, the systems are able to understand absolutely free and easy NL addresses. On the other hand, the keyboard as an input device is unnatural and difficult to use. The only natural way to input NL texts is that used in usual man-to-man communication, i.e. oral speech.

One can distinguish three relatively independent stages of the transition from the keyboard to oral speech input:

Stage 1. A correct understanding and interpretation of a text.

Stage 2. Overcoming possible deviations from the language standards: misprints and misspellings in written texts and individual or regional pronunciation peculiarities, as well as noise, in oral speech.

Stage 3. An acoustic recognition of oral speech, i.e. converting a perceived sonic sequence into a character string, and separating it into words in case of continuous speech.

Everyone knows it is impossible to cross a gap in three jumps. Consequently, it is no use attracting the user's attention to NL man-to-computer communication facilities until all the three mentioned stages are worked out and merged into a whole.

All the aforesaid about orientated linguistics is mainly concerned with Stage 1.

The problem of overcoming deviations from the language standards (or the problem of errors, Stage 2) is as old as the computer NL understanding problem itself. The traditional approaches to this problem basically gravitate to the information transmission theory. In terms of practice, the wellknown PC spelling checkers should be mentioned. Though the problem seems to be well studied, orientated linguistics still has some new clues.

The problem of errors is seen at quite a new angle in case of man-to-computer communication. In fact, the purposes of the NL text processing considerably depend on whether a text is meant to be read by a man or a computer. If addressed to a human being, a text has to comply with the requirement of grammatical accuracy, to say the least. Therefore, all spelling violations must be detected and corrected. At the same time, a computer-addressed text should provide nothing more than an adequate interpretation of the text message and, as a result, an adequate reaction to this address: all errors may be just ignored.

In this book we present a model of ignoring errors in written (printed or entered from the keyboard) texts. We proved several theorems that made it possible to invent special model-adequate tools of processing texts with errors — the so called q-tables with μ-chains in them.

The book covers both theoretical and algorithmic aspects of dictionary retrieval in case of garbled texts. The problem is to reduce the list of dictionary words and word combinations that can be parts of the input text. This is another application of the pre-recognition. The developed pre-recognition method classifies a dictionary in a certain way and searches for a word by means of a special function. Though this function is not a distance in the literal meaning of the word, a proved theorem says that it effectively truncates the dictionary areas where any further search is inexpedient.

The oral speech input problem (Stage 3) is known as one of the most difficult problems in the field of Artificial Intelligence. Even a very sophisticated speech recognition algorithm cannot guarantee a completely correct understanding because of homonymy, polysemy and some other phenomena. Thus, one is inclined to think that the correct recognition probability is physically limited to the level of 97% for speaker independent large dictionary systems. Nevertheless, orientated linguistics discovered a way to surpass this limit, thus obtaining a higher correct recognition probability. We prove an appropriate theorem at the end of the book.

Chapters 1–16, 21–26 and 28 of the book are written by Prof. V. Fain and chapters 17–20 and 27 are by Dr. L. Rubanov.

The authors would like to acknowledge Prof. Irene Stern (Kiev University), whose valuable comments were of much help. We wish to express our special gratitude to Gregory L. Toprover, an active participant of our today's research work, who carried out the main burden of translating into English, assembling and editing the book. We would also like to thank Samuel V. Fain who took part in translating the book.

Part I

THINKING, ACTIVITY, DIALOGUE

Chapter 1
PRAGMATIC THINKING IN THE COURSE OF "SUBJECT–OBJECT" INTERACTION

1.1 Activity and pragmatic thinking

Thinking is a superior display of the vital functions of living matter. At the same time it is the most complicated and alluring scientific problem.

Science tries a great variety of approaches to the problem of thinking: a psychological (phenomenological and experimental) approach, a physiological approach (mainly, researches into electric-chemical activities of neurons and neuron groups), a model approach (in particular, studies of the behavior of large nets of neuron-like trainable elements) and others. It is typical of all the approaches that their investigation subject, i.e. thinking, lacks an accurate formal definition as well as many other concepts connected with the explorations into intellect.

This can be partially explained by an extreme diversity and complexity of what we connect intuitively with the whole notion of "thinking". Therefore, it is natural for science to highlight an area of thinking which is narrow enough to be observed as a formal model and at the same time expressive enough to be of any theoretical and practical interest.

Following this idea, we shall focus on those parts of thinking that comply with the following statement: a subject's thinking is a means of arranging the subject's activity to optimize some criterion of his prosperity. The approach to the problem, derived from the said idea, is naturally named *pragmatic.*

The essence of this approach can be revealed by the following reasoning. The subject's arranging his activity in a particular environment can be nothing other than raising and solving problems which form his interaction with the environment. Therefore, it is *raising and solving problems* that form the essence of pragmatic thinking. Although the subject picks up these problems and establishes their succession rather subjectively, the initial sets of plausible problems and solution methods are objective, which is what makes the thought process reflect upon these sets adequately. Thus, to know the structure of these sets means to know what thinking is in the aspect that concerns us. This is the essence of the pragmatic approach.

The above text describing the problems of establishing some interaction with the environment needs more explanations. The point is that when solving a problem, the subject can affect himself as well as the environment; this ambiguity of the action addressee can confuse the issue. We shall avoid this if we take account of the two aspects of the subject's nature simultaneously. The first aspect is the subject's "intellectual" side, which enables him to perceive the environment and his own biological or cybernetic structure and to plan a reaction to them. The second aspect is represented by this very biological or cybernetic structure, and there the subject is just a part (element) of the environment. We shall keep this issue clear if we "isolate" the subject's biological or cybernetic essence from his intellectual (informational) essence by adding it to the environment. For example, we shall consider the subject's indisposition towards a spontaneous change of the environment in which his intellect is functioning, as if his body were just a container for his intellect and a part of the environment. So, when speaking about the "subject", we shall be referring only to the intellectual aspect of the subject's activity.

Once accepted, this interpretation of the interacting parts calls for an integration of the environment and the subject's "body" into a single concept. This new concept is opposed to the subject as the environment was opposed to him earlier. The word "object" seems a natural term for this concept. In this case, the question of the subject's activity in the environment can be discussed in the very convenient terms of "subject—object" interaction. Furthermore, and this is especially helpful for constructing formal models, any problem under the subject's consideration gets a *regular statement*, namely, *to change and/or clarify the object state.*

A mathematical simulation of the aforementioned situation will not be significantly altered if the environment and the subject's "body" are integrated into the general notion of "object". In fact, whatever is investigated it can be finally represented by values of certain properties or characteristics. Thus, if we unite characteristics of both the environment and the subject's "body", we shall obtain a set of characteristics of the object, and the values of these characteristics will describe the object state.

A change in the state of the object, if a result of the subject's solving his next problem, will be called *purposeful.* Certainly, the object can change for its own reasons, independent of any actions of the subject. We shall call a change in the object state *spontaneous* if not initiated by the subject.

There are both differences and similarities in the subject's activities connected with purposeful or spontaneous changes of the object. In the next section we shall consider how those differences and similarities manifest themselves.

1.2 Subject's activity in purposeful and spontaneous changes of the object

Let us designate the subject S and the object Q. A moment of time will be denoted as ν, and the object state at the moment ν is $Q(\nu)$. The triad $(S, Q; \nu)$ is labelled as the situation at the moment ν.

S does care about changes in the object state because in general they affect his own state. Therefore, the main characteristic of the subject S's attitude to the object Q at the state $Q(\nu)$ is the degree to which S's needs are satisfied by the situation $(S, Q; \nu)$. We shall denote this degree of satisfaction as $E(\nu)$. It is enough for our purposes to distinguish two values of $E(\nu)$: $E = 1$ ("satisfied") and $E = 0$ ("dissatisfied").

S's actions in some situation $(S, Q; \nu)$ depend on how he estimates $E(\nu)$ for the object state $Q(\nu)$.

If $E(\nu) = 1$ then S does not make any effort to change Q. In this case the situation $(S, Q; \nu)$ is called "quiet".

If $E = 0$ then the situation $(S, Q; \nu)$ is called "tense". In this situation, S investigates his opportunities of improving it by changing $Q(\nu)$. With a positive result of the investigation, S acts to obtain the desired change.

This means that there are *three kinds of the subject's activity* that affect the object.

Activity of the first kind could be named "informational". It refers to collecting information about the state of Q and can be divided into two subkinds depending on whether the information concerns the current or a projected state. In the former case S's activity is called "post-transitional", and the information obtained is called "post-information". In the latter case the activity is "pre-transitional", and the information is named "pre-information".

The second kind of activity is referred to as "selective". It occurs when post-transitional activity in a tense situation suggests more than one way of changing the object to improve $(S, Q; \nu)$. This activity selects the best option in terms of common sense.

It is obvious that the informational and selective activities together make up the subject's raising a *problem* of changing Q.

Activity of the third kind can be termed "operative". It includes direct actions to accomplish a projected change of $Q(\nu)$.

Therefore, operative activity represents *solving problems.*

Now we can specify common features of, and differences between S's activities in the course of purposeful and spontaneous changes of $Q(\nu)$.

Let us consider S's activity after a change of $Q(\nu)$. It is clear that the same stage comes first no matter whether the change was purposeful or spontaneous. It is post-transitional. At this stage the values of the characteristics of Q, that are the result of the last change (the "current" values), are taken into account to evaluate an absolute level of S's satisfaction in the new state of Q. They are compared with another collection of values of the same characteristics which is called "basic".

The essence of this comparison is the same in the cases of both purposeful and spontaneous changes. It is intended for estimating the rate of changes in addition to the absolute level of satisfaction. However the semantics of the basic collection depends on whether the change was purposeful or spontaneous. In fact, if the change was spontaneous, then S's decision about the value of $E(\nu)$ is influenced by whether the situation of his needs is better than or worse than or the same as the previous state of the object. Of course, the role of the basic collection is then played by the values of the characteristics of the previous state. However if the change was purposeful, it is natural to take the expected and predicted values of the characteristics as the basic ones. Comparing them with the current values, S can judge whether the change of Q he planned and carried out, has justified his hopes.

This is the sole difference between S's activities after a purposeful or a spontaneous change of Q. As we can see, it concerns only informational activity. In both cases the result of the post-transitional stage is one or another value of $E(\nu)$, and the further events in the S—Q system depend on that value.

If $E(\nu) = 1$, i.e. the result situation of the occurred change of Q turns out to be quiet, then S stops acting. He will continue only if a new spontaneous change of $Q(\nu)$ arises.

However if $E(\nu) = 0$, i.e. if the current situation is tense, then S starts pre-transitional activity.

In so doing, S considers plausible changes of Q and estimates them according to the following criteria:

1. Whether $E = 1$ in Q's new situation brought about by the projected change.

2. How great his expenses (calculated by some generalized formula) for the change will be.

These two estimates give some general value of the potential profit of the change. Certainly, in a more detailed consideration we would use $E \in [0,1]$ instead of $E \in \overline{0,1}$ and would obtain a non-quantized result value of E; but a draft of S's activity works fairly well here.

A projected change which is satisfactory according to the general estimate, is called "potentially favorable".

If the described pre-transitional activity exposes no potentially favorable changes of $Q(\nu)$, S's activity stops as well. If only one potentially favorable change is foreseen, S immediately passes onto the stage of operative activity. Lastly, if more than one favorable change is exposed, S engages in selective activity and then operative activity, the selective activity now having finished.

In this way, we have shown the possible kinds of S's activities in the S—Q system. It allows us to clarify the fields of our further investigation.

1.3 Further investigation

Let us specify the nature of this further consideration.

First of all, let us compare S's activity in a spontaneous versus a purposeful change of Q. As we saw above, the only post-transitional subkind of activity was connected with spontaneous changes. As opposed to this, in a purposeful change all the considered kinds and subkinds of activity are present, including the aforementioned post-transitional one, though with some non-principle semantic differences as considered earlier. From this it follows that we may focus on purposeful changes to observe the whole picture of S's activity. A special study of spontaneous changes is not necessary.

Furthermore, the variety of kinds and subkinds of activity does not each require a separate and equally thorough investigation. In order to settle this idea, we should pay attention to the "technological" trait peculiar to all the kinds of activity; namely the applicability of the notion "algorithm" to each of them.

Let us start with informational activity. It is obvious that there are three ways of obtaining information about the values of object characteristics:

(a) measuring;

(b) reasoning exactly or approximately;

(c) addressing an information store like a data/knowledge base.

All the three ways are equally good a priori but, as for obtaining post-information, (b) and (c) are likely to prevail, because the future is concerned. Here it is important to note that any of the above ways probably demands several actions (operations) to acquire information about a single value of a single characteristic. For example, a characteristic value measurement in accordance with method (a) includes at least the delivery, installation and verification of a certain measuring device. This statement is still more obvious with methods (b) and (c). It is this sequence of operations that is called "algorithm". This notion will be explained in detail below.

Selective activity imparts a direct mathematical meaning to the idea of algorithm as a sequence of more than one operation. It is the mathematical problem of a multi-option, multi-criteria choice, which has wellknown solution methods. All these methods lead to algorithms made up of more than one operation.

In operative activity an object change projected as a single action also requires a sequence of more than one independent action as in the aforementioned example of measuring. It is the symbolic representation of those actions and the structure arranging their execution, that are usually referred to as algorithm.

Thus in formal terms, any mentioned kind or subkind of activity is performed according to the same pattern, that is by means of an algorithm, which usually contains more than one operation. Therefore, our study of activity can be largely independent of the kind of activity studied if the field of this study is the very essence of activity. Namely, this essence is the relationship between a projected result (which can be either the information acquisition or the object change selection or the change accomplishment) and the algorithm to achieve that result.

The pointed uniformity of the different kinds of activity allows us to carry out a detailed study which is, first of all, a study of relationship between a sought-for result and the appropriate algorithm by means of probing into only one kind of activity. We shall implement a study of this sort for *operative* activity. This choice gives us a hope of obtaining the most general results because of a great variety of the practical displays of operative activity and rather a low degree of its formalization in comparison with that of the other kinds of activities.

We shall consider operative activity in the next chapter.

Chapter 2
SUBJECT'S OPERATIVE ACTIVITY

2.1 A model of the subject's operative activity affecting the object

Let the object Q be described by q numbers $x_1, \ldots, x_q$, and let X symbolize a bounded set of those numbers characterizing Q (the characteristics of Q). For the sake of simplicity, we shall consider the characteristics from X as having continuous scales though the reasoning below remains true with discrete scales.

If X is provided with a proximity measure, it becomes a q-dimensional space with X as its basis. This space will be designated by Σ, and the object Q is pictured in this space as a point $x = (x_1, \ldots, x_q)$. It is suggested that the object Q can not change its state by null-time leaps. Therefore, its changing in time is represented in Σ as a continuous trajectory $x(l)$, where l is the length of the way along the trajectory from a certain starting point.

The state of Q can change either spontaneously or as a result of some purposeful actions associated with the subject S. We noted above that it was purposeful actions that were of interest to us.

In our model any change in the state of the object Q manifests itself as a change in the values of its characteristics from the set X. Our study on the subject's purposeful actions distinguishes two kinds of changes in the characteristic x_i, called *purposeful* and *free.*

A purposeful change of x_i is a result of some influence on this characteristic and/or the other characteristics. In other words, a purposeful change of x_i may take place as a result of either *direct* or *indirect* influences on it. Indirect influences are possible because different characteristics can be correlated inside the object Q.

The characteristics of the object Q can also change in the absence of any influences or, more exactly, within a time interval between two successive influences. "Mental inertia" suggests naming such a change *free.* Here purposeful changes will be of prime interest to us.

Generally, a purposeful change can affect not only a single characteristic x_i but a set of characteristics (designated X_a, $X_a \subset X$ and called a *goal set*) simultaneously. The goal set X_a can serve as a basis of some space Σ_a called a *goal space.* If the proximity measure of Σ_a is imported from Σ, the space Σ_a may be treated as a subspace of the space Σ. Note that the set X of all possible characteristics is static and stable, whereas X_a is dynamic: its composition varies from one purposeful change to another. Moreover, *all* the characteristics from X_a must change simultaneously by the definition of this set. The timed process of a change pictures itself in Σ_a as a trajectory that we shall designate $x_a(l_a)$. Let the considered purposeful change start at the moment ν' and finish at the moment ν''. We may specify this in the goal set notation and write down $X_a\langle\nu',\nu''\rangle$. If the object Q has a point x'_a as its projection onto the space Σ_a at the moment ν', and x''_a as that at the moment ν'', the segment $\langle x'_a, x''_a\rangle$ of the trajectory $x_a(l_a)$ represents the considered purposeful change in Σ_a. We shall call x'_a and x''_a the *initial* and *goal points* of the segment $\langle x'_a, x''_a\rangle$ respectively.

The points x'_a and x''_a are also called *special points* of the trajectory $x_a(l_a)$. The segment $\langle x'_a, x''_a\rangle$ will be referred to as *purposeful change segment* in the space Σ_a or briefly *p-segment*, if its length (measured along the trajectory $x_a(l_a)$) is not less than some limited constant ε. The latter condition was set because in this model we associate purposeful changes of the object Q with actions of the subject S, who distinguishes states of Q by means of tools of a limited resolution. Poor resolution displays itself in each point x_a being surrounded in Σ_a by a finite domain $\sigma_a(x_a)$, within which S can not tell states of Q from each other. For instance, a simple formulation of this condition is as follows:

$$\varepsilon > 2\sigma_a\,.$$

It enables the subject to say with all certainty whether some segment of the trajectory $x_a(l_a)$ is a p-segment. The domain $\sigma_a(x_a)$ is termed a *subjective image of the object* Q in the space Σ_a or briefly *s-image.*

A p-segment $\langle x'_a, x''_a\rangle$ is called a *purposeful change link* or, briefly, a *p-link*, if it has no special points between the initial point x'_a and the goal point x''_a, i.e. if x'_a and x''_a are neighboring special points on the trajectory.

Now let us introduce the important notion of one-link purposeful transition the object Q makes from a state x'_a to a state x''_a.

A change in the state of Q is called *one-link purposeful transition (OPT)* in the space Σ_a if the following conditions are satisfied:

C2.1. There exists a non-empty goal set $X_a\langle\nu',\nu''\rangle$.

C2.2. The segment $\langle x'_a, x''_a\rangle$ of the trajectory $x_a(l_a)$ is a p-link.

C2.3. $\sigma_a(x'_a)\cap\sigma_a(x''_a)=\varnothing$.

Condition C2.1 means that only a purposeful (not free) change can be a purposeful transition. C2.2 means that a change can be a one-link transition in Σ_a only if the segment $\langle x'_a, x''_a\rangle$ has no special points except x'_a and x''_a. Condition C2.3 gives S an opportunity of both planning a change and estimating its results.

A finite chain consisting of OPT's is named a *purposeful transition (PT)*. It is natural to study a PT by studying links of which it consists, i.e. OPT's.

2.2 Transition and its realizing algorithm

Now let us consider an OPT $\langle x'_a, x''_a \rangle$ with $X_a \langle \nu', \nu'' \rangle$ as a goal set. In order to make this transition, S undertakes a *sequence of actions (operations)* called *algorithm* because we do not have any other term to express the idea better. It is designated by $A(x'_a, x''_a)$.

Let us define the notions of "operation" and "sequence" used above.

As it has already been noted, any S's action to affect Q is displayed in this model as operations over characteristics from X. In this connection we shall define two types of operations over these characteristics, calling them active and test operations.

Consider a set of characteristics $X_{am} \subset X$ and a space Σ_{am} with X_{am} as its basis. The proximity measure in Σ_{am} is considered to be imported from Σ.

By the *m-th active operation* $\alpha_{am}(x'_{am}, x''_{am})$ we mean a change of the object Q's state, which is caused by a purposeful change (started at the moment ν'_m and finished at the moment ν''_m) of all the characteristics from the set X_{am} and which produces in the space Σ_{am} a purposeful change segment $\langle x'_{am}, x''_{am} \rangle$ of length $\geq \varepsilon$ along the trajectory $x_{am}(l_{am})$.

We shall speak of the active operation $\alpha_{am}(x'_{am}, x''_{am})$ that it "occurs in the space Σ_{am}". The special points x'_{am} and x''_{am} of the segment $\langle x'_{am}, x''_{am} \rangle$ are also called the special points of that operation.

The term *test operation* is used in reference to any act of testing the compliance of the results of the previous active operation (operations) with a certain condition. As before, one can test either some characteristics from X or some other quantities calculated from them.

Active and test operations are united by the general notion of *operation.* It is known that any algorithm can be represented as a sequence of active and test operations only [1].

Since test operations do not move the point x in Σ, only active operations are responsible for purposeful changes in its location. Therefore, in this segment only algorithm active operations will be enumerated and supplied with the appropriate index m.

A collection of M active operations is called a *sequence* if

$$\forall m \in \overline{1, M}: \quad \nu'_{m+1} \geq \nu''_m .$$

The sign $\geq$ is used on account of a free change (or an invariability interval) between two forced changes of Q.

Since only active operations can change the object Q purposefully, it is natural to admit that a change of Q in the OPT starts together with the first active operation of the algorithm $A(x'_a, x''_a)$:

$$\nu' = \nu'_1 . \tag{2.1}$$

Similarly, it is hardly possible to say that the OPT finishes before the last (M-th) operation of the algorithm. It means

$$\nu'' = \nu''_m \,. \tag{2.2}$$

This is our model of transition and its realizing algorithm.

2.3 The OPT and the active operation. The OPT recursion theorem

Now we can open a discussion about the important statement that discovers a sort of recursion in the structure of algorithms. Namely, active operations are governed by the following statement:

Theorem 2.1 *(The OPT recursion theorem)*
Let $\langle x'_a, x''_a \rangle$ be an OPT in the space Σ_a and this OPT is realized by an algorithm $A(x'_a, x''_a)$ made up of more than one active operation. Then the algorithm's m-th active operation is itself an OPT in the space Σ_a, and

$$X_{am} \cap X_a = \emptyset \,. \tag{2.3}$$

Proof: To be an OPT, an active operation $\alpha_{am}(x'_{am}, x''_{am})$ should comply with Conditions C2.1–C2.3. Let us prove that those conditions are fulfilled as applied to $\alpha_{am}(x'_{am}, x''_{am})$.

Condition C2.1 is fulfilled by the definition of active operation.

Condition C2.2 is fulfilled because the active operations of the algorithm form a sequence. By definition it means that the moment ν''_{m-1}, when the change caused by the $(m-1)$-th active operation finishes, comes before the moment ν'_m, when the change caused by the m-th operation starts, and the moment ν'_{m+1}, when the change caused by the $(m+1)$-th operation starts, comes after the moment ν''_m, when the change caused by the m-th operation finishes. From this it follows that within the time segment $[\nu'_m, \nu''_m]$ no change starts or finishes except for the change caused by the m-th operation. Consequently, there are no special points within the segment $\langle x'_{am}, x''_{am} \rangle$ of the trajectory $x_{am}(l_{am})$ other than x'_{am} and x''_{am}. So, $\langle x'_{am}, x''_{am} \rangle$ is a p-link.

Condition C2.3 is fulfilled too. In fact, the active operation $\alpha_{am}(x'_{am}, x''_{am})$ is S's purposeful action. Thus, it complies with the "macro-scale" requirement, that C2.3 imposes on changes.

Now we shall prove that $X_{am} \cap X_a = \emptyset$. Since there are more than one active operation in the algorithm, from Eq. (2.1) and Eq. (2.2) it follows that the change caused by $\alpha_{am}(x'_{am}, x''_{am})$ either starts after the OPT $\langle x'_a, x''_a \rangle$ starts, or finishes before this OPT finishes, or both. Therefore, at least one of the moments ν'_m and ν''_m corresponding to the start and the finish of the operation $\alpha_{am}(x'_{am}, x''_{am})$ lies *within* the time segment $[\nu'_a, \nu''_a]$ occupied by the transition $\langle x'_a, x''_a \rangle$. This transition is a one-link transition. Hence, by the definition of p-link, *none* of the characteristics from the set X_a can have its special point within the time interval (ν'_a, ν''_a). It has just been shown that the projections of special points onto *all* the characteristics from X_{am} are located within the same time interval. Therefore, the sets X_a and X_{am} have no elements in common, and Eq. (2.3) is true, Q.E.D.

In the next chapter we shall interpret the most important results of the theorem.

Chapter 3
ACTIVITY MODEL INTERPRETATION

3.1 Dialectics of relation "transition–algorithm" and the Indirect Action Principle

Let us consider the methodological aspect of the relation between the object transition from a state x'_a to a state x''_a and the algorithm that realizes this transition. When comparing this relation with relation "goal—means", we naturally associate the transition with the goal and the algorithm with the means of reaching it. At the same time, Theorem 2.1 says that any active operation of the algorithm is a transition too. Therefore, the operation takes on the role of goal with respect to its "own" algorithm, whereas the latter becomes a means of realizing it. Thus, the considered relation finds its dialectics in the *role duality* inherent in either of its parts: they appear to be the goal and the means simultaneously.

Furthermore, Eq. (2.3) states that within the accepted idealization a desired change of the object can be made only by an *indirect* influence on certain characteristics, not by a direct one. Looking paradoxical at first sight, this fact turns out to be quite natural. For example, imagine a lieutenant-colonel whose goal is to be promoted colonel. Apparently, this promotion is a one-link transition, because these two ranks are adjacent. The goal set X_a in this case may contain the characteristics "power and respectability", "an office car at one's disposal", "an aide-de-camp at one's disposal" and so on, but the fact is that direct physical actions such as "getting more power" or "getting an aide-de-camp" *do not* exist at all! The algorithm of the promotion to the desired state comprises operations which make our lieutenant-colonel handle characteristics from beyond X_a. Among them there may be "increasing one's zeal", "improving one's commanding skills", "looking smart in the eyes of one's superiors" and so on. The aforesaid suggests calling the phenomenon established by Theorem 2.1 the *Indirect Action Principle.*

When we take into account the semantics of the characteristics from the goal sets $X_a, X_{am}, \ldots$, we shall have to consider the spaces $\Sigma_a, \Sigma_{am}, \ldots$ together with special points in them as "object domains". We shall elaborate this term below, and here we would like to give another explanation for the duality mentioned. The matter is that the goal and the means practically always belong to different object domains. It will be proved in the next section.

3.2 Declarable and executable operations

The Indirect Action Principle establishes the structure of the goal reaching process. This structure implies a certain *recursiveness* (or reflexiveness) which comes from the role duality mentioned: the transition is realized by a collection of active operations, and each of them is a transition itself, being realized by a collection of active operations, and each of them is a transition itself, being realized by .... Since the model under consideration relies on the very general assumptions about the object Q and its characteristics, the recursiveness in question is likely to be typical of various kinds of activities. Therefore, it is of great practical significance to regard it.

In this connection a natural question arises: what limits this recursion (reflection), and how deep is it? Theorem 2.1 offers the following answer: the recursion deepest level is reached when the OPT of the previous level is realized by an algorithm which is made up of *a single active operation.* It is easy to prove that this is the only case when a direct action can occur.

The aforesaid suggests introducing two kinds of active operations: declarable and executable. An active operation $\alpha_{am}(x'_{am}, x''_{am})$ is called *declarable* if its realizing algorithm comprises more than one active operation. As we have seen, $\alpha_{am}(x'_{am}, x''_{am})$ can not be executed directly in this case. Contrastingly, an *executable* operation is realized by an algorithm made up of a single operation which makes this algorithm.

It is not a universal principle but an *agreement* that answers whether the active operation is single in an algorithm given, i.e. whether the operation is executable. For example, one can go from one room to another executing a sequence of operations, each of them is a step. An agreement can declare a step to be a direct physical action; in this case the step realizing algorithm consists of the single operation that is the step itself, and the recursion stops here. This example also illustrates the expression "practically always" used at the end of section 3.1, as it demonstrates a degenerated situation of goal and means object domains matching. Other circumstances can demand a further decomposition of the step into the operations "foot down", "body motion", "foot up", etc. Naturally, it makes the recursion deeper. The situation looks like answering the question "what is a thing made up of?". Depending on the agreement the answer can be: "of parts", "of molecules", "of atoms", "of nuclei and electrons", "of protons, neutrons and electrons" and so on. If the concept of a practice-motivated agreement were removed, it would make the recursion as deep as the world of microparticles.

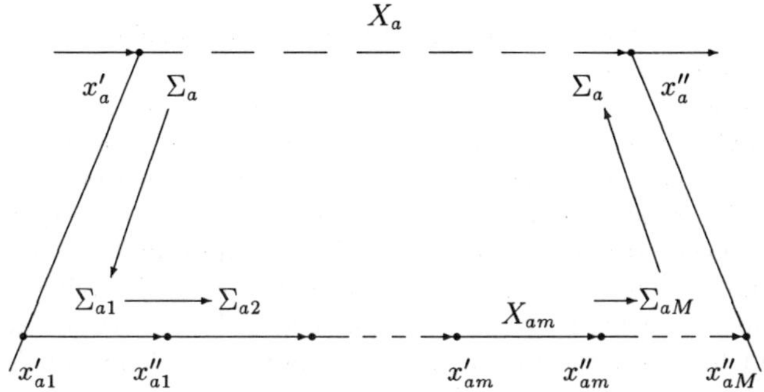

Figure 3.1

3.3 A standard structural element of the process of changing Q

The recursive nature of the transition realizing process imparts a certain homogeneity to the structure of the transition and makes it possible to reveal its standard structural element. The couple "transition — its realizing algorithm" forms this element. It is convenient to represent the couple graphically as a trapezium (see Fig. 3.1) in which the upper base represents an OPT and the lower one depicts the realizing algorithm. For the simplicity sake, the algorithm is shown as a linear sequence of operations (with only active operations numerated), but it can be ramified if test operations are included. Yet, it does not obscure our conclusions because any algorithm has one input state and one output state at any rate.

The dashed arrow, forming the upper base of the trapezium, symbolizes that it is a declarable, not executable, operation. It is simply the goal of the action, a task for the transition, but not the transition itself: by virtue of Theorem 2.1 a transition cannot be realized by a direct influence on X_a. The sides of the trapezium display that in accordance with Eq. (2.3) object domains change when the transition goal (task) formulation gives way to the task realizing algorithm as well as when the process returns from the algorithm to the expected result of the transition.

3.4 The symmetry of the considered hierarchy. OD and OSD

In Fig. 3.1 the horizontal arrows, one entering the point x'_a and the other starting from the point x''_a, show that the considered OPT $\langle x'_a, x''_a \rangle$ can be just an element of a chain termed purposeful transition (PT) at the end of Section 3.2. Now we can specify the notion of PT, describing it as a limited *sequence* of OPT's. And the term "sequence" keeps the meaning defined in Section 3.3.

Now the OPT $\langle x'_a, x''_a \rangle$ looses the shade of uniqueness connected with its representing the highest level of the recursive hierarchy. This shade was also stressed by the fact that there were edges going down and to the sides from the upper base of the trapezium in Fig. 3.1 but no edges going up. It damaged the recursive structure symmetry.

Considering an OPT as a PT element removes this feeling of imperfection. A chain of OPT's is then a sequence of active operations, and this sequence serves as a means of realizing an OPT of a higher level in another object domain. Thus the hierarchy in question acquires a *complete symmetry*; its expansion upwards as well as downwards (discussed above) is limited exclusively by an *agreement*. For example, when a young man, S takes the goal of "living a worthy life" as his upper-level OPT. With years passing, S looks forward and revises his standpoint to pursue the goal of "maintaining and developing one's family honor and prosperity founded by one's ancestors for future generations". Then the former upper OPT of the earlier age becomes an active operation in the sequence realizing the upper level OPT of the mature age. Further movement upwards is also possible, for example, if S pursues goals connected with the prosperity of his country, or with the ecological prosperity of the whole planet. Even the Universe may be concerned if some "Universal Mind" acts as S. With no limiting agreement accepted, this movement can be as infinite as the Universe itself.

Now we can specify the use of the notion "object domain". *Object domain* (OD) terms a space Σ_M with the set

$$X_M = \bigcup_{m=1}^{M} X_{am}$$

as its basis, together with special points in this space. Thus, the space Σ_M is comprehended as the object domain where some OPT realizing algorithm is working. The space Σ_{am} with its special points, dealing with a single active operation of this algorithm, can be named an "object subdomain" (OSD).

The space Σ_a of the transition (or, more exactly, OPT) $\langle x'_a, x''_a \rangle$ realized by the mentioned algorithm is also an OSD because this OPT, as it has been said above, is simultaneously an active operation of the algorithm of the next (that is one step higher) level. However, when our consideration stays within the limits of a single OPT—algorithm couple (one "trapezium"), we shall sometimes use both terms "OSD" and "OD" with reference to Σ_a. In this way we shall be able to speak about changing object domains, thus stressing that the OPT and its realizing algorithm form a couple. In particular, we used this possibility in Section 3.3 when considering "switches" of object domains between the trapezium bases.

Let us add that from

$$M > 1 \Rightarrow \forall m: \; X_m \cap X_a = \emptyset$$

also follows

$$X_M \cap X_a = \emptyset$$

which means that like any operation of an OPT realizing algorithm, the whole algorithm is situated in another OD than the OPT.

3.5 The non-uniqueness of correspondence "transition—algorithm"

In the discussion about the OPT—algorithm couples we tacitly supposed the algorithm to be unique. In general, it is natural to assume that an OPT can be realized by more than one algorithm. For example, S has three options to accomplish the OPT "Obtaining the Ph.D. degree": he may either become a postgraduate, or work at his thesis independently, or present a collection of his papers published.

The reverse situation is also possible: one algorithm (maybe with different values of its arguments, see below) can be utilized to realize different OPT's. For example, the promotion algorithm that works to turn a lieutenant-colonel to a colonel, essentially works with the transition "major → lieutenant-colonel" or even the transition "lab assistant → senior lab assistant".

From what has been said it follows that the considered hierarchy should be shown by a spatial, not plane structure which can be a result of multiplying the plane trapezium of Fig. 3.1. A possible fragment of this structure is pictured in Fig. 3.2. For the simplicity sake, the initial and purpose points of all the OPT's shown are numbered. Edge $\langle 1,2\rangle$ illustrates the case when OPT can be realized by two different algorithms: $\langle 5,6\rangle$ and $\langle 7,10\rangle$. The same concerns OPT $\langle 8,9\rangle$ (algorithms $\langle 11,12\rangle$ and $\langle 13,14\rangle$). At the same time, algorithm $\langle 11,12\rangle$ can realize two different OPT's: $\langle 8,9\rangle$ and $\langle 9,10\rangle$ represented in Fig. 3.2 by trapezia 11–8–9–12 and 11–9–10–12 (the cases "major → lieutenant-colonel" and "lieutenant-colonel → colonel", both OPT's from the same OD). Algorithm $\langle 5,6\rangle$ can realize two OPT's too: $\langle 1,2\rangle$ and $\langle 3,4\rangle$ (they are from different OD's, like in the examples "major → lieutenant-colonel" and "laboratory assistant → senior laboratory assistant"). Note that pre-information can direct Q from state 1 not only to state 2 but to any other a priori favorable state as well, for example state $2'$ or $2''$. And if another OPT had been chosen on the selective activity stage, it would have been supplied with a structure as branched as that shown in Fig. 3.2. We do not draw it as to not overload the picture.

3.6 Polytrapezium and its tail

A spatial graph illustrated by Fig. 3.2 can be called a *polytrapezium.* It shows an OPT of the agreed highest level and its realizing algorithm. The same graph without the edge of this OPT is called *the OPT tail.* Just the same, a sub-graph representing the algorithm of some operation $\alpha_{am}(x'_{am}, x''_{am})$ (not including the edge of the very operation) is called *the operation tail.* Any tailed operation is certainly declarable.

As it was stated above, the OPT tail is limited by the mentioned agreements. Thus the number of levels is finite in the upper-level OPT tail (later we shall call it the "upper OPT") as well as in the tail of any operation from the upper OPT tail. Furthermore, the number of operations in the lower base of any level trapezium of the tail is finite (because the algorithm is executable), as

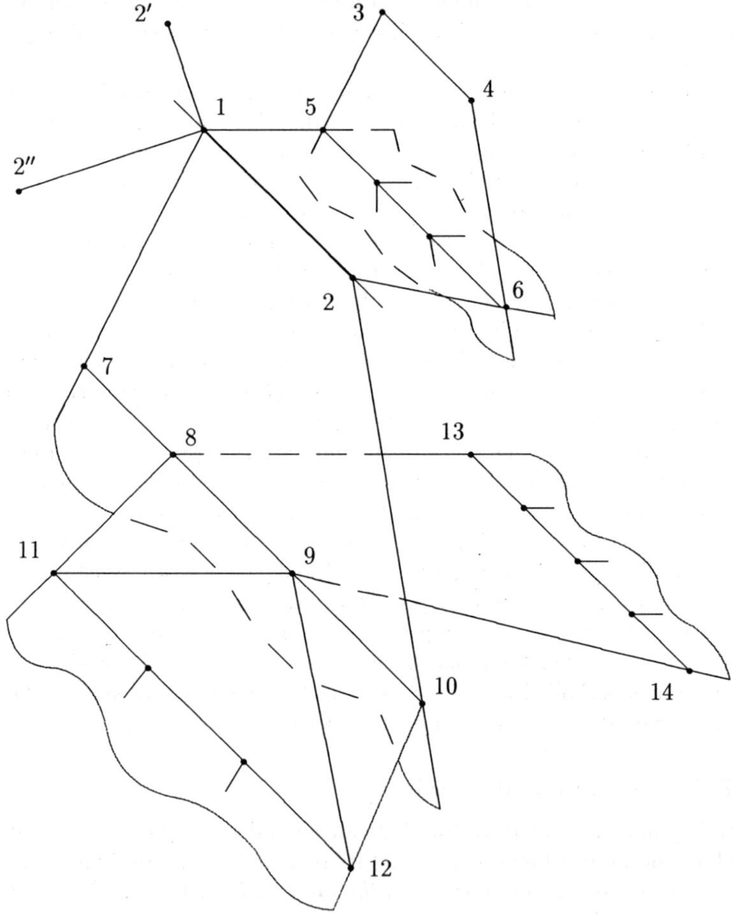

Figure 3.2

well as the number of branches in cases when an intermediate level OPT can be accomplished by more than one algorithm.

It means that the general number of operations (active and test ones) in the upper OPT polytrapezium is always *finite*. We shall designate the bounded set of all operations of the polytrapezium as $\{\alpha\}$ and the number of its elements as κ.

Within the framework of this study we shall consider *the topology of any polytrapezium to be fixed.*

Let us note now that some operations in the set $\{\alpha\}$ can be similar, or equivalent to each other. Two operations are called *equivalent* if formal representations of their tails differ only in values of the arguments. Equivalent operations can be found either at the same level or at different levels of a tail. For example, the operation "unscrewing a bolt" can be found in the car maintenance polytrapezium both at high (disjoining whole units from the chassis) and low levels (separating small parts). At all these levels the operation has the same (except for the values of the arguments) tail: "removing dirt, soaking rust, taking a suitable wrench, etc.", but the values of the arguments (the bolt location, the wrench type and size, the force to be applied and so on) may differ.

The set $\{\alpha\}$ includes the subset that involves all the polytrapezium operations equivalent to some operation $\alpha^{(k)}_{am}(x'_{am}, x''_{am})$. This subset will be called the k-th equivalence class in $\{\alpha\}$ and designated $\{\alpha\}_k$. The introduced equivalence relation breaks $\{\alpha\}$ into $\widehat{K}$ equivalence classes ($\widehat{K} < \kappa$, $\widehat{K}$ is finite, of course). The set of all those classes (the factor-set of the set $\{\alpha\}$ according to the equivalence relation considered) is denoted by $\widehat{A}$. By the definition of equivalence, all operations from the k-th class have identical (except for the values of the arguments) tails, i.e. they are realized by the same algorithm. Thus the set $\widehat{A}$ of classes is mapped in the one-to-one manner on a collection of $\widehat{K}$ algorithms. The set $\widehat{A}$ itself can be spoken of as a collection of "prototypes". This collection should be powerful enough to form the whole set $\{\alpha\}$ by varying arguments and then to reconstruct the whole tail of the upper OPT on the base of $\{\alpha\}$.

Thus we have represented the structure of activity in the OD of an OPT as a polytrapezium with this OPT as the upper one. However, we considered polytrapezium algorithms as existing and known. It is high time we set the following questions: where do those algorithms come from? Who creates them? When? How? Answers to these questions are dictated by an important property inherent in the environment where the activity is performed. This is the property of the environment being stationary and we shall consider it in the next chapter.

Chapter 4
ACTIVITY IN A STATIONARY ENVIRONMENT

4.1 "Problem" and pragmatic thinking

Let us define the notion of "single address to Q".

Naturally, the subject S's changing the object Q or getting clear the current values of its characteristics (in this section we shall refer to both actions as "addresses" to Q) can concern not the upper OPT of the whole polytrapezium or "the top OPT" as we shall call it. Generally speaking, a desired address may be corresponded by any operation of any level of the tail; this operation obviously works as a "local" upper OPT for the given address. For example, suppose that "Putting a car in order completely" is agreed to be the top OPT. Then a single address for curing a wheel pin hole is corresponded by some local upper OPT, represented as an operation in the top OPT tail. This operation is likely to lie considerably lower than the top OPT itself.

The polytrapezium operation that makes the upper OPT of an address is termed as *goal operation* and marked with an asterisk, for example, $\alpha^*_{am}(x'_{am}, x''_{am})$ or simply α^*_{am} or α^*_a. Thus any operation from the tail can simultaneously be a goal operation and just an operation of the algorithm that it belongs to.

S interacts with the polytrapezium of plausible actions over Q in the two stages: "informational" and "working". At the first stage S forms his intention as a description of the desired operation. It can be either changing Q in case of an active operation, or figuring out the values of characteristics of Q in case of a test operation. Formally, a description is the two (x'_a, α). x'_a is still a collection of the current values of characteristics from the goal set X_a, i.e. the values that S wants to find out or change by his next address to Q. α is a collection of data (see below) about the operation that must give the desired result. Having formulated his intention, S scans the polytrapezium for an operation to affect the characteristics from the set X_a so that they meet the description (x'_a, α). This operation, say α_{am}, acquires the goal operation status with the symbol α^*_{am} designating it. Thus the goal operation reveals its tail, and S proceeds to the working stage of the process, i.e. to the execution of the operation affecting Q.

At the working stage, the way down the tail to the very bottom leads to the first and the last executable operations of the given address. Those operations are called the a^*_{am} *starting* and *finishing operations* respectively.

A *single address* to Q terms carrying out a sequence of operations completely, i.e. from the α^*_{am} starting operation to the α^*_{am} finishing operation. Another name of this is *the OPT α^*_{am} execution act.*

It is obvious that any single address to Q is actually the process of solving a *problem* raised by the subject S. Such a problem concerns the object Q and the environment as a part of it. In fact, any single address consists by definition of active and test operations, i.e. of operations intended for changing Q or figuring out its state. And it was noted in Section 1.1 that the problem of accomplishing a sequence of operations was just an ordinary problem of S's activity. The problem solved by the n-th single address (counting from a certain moment) is designated as z_n. It is just raising and solving problems z_n that form *pragmatic thinking* considered in Section 1.1. Each problem has a goal operation α^*_{am} in the polytrapezium and the description (x'_a, α) of this operation can be regarded as a formal representation of the problem z_n formulation. As we remember, the tail of any declarable operation completely represents the realizing algorithm. In this connection we shall say about the tail of the goal operation chosen to solve the problem z_n that it is the *problem z_n solution algorithm.*

Taking problems z_n into consideration allows us to pass on to the question of polytrapezium and environment stationarity. We shall consider this question in the next section.

4.2 Polytrapezium $\widehat{K}$-stationarity and environment K-stationarity

When considering the question of stationarity, one should remember that a polytrapezium may have different sets $\hat{A}$ of classes of operations from the set $\{\alpha\}$ even if the polytrapezium topology is fixed. Let Z denote the sequence of problems z_n the subject S has solved since he started his work with some given polytrapezium. N is the number of problems in the sequence Z or (which is the same) the number of single addresses to Q during the mentioned period.

Let us consider the sequence

$$Z = (z_1, \ldots, z_n, \ldots, z_N)$$

of all the problems risen from the initial moment (when the problem z_1 emerged) till the moment when the last (N-th) problem emerged. Let these N problems have required $\widehat{K}$ different algorithms to solve them. Then

$$\widehat{K} < N$$

is possible if some problems in Z were of the same type, i.e. called for the same algorithm from $\hat{A}$.

Let us assume that each problem occurred after some $N = \widehat{N}_0$ appeared to be of the same type as one of the preceding problems. Then the problems stopped calling new algorithms and this means that the condition

$$\forall N \geq \widehat{N}_0 : \ \widehat{K} = const \tag{4.1}$$

was satisfied. A polytrapezium which complies with condition Eq. (4.1) is named $\widehat{K}$*-stationary.*

All the N single addresses to Q having been processed, all the called goal operations might turn out to be not from all the $\widehat{K}$ classes but from some subset A of classes, $A \subset \widehat{A}$ and the cardinality of A was K,

$$K < \widehat{K} . \tag{4.2}$$

It means that S's intentions never exceeded the limits of the K classes that establish the set A. And in most applications S's intentions are determined neither by his imagination nor by an arbitrary choice. Those intentions arise as a result of the necessity to react to one or another situation in the environment that S is working in. In this aspect, a stable demand for operations from only K classes reflects not so much the properties of the application computer system (i.e. the polytrapezium) or of the subject himself, as the *environment objective property* of offering problems of only K types thus being satisfied with only K algorithms (among $\widehat{K}$ available).

Certainly, a disintegration of the community's activity into isolated environments is rather conditional and arbitrary, but it does not confuse our consideration. In this way $\{\mu\}$ will letter a set (bounded) of all environments formed in some community, and μ_m denotes the m-th element of the set $\{\mu\}$, $m \in \overline{1, M}$; M is the cardinality of $\{\mu\}$. It is natural to think that

$$M \gg 1 . \tag{4.3}$$

So, if solving problems in the environment μ_m gives that

$$\exists\, N_0 : \qquad \forall\, N \geq N_0 : \; K = const , \tag{4.4}$$

the environment μ_m is called K*-stationary.* If the problems are solved by means of a polytrapezium which meet conditions Eqs. (4.1) and (4.2), the environment μ_m is called K-stationary with respect to this polytrapezium.

Note that we should have spoken here not about the environment but rather about the entire object Q, because earlier we conjoined the "body" part of S and the environment. However, the opposition "subject—environment" seems to be more habitual in this context; besides, it provides a terminological compatibility with our previous works (see [2], for example).

Of course, environments beyond the definition of K-stationarity should be taken into account too.

We say an environment is *non-stationary* if it does not meet condition Eq. (4.4). For such environments

$$(N \to \infty) \;\Rightarrow\; (K \to \infty) . \tag{4.5}$$

Implication Eq. (4.5) is characteristic for a non-stationary environment and can be its definition.

Coming back to K-stationary environments, we should like to emphasize that the set A consists of those K classes of equivalent operations (among the general number $\widehat{K}$ of classes of the given top OPT polytrapezium), which involve no less than one goal operation each. Let $\{\alpha^*\}$ symbolize the set of these operations. Sometimes the same letter A will be helpful to denote the set of K problem solving algorithms which is mapped one-to-one on the mentioned set of K classes of operations. Then A will be understood as a collection of K *ready-to-use algorithms* (one algorithm per class of problems), even if they contain similar blocks, but not as a collection of K blocks to construct those ready algorithms.

We shall refer to the set A as the *finite problem domain* (FPD) of the given top OPT (please, do not confuse them with *object* domains and subdomains introduced above!). Of course, if state 1 (see Fig. 3.2) were continued to another top OPT (e.g. $\langle 1,2' \rangle$ or $\langle 1,2'' \rangle$) it would form another FPD. For example, imagine a person who wants "to make a career". If a military career is concerned, the FPD involves entering a Military College and a General Staff College, getting a command post in the Army, etc. A political career suggests another FPD, a scientific career suggests still another and so on.

We have seen that the $\widehat{K}$-stationarity of a polytrapezium and the fixedness of its topology are crucial for organizing, structuring and, in a way, standardizing S's activities. We have also seen that those properties come from the K-stationarity of environments. Therefore, if we want the further investigation to lean upon the said properties and not to loose its practical significance, we must make sure that K-stationary environments are not exotic. The next section is devoted to that particular problem.

4.3 Are real environments stationary?

For this question to be answered, we had to make familiar with the histories of many problem domains. We did study some of them ourselves (oil-products distribution, trade and deliveries of oil-chemistry articles, medical service, traffic police, bibliographical service, etc.). The others are known from the literature. If a problem domain is already equipped with computer systems (DBMS, expert system, etc.), we used a description of that system.

The studies indicated that a great variety of problem domains have *two states* of their functioning. That is in complete accordance with the wellknown philosophical principle of the development dialectics.

One of the states represents time periods of a problem domain explosion-like development. As $\delta\nu_e$ we shall designate a duration of this period. An explosion-like period lasts for a relatively short time but during this period the domain suffers qualitative changes: obsolete establishments vanish, new kinds of activity and new problems appear and demand new methods to handle them. This period is commonly provoked by dramatic social or technological progress, for example, legislation reforms or a major scientific discovery. It raises problems of such complexity and entanglement that only talented and experienced people can work them out; it seems hardly possible to speak about charging a computer system with that kind of activity in the near future.

An explosion-like development period makes way for a stable, stationary state of the problem domain when it functions in a settled, "normal" mode. $\delta\nu_r$ symbolizes a duration of a stationary period which is always *much longer* than an explosion, i.e.

$$\delta\nu_r \gg \delta\nu_e . \tag{4.6}$$

The nature of activity during a stationary period is rather *routine*; absolutely new problems arise rarely and a large body of current problems is satisfied by the assortment of methods created during the explosion. An important point is that this assortment is sure to be *finite* in every domain because created by a finite number of people within a finite period of time. From the fact that the finite assortment of methods mostly serves the practice of the problem domain during the entire routine period it follows that problems arising in this period are mainly of the *finite number of types* and this number matches the number of methods in the mentioned assortment. Since this period is usually very long, the conclusion comes that *any* problem domain in a routine period of its existence makes an environment *with the K-stationarity traits.*

To complete the description we must make another note. As time elapses, the portion of problems for which there are no satisfactory methods in the established assortment, starts increasing. It indicates the forthcoming end of the routine period, followed by the transition to a new explosion and so on and so forth.

The said suggests an answer to the question of how wide-spread K-stationary environments are. Really, let us fix some characteristic state of an environment, for example its state in the moment when it starts its transition from an explosion-like period to a stationary one. Apparently, the moment of its getting to this state is a random value for an observer who chooses the environment at a guess and has never considered it before. Let us suppose this random value to be evenly distributed along the time axis. Then the probability P_r of finding the environment in a stationary state at any moment of time is

$$P_r = \frac{\delta\nu_r}{\delta\nu_r + \delta\nu_e} ,$$

which is very close to 1 because of Eq. (4.6). In other words, at any moment of time an overwhelming majority of considered environments appear to be K-stationary. Therefore, an investigation and use of the potentialities of K-stationarity prove to be quite beneficial.

The phenomena inherent in routine periods of action affect the organization and work of existing computer systems in an especially obvious way. Any existing system, whatever it is intended for, can be actually equipped with no more than a finite collection of problem solving methods, which is with a *finite number K of algorithms*. However, despite this restriction the system satisfies its problem domain for a very long time (for years usually). It means that the problem domain is going through a routine period of its existence and the established environment is K-stationary. For example, one of our industrially applied systems (that is the below described management information system "Oil-products" for the transportation and distribution of oil-products) used to get an average of 150–200 addresses per day which gives $N \approx 500\,000$ for the ten years long exploitation of the system with the practically invariable collection of algorithms. At the same time the number K of algorithms was rather small (about 20).

If one adheres not to the letter but rather to the spirit of the formal definition of K-stationarity, they can notice that this phenomenon expands much wider than the human purposeful activity considered above. In Introduction we have already emphasized that the great extent and role of reflexive and instinctive activities in the fauna, the prevalence and profitability of prolonged, large-serial production in industry, the professional specialization of people's knowledge and skills in society illustrate how deep and wide the considered phenomenon penetrates the surrounding life.

Of course, the "habit" of stationarity becomes harmful during a period of changes: some species of animals get extinct, some industries demand radical reforms, some staff need retraining and so on. Nevertheless, when the next stationary period comes, it enforces the functioning principles of the stable mode again, i.e. it returns the universally used opportunity of reaching a high efficiency of activity due to K-stationarity.

In this way the section has shown that K-stationary environments exists "almost everywhere" which means that K-stationarity is a very wide-spread phenomenon. Therefore, it is reasonable to take K-stationarity as the base for the following consideration of how to use and develop algorithms that form a polytrapezium.

Chapter 5
PRODUCTION AND USE OF ALGORITHMS IN A K-STATIONARY ENVIRONMENT

5.1 Providing an algorithm to solve the problem z_n in a K-stationary environment

If an environment is K-stationary, i.e. it does not raise problems from beyond K known classes for rather a long period, it allows preparing K appropriate algorithms in advance instead of developing heuristically a new algorithm for every coming problem. Therewith a switch between problem classes causes a change of the algorithm, whereas a switch between problems of the same class alters only the values of the algorithm arguments.

It is this possibility of always staying within the boundaries of a fixed collection of beforemade algorithms that makes the specificity of the algorithmic support for solving problems from Z under the K-stationary conditions. As for the advantages of using ready algorithms and not designing them *ad hoc* for every coming problem, they are quite obvious. Here we are pointing out the most essential ones.

1. Training psychology and everyone's individual experience show that it takes *far less power, time, ingenuity*, etc. to solve a problem by means of a familiar method rather than do it from the very beginning. The heuristic approach treats the process of solving problems as if each problem were handled for the first time. Since a solver's heuristic talent is limited, in Z there can appear problems which find *no solution* if treated heuristically. This observation is crucial because in some problem domains a failed search for a solution can destroy the very system or its user.

2. In reference to the mechanized solving, the heuristic approach requires a machine solver intellect (that is its knowledge and its capacity of associations, reasoning, discoveries, etc.) to be a priori powerful enough as to solve any possible problem, even the most difficult one. The experience of machine problem solvers and theorem provers (see for example, [3, 4]) indicates that the "intellectual power" of those systems cannot be even distantly compared with that of a human expert. What is more, this situation is sure to remain the same in the near future. However, if a ready

algorithm is selected among the $K < \infty$ algorithms of the collection A, *there are no restrictions on the problem complexity, except those inherited from the man.* In fact, each new type problem can be redirected for a highly competent human expert to invent a solution algorithm. His work being finished, the ready algorithm just will be fed into the computer.

3. The fact that K-stationarity permits utilizing beforemade algorithms to solve any problem from Z, suggests quite an obvious way of developing an *automatic problem solver.* This way demands two things automated:

   (a) the problem statement driven selection of a proper algorithm among K available ones;

   (b) the problem statement driven evaluation of its arguments.

   In Section 5.4 we shall consider the possibilities of implementing this automation.

Besides the properties of stationary environments allow using beforemade algorithms, they considerably facilitate their development. It will be discussed in the next section.

5.2 Using the environment stationarity to produce algorithms of the set *A*

If some OPT is realized on the computer, the term "OPT realizing algorithm" naturally denotes a software system that implements the sequence of operations of the OPT tail. The previous section asserted that inventing algorithms from the set A was a highly competent expert's prerogative. This comes in contradiction with the wellknown programming automation paradigm that expects a computer to design a problem solution program independently, proceeding from the problem initial premises and data about the sought-for result.

In our opinion, this orientation of the programming automation meets a user's practical interests not quite correctly. If one studies experts' activities in various application areas and discusses those activities with them, he will discover the following.

A user who is an expert in some applied field really wants to be emancipated from the obligation to know and follow accurately the present-day programming languages with their sophisticated syntax and unnatural lexicon, to learn all the details of operating systems.

But he declines to give up inventing a problem solution *idea*, searching for a pipe-wretch approach. Quite the reverse, it is these things that he usually considers as his professional destiny and gets his creative satisfaction from.

Thus, as for psychology, the automatic production of algorithms is badly grounded in case of real nontrivial problems. In the implementation aspect it is not grounded either, because formulating a problem (composing the totality of its initial premises) and searching for a solution are usually interlaced and come "hand in glove" in real life. For example, one can hardly estimate whether the set of problem initial premises is complete, until he has a clear solution method. That is likely the reason for why a real automatic problem solver has not been created yet. Besides, in practical situations there appear extraordinary difficulties connected with the combinatorial nature of the theorem machine proving methods that support most programming automation projects. For instance, the Robinson resolvent method [4] offers either an intolerably huge exhaustive search or an intolerably high failure probability due to truncating the exhaustive search tree.

Thus, there is no use automatically generating new solution algorithms for serious practical problems. Yet, a certain degree of the object stationarity gives the opportunity of a profitable labor division between the object domain human expert and the computer. Then the expert would carry out only creative pieces of work thus forming a problem solution method and the computer would shape that method as a program by means of a dialogue with the expert in the expert's professional natural language.

Let us prove that the said labor division opportunity exists for real in case of a certain kind of environment stationarity.

In fact, let there be a couple "author of the method — executor of the method realizing program". The author of the method ("the author" below) is supposed to be a highly competent person. As for the program executor ("the executor" below), our task is to show that if the environment is stationary, this part can be carried out by a computer as well.

Let a problem z_n come from the environment and have no ready algorithm yet. In terms of our model, the situation acquires the following interpretation. The problem coming means that a single address to Q is necessary. The initial premises of the problem z_n and a description of its sought-for result establish an OPT. To solve the problem z_n is to construct its OPT tail.

This is the couple "author—executor" who must do it. Therewith the following demand is imposed on the construction procedure:

Demand D5.1 *The author should carry out those steps of the procedure which want new solutions to be invented. The executor gets a step only if this step already has a realizing method.*

Apparently, this demand reflects the above discussed reason for involving the author—executor couple into the process of creating algorithms as well as the labour division between them.

Generally, the participants of the couple interact as following: a problem z_n being received, the author invents an approach to solve it and describes the solution in some convenient language: formal, graphic, natural or their combination. The description being ready, the executor converts it into a computer-implementable calculating program.

Let us specify some aspects of that interaction.

Whatever form and language the author describes the invented approach in, within the boundaries of our model the description in its essence can be nothing but a totality of descriptions of tail elements. Those elements can be of two types: (a) operations themselves (active and test ones); (b) data on their respective locations and interconnections in the polytrapezium. It is natural to anticipate that each element of the tail finds a semantically complete part of the author's description, i.e. a part which contains all the author has said about a single element of the tail. Those semantically integral parts of the description will be termed fragments.

However, the content of description fragments depends not only on the essence of the algorithm invented by the author but also on the executor's knowledge level. In fact, Demand D5.1 says the executor can handle only *ready knowledge* and different executors may possess different generalization levels of that knowledge. The higher is the executor's level, the lower is the average "refining" of the description he needs and the higher is the polytrapezium levels that hold tail elements he is familiar with. We call a tail element familiar if the executor has ready knowledge and skills to translate it into appropriate program blocks. The author, who is interested in the extreme laconicism and realizes the executor's knowledge, will construct the description out of fragments corresponding to the tail highest elements familiar to the executor. For example, if the executor is competent enough as to be familiar with the matrix calculations, the author can limit the description by a fragment like "Now invert the matrix Y", the proper OPT lying rather high in the polytrapezium. But for a less competent executor the author has to describe the OPT trapezium bottom base that is to explain in every detail the sequence of low-level operations to perform the matrix inversion.

Another interesting remark is that the *agreement* mentioned in Sections 3.2 and 3.4 takes place here between the author and the executor. That agreement allows the author to consider any fragment of the description as an "executable operation": for the author each fragment is an ultimate product and no further tail-like explanations are required *from him.* As for the executor, the same fragment always acts as a "declarable operation": he treats an executable operation as a physical process of computer calculations, whereas the author's description fragment cannot be of this sort by its very nature because it is presented symbolically and not in the form of a physical process.

From the said it follows that actions of the couple "author—executor" fall into the scheme of the problem-to-subproblems reduction. The author expresses a problem solution as a group of subproblems stated by the description fragments and the executor provides solutions for those subproblems.

Let ζ_n designate a subproblem (just a problem below) of translating the next (n-th) fragment of the author's description into a program block, and let $\mathcal{Z}$ symbolize the set of all problems the executor solves for all description fragments of all problems from Z ($\mathcal{N}$ letters a cardinality of the set $\mathcal{Z}$). It is clear that the number $\mathcal{N}$ of fragments can be very great for even a single problem z_n. And if the author deals with an arbitrary number N of problems z_n, it is natural to consider the cardinality $\mathcal{N}$ of the set $\mathcal{Z}$ of fragments (and therefore of problems ζ_n) unlimited:

$$\mathcal{N} \to \infty$$

Leaving the level of problems z_n for the level of problems ζ_n, we can set ourselves at the question of environment stationarity for the problems ζ_n, i.e. for the set $\mathcal{Z}$. Let us assume that the environment generating problems ζ_n, is Ξ-stationary. As we remember, it means by definition that the set $\mathcal{Z}$ is subdividable into a finite number Ξ of classes so that problems from the same class can be solved by means of only one algorithm with variable arguments. If so, it is enough to have a collection of Ξ algorithms to solve all the problems from $\mathcal{Z}$.

And from the finiteness of Ξ it follows that all algorithms of the collection can be prepared in advance and used by the executor as ready-to-use. Thus, Demand D5.1 will be satisfied.

Therefore solving a problem ζ_n in a Ξ-stationary environment, one may act as if he were solving a problem z_n in a K-stationary environment, which includes the selection of one proper algorithm among Ξ available and the proper evaluation of its arguments.

Now there are two articles for a complete automation: 1) solving problems from Z in a K-stationary environment and 2) the executor's activity when the author—executor couple is forming algorithms in a Ξ-stationary environment. The feasibility of this automation depends on the answer to the following question. Can the two mentioned actions, i.e. selecting a proper algorithm and evaluating its arguments, be executed automatically in environments of this type? We shall try to answer this question in Section 5.4. And in the next section we shall consider the urgent and methodologically important question of the stationarity "strength".

5.3 Weak and strong stationarity of environment

In this section we shall pay attention to relative strengths of environment stationarities. A scale of the stationarity strength can be introduced just as topology strength scales exist for comparable topologies. Namely, one of two types of stationarity will be considered stronger if its existence tugs the existence of the other. In the present case, from the finiteness of the number K of algorithms in the collection A and the finiteness of their lengths it follows that the number and lengths of all possible polytrapezium tails are finite too, i.e. Ξ-stationarity follows from K-stationarity. The reverse would be false. In fact, with no limits on lengths of constructed algorithms, a finite number of polytrapezium elements does not ensure the finiteness of the number of algorithms formed out of them.

Constructively, the introduced notion of stationarity strength results in that the stronger is the stationarity, the larger are program blocks that form an appropriate collection of algorithms but the less universal is the algorithmic set that can be made out of them. For example, the present software tools for statistic data processing include fairly large program blocks, but those tools help to develop algorithms for environments with only statistic problems. At the same time, algorithms like these can be designed by means of any universal programming language (C, Pascal, PL/1 and so on) but it takes much more efforts. The successful use of high-level programming in universal languages proves that the environment stationarity with respect to the translators of those languages takes place almost everywhere, but this stationarity is considerably weaker than the stationarity stipulating the use of special tools.

It should be thought that though the weakest but inevitably existing stationarity is inherent in natural language just like in any communications symbolic system in general. The matter is that any symbolic, in particular natural-language, fragment implies a foreknown interpretation. The lowest strength of natural language stationarity is a natural tribute for its universality which allows discussing any problem in any domain. But as soon as even a slight specialization appears and even subtle object and problem domains emerge, the general use tries to exploit the resulting stronger stationarity to operate larger blocks, introducing new words and terms into the language to facilitate operating those blocks.

The adduced reasons give a chance to what we named in [51] "programming humanization". We mean an environment which is stationary enough to rely on a set of few in number and rather large blocks, with the author making descriptions in natural language. The computer being equipped with some means to convert a natural language description fragment into an appropriate program block or an interblock link and to determine argument values, the "programming humanization" will be implemented. It would make a human expert free of all his duties except for inventing an algorithm idea and formulating its structure in natural language. Here we are coming up to the problem of computer understanding of natural language addresses, which will be discussed later. At the present moment we must return to the question raised in Sections 5.1 and 5.2. That is the automatic selection of an algorithm among the available set and the evaluation of its arguments.

5.4 The pattern recognition problem as the core of activity in a stationary environment

As we could see in Sections 5.1 and 5.2, an environment stationarity would be of more utility if a proper algorithm were selected and its arguments were evaluated automatically for any problem z_n or ζ_n. Let us probe into this. For definiteness sake, we shall consider problems z_n in a K-stationary environment.

When a subject receives a problem sequence Z from the environment and relates each of these problems to a solution algorithm from A, he obviously *maps* the set Z of cardinality N onto the set A of cardinality K:

$$Z \mapsto A\,. \tag{5.1}$$

And an algorithmic implementation of this mapping under conditions Eqs. (4.4) and (4.5) (i.e. in a K-stationary environment) is the *pattern recognition problem* by definition.

With a specific nature of the sets shown in Eq. (5.1) this fact can be particularized.

Taking into account that in a K-stationary environment the set A consists of K beforemade algorithms for problems of all the K plausible types, we must state the following. The subject S who "holds" the algorithms, can react to any problem from the sequence Z, say to the problem z_n, in the only way. This is to choose the algorithm adequate the problem z_n (this algorithm always exists and is unique by force of the K-stationarity) and to launch it.

As for a well-grounded choice of the algorithm adequate to the received problem z_n, S has the only way as well. He has to compare the problem wording (the totality of the initial premises) with possible wordings of the problems from each of K classes and to choose the algorithm of the class (let it be the k-th class) that has the maximal and sufficient likeness in terms of the mentioned comparison. Apparently, this is also nothing other than solving the pattern recognition problem.

Thus K-stationary environments lead us to the following paradox-like conclusion: to solve a problem z_n one should not solve the problem z_n at all. Instead, in every case (with $\forall n$) it is necessary to solve *the only problem* of figuring out the index k of the z_n-adequate algorithm from A by means of the problem z_n wording. It means solving the pattern recognition problem. The index k being ascertained, the argument set of the k-th algorithm comes openly to surface and it brings us to the second part of the pattern recognition problem, which is the evaluation of the parameters of the problem z_n within its (the k-th) class. In other words, it is an extraction of values of the algorithm arguments from the wording of z_n (and from some other sources, see below). Thereafter the algorithm with the evaluated arguments is ready to be launched, which necessarily solves the problem z_n.

So, an environment being K-stationary means that the infinite set Z can be mapped onto the bounded set A without losses.

This kind of correspondence plays a crucial part in mathematics: the entire continuous mathematics and calculus are based on the compact continuum representability as a finite ε-net. This analogy illustrates the significance of the environment K-stationarity in solving problems from sets Z.

In this connection we would like to mention one very interesting work [5]. Neither advancing nor formulating general principles, the author constructs an automatic solver for a finite number of classes of combinatorial problems (like the problem about a commercial traveller, the transporting problem, painting a graph, making up a train time-table and so on). The solver functions as follows. A computer is equipped in advance with a set of programs for solving problems of the mentioned classes. The set is created by the author who is a highly competent mathematician. A high level formal language (ALICE) is designed to feed problems of those classes into the computer. There is a program to recognize the class of a proposed problem (and correspondingly, the necessary solution program) by its wording in that language. From the same source the program extracts values of the solution program arguments. The author reports that the system solves problems much more effectively and competently than if solution programs were written *ad hoc* by an average mathematician. No wonder, because the level of the system programs corresponds to the author's high competence.

As we can see, an extraordinarily effective (though spontaneous and connected with the sole FPD) use of K-stationarity takes place here. At least partially it illustrates its powerful potentiality considered in Section 5.1.

We dare say once more: it is very important that the search for an algorithm and the evaluation of algorithm arguments appear to be pattern recognition problems. And the above pointed fundamental phenomenon is not the only reason for that. Another reason is that the pattern recognition possesses and suggests very efficient constructive concepts, the concept of training set among them. We shall consider those concepts in one of the following chapters. And in the next chapter we shall continue considering the author and executor's joint activity. In particular, we shall set focus on a dialogue between them.

Chapter 6
SUBJECT, DIALOGUE, NATURAL LANGUAGE

6.1 The subject's structure and how a dialogue arises

In Chapters 1–4 the subject S was tacitly presumed to be unique and integral, in a way. That presumption allowed us to clarify the "subject—object" interaction and helped to investigate it. However, in Chapter 5 we discovered that activities during the time period between setting a problem and launching its calculating program might involve two participants. They are the author and the executor of the problem solution, and at least a one-way dialogue takes place between them, where the author lets the executor know of the solution he developed.

This "bifurcation" of the subject occurs probably not only in the situations when his activity results in a computer program. It is natural to touch on the general case, when S appears to be compound in any kind of activity. Here we are going to consider the simplest variant of a compound S, namely, his incorporating a couple "goal manager—task executor".

The "goal—means" duality suggests that up to now the subject S model has been rather arbitrarily combining two quite different functions: formulating a goal (drawing up a task for a transition) and executing operations to reach this goal (fulfilling the task and accomplishing the transition). In this aspect the subject's setting a task to himself and fulfilling it look rather like a particular case. The general case will distribute the mentioned functions among two (and more) "sub-subjects", either specializing in his own function. With two sub-subjects, we shall designate the goal manager as S_G and the task executor as S_A. Of course, the goal—means duality cannot help affecting our sub-subjects, thus provoking a duality of their roles. In fact, on getting a task from S_G a sub-subject turns out to be S_A with respect to this S_G. Then he can decompose the task into a number of subtasks to his subordinates, thus acting as S'_G with respect to them.

The methodological aspect of S's division into S_G and S_A displays itself in a *dialogue* which arises between S_G and S_A. This fact is crucial for the considered part of the subject's activity. The practical significance of this division is that it characterizes the relations between the parties in many cases of the problem solving activity and, in particular, in a *man-computer* system.

Suppose there is an environment that raises problems to be solved via a dialogue between S_G and S_A. A dialogue of this kind has a very important feature: the texts of its addresses have special properties that reflect the stationarity degree of the environment. Let us be more specific about this. We have been considering the environment K-stationarity as a property of solutions of problems z_n from the sequence Z. But in the $S_G \leftrightarrow S_A$ dialogue each (say the n-th) S_G's address to S_A, if interpreted as a "single address" (Section 4.1), represents a problem z_n. Therefore, the environment K-stationarity can be considered as a property of *reactions* to a sequence of addresses. Thus, within the process of solving problems via a dialogue, the notions "environment producing problems" and "environment producing reactions to S_G's addresses" may be not distinguished. This observation is helpful when one studies an environment and its problems indirectly, by studying the texts of the $S_G \leftrightarrow S_A$ dialogue. In particular, we shall see a situation of this sort in Chapter 14, where we shall be considering lengthy texts of man-to-man interaction and where the notion "environment of reactions to the author's texts" will be introduced.

Hence S's division into S_G and S_A calls for an analysis of their interaction. If S_A is a computer or computer system, a *formal* analysis becomes all the more necessary.

S_G and S_A can communicate by various means: fixed addressing formats, formal languages, etc. Among those means there may be natural language (NL). This case seems to be especially important and interesting. The reasons for this statement are known [51]; we shall briefly refresh them in the next section.

6.2 A natural language dialogue with the computer

Let us indicate the fundamental reasons for our special interest in the NL man-to-computer dialogue.

1. To use computers effectively and competently, one should be gifted in mathematics, in discrete mathematics better. Of course, people who lack such a gift, for example those of nonmathematical mentality, can be taught formal and format means of computer communication. But the experience proves that this knowledge remains alien to them: they acquire it reluctantly and use it with uncertainty and allow it to evaporate from their memory on any occasion, just like schoolboys do with an unfavoured subject, the exam being passed. If nothing is done to meet those people halfway and make the computer understand their professional natural language, the computerized sphere will loose a lot of important branches: medicine, design, law, criminology, agricultural technology, pedagogy, etc.

2. Even people of scientific mentality (engineers, designers, technologists, etc.), who are potentially capable of addressing the computer in the formal manner, usually hate to do it. They consider computer skills accessory with respect to their main professional knowledge and, besides, hard to

acquire. School computer classes can be very helpful but cannot substitute the computer NL addressing facilities: natural language, once learned in childhood, can be used during the whole life in any field of activity, whereas the computer communication formats differ from one branch to another; they grow more and more enhanced and sometimes even give way to new ones.

3. Those who deal with computers know how format addressing skills dwindle in one's memory if one breaks up his work for a more or less long period, e.g. for a year. This never happens to NL: this knowledge is steady and used regularly.

It seems that the above arguments, though not exhaustive, make sufficient grounds for our primary interest in NL dialogues.

If we consider an NL dialogue between the man and the computer, i.e. a dialogue of asymmetrical participants, the orientation of our interest in such a dialogue should be more specified. We should take into account that the man-to-computer addressing needs natural language to a much greater extent than the backward process. This asymmetry is of psychological nature. It is stipulated by the fact that a human being comprehends information in an unfamiliar form (for example formative computer data) much more readily than produces information in such a form himself; just recall studying a foreign language. If we also take into account the great difference between the technological patterns of information production and perception (what is a consequence of the fundamental difference between the active and passive bases), we shall come to the conclusion that there is no point in connecting these two cases and developing them jointly. Therefore we should pay predominant attention to that part of the dialogue where the man addresses the computer, i.e. to the problem of *computer natural language understanding.*

This problem wants another refinement. Potential users, people of non-computer professions, usually oppose any attempts to thrust on them various versions of "almost natural" or "truncated natural" language as a means of computer addressing. They do it on every excuse, preferring sometimes even a completely "unnatural", i.e. formal language. The origin of this phenomenon is clear: restrictions imposed on the "almost natural" language grammar (for example, on plausible case forms or syntactic constructions), run counter the very strong habit of everyday free and easy natural language use. Therefore, the psychological burden of memorizing and applying the mentioned restrictions appears even harder than that of mastering a format addressing system which at least does not hurt one's habits.

Therefore, if computer addressing is associated with NL then this NL must be a language with *no exterior restrictions*; there must be *no instructions* on how a user should arrange his texts and how he should not.

Of course, it does not mean that this absence of restrictions will immediately make the entire NL infiltrate into the work of a man-computer system. When inside his professional environment, a person unconsciously sets for himself some extremely hard topical restrictions which fact is used in our further consideration (as well as in publications by some other authors, see [6], for example).

Thus, it is expedient to consider *the problem of computer understanding of free and easy NL texts* as the main problem in the $S_G \leftrightarrow S_A$ dialogue implementation. However, we can particularize this problem by saying that the first three parts of this book will deal not with any NL texts, but with relatively short addresses made up of one or several sentences. Such addresses are typical of NL free and easy *operative business dialogues*, and especially man-to-computer dialogues.

It is natural to begin discussing the problem of man-to-computer NL dialogues with a review of its present state. We shall do this in the next section.

6.3 The present state of the man-to-computer NL dialogue problem

The NL understanding problem, i.e. the problem of interpreting some sense enclosed in an NL text, is commonly thought an issue of conventional, classical linguistics. No doubt, this linguistics is an important and profound scientific branch.

However, as for computer NL understanding systems, conventional linguistics has got "stuck": no really good commercial system of the kind has been developed on its base so far. No system can admit of the complete naturalness and freedom of input texts, i.e. the complete absence of any restrictions on their structures, with the correct and full sense interpretation highly guaranteed. On top of this, those systems are too bulky and complex, they are usually connected with excessive computational resources [7].

This situation induces a feeling that the existing approach to the computer NL understanding problem is inadequate. It seems necessary to analyze how this inadequacy arises and manifests itself, and then, if possible, propose and substantiate some ways of neutralizing it.

It is clear that a deeper study of NL and linguistic psychology can scarcely bring any success to the investigation: we are unlikely to go deeper than the existing linguistics and linguistic behavior psychology. It is no use probing into pure computer science either: if this way could give an answer to our question we would already have got it.

Apparently, the roots of the mentioned inadequacy should be sought via ascertaining fundamental regularities of the man-to-computer natural language interaction. The computer is a precise calculating tool, whereas NL in people's use is an extremely flexible and fuzzy informational channel. It is an intersection of these specificities that can explain the failures of conventional linguistics and suggest successful approaches to the man-to-computer NL communication problem. In the next section we shall consider some phenomena existing due to the pointed "intersection of specificities".

6.4 Specificity of NL interaction in a man-to-computer operative dialogue

Even at the present stage of our investigation one cannot help seeing some fundamental manifestations of the NL man-to-computer interaction specificity in an operative business dialogue. We mean the following three manifestations.

1. The distinct asymmetry between the man and computer in their capability of grasping and interpreting all nuances and aspects of sense an NL dialogue address conveys. In particular, the computer cannot grasp any emotional, ethic, aesthetic sense nuances that the man grasps and interprets easily without even noticing that. This phenomenon will be considered in detail in Section 8.4.

2. Though there are no formal restrictions on the contents and forms of NL addresses, the man takes into account (in part consciously and in part unconsciously) that his interlocutor is a "cold-blood machine". He can not eliminate unnecessary emotional and similar aspects from his text (because of the firm skills of free man-to-man NL interaction), but his allowances for the interlocutor's "computerness" leave their imprint on the texts of his addresses. This fact is crucial for the choice of an approach to the analysis of NL texts of operative business dialogue addresses. We shall consider this in Section 8.3 and further.

3. A relatively short length of operative dialogue addresses and the necessity of the interlocutor's reaction to each address establish a peculiar rhythm of the execution of reactions. This allows us to introduce and use the notions "the starting moment" and "the finishing moment" of a reaction to the current address. Free man-to-man communication with lengthy NL texts usually lacks such timing of reactions: different components of reactions may have different duration, may start and finish at different moments. This peculiarity is very serious, and we shall have to take it into account in our further investigation, in particular in Section 14.3 where it will be put into the basis of the notions "synchronism" and "asynchronism" of reaction components.

The described differences (as well as some others, see below) in the properties of NL used in man-to-computer or man-to-man communication are so dramatic and deep that often it is more convenient to speak about *two different languages*: the language of usual man-to-man communication and the "language of operative business dialogue addresses".

In the next chapter we shall see that the specific properties of the latter language are important not only in the philosophical and theoretical aspects. They also play a decisive practical role. We shall begin the second part of the book with this consideration.

Part II

COMPUTER UNDERSTANDING OF NL TEXTS IN CONVENTIONAL LINGUISTICS

Chapter 7
POSSIBILITIES TO USE NL IN A MAN-TO-COMPUTER DIALOGUE

7.1 On setting the problem

Let S_A be a computer and let there be a dialogue between S_G and S_A who are solving a problem z_n. Considering the dialogue we shall proceed from the following assumptions:

(a) we shall always associate the problem solution development with S_G and the solution realization with S_A;

(b) we shall think that S_G is always able to find a correct method to solve any received problem;

(c) S_G lets S_A know of his idea how to solve z_n by means of a dialogue.

Let us specify the notion "address language" mentioned in Section 6.4. We shall call S_G and S_A "parties to a dialogue". The parties exchange information. When one of the parties stops his information transmission and gives way to the other party, an event like this is called a party alternation act. A dialogue is considered to consist of addresses. An *address* is a data sequence that one of the parties gives between two successive party alternation acts. We shall designate an address by t. The language, a party uses to form its dialogue addresses, is called the *"address language"* of this party. In particular, any NL can work as an address language. Besides the notion "address language" clarifies the presented ideas, it is fundamental for the considered problem, as we shall prove below.

Note that assumption (b) itself does not guarantee a successful solution of any received problem. In addition to this, S_A must correctly understand all addresses of S_G (and vice versa) in the process of their dialogue .

According to the second part of assumption (a) the dialogue results in a sequence of operations for S_A to solve the problem z_n. This sequence was named a problem solution algorithm. Let the symbol $f_k(a^{(n)})$ denote it. Here f_k stands for the algorithm body, and $a^{(n)}$ expresses the vector of its arguments. The algorithm $f_k(a^{(n)})$ is said to be fixed if its body f_k is invariable. Now the idea of one-type problems (Section 4.2) can be specified: two problems z_n and $z_{n'}$ are of the same type if their solution algorithms are $f_k(a^{(n)})$ and $f_k(a^{(n')})$ respectively, i.e. if they have the same body and differ only in the values of the arguments.

Let T_G and T_A designate the sets of all possible (in the given couple S_G — S_A) addresses by S_G and S_A respectively.

Any dialogue address t provokes some reaction of the interlocutor. Therefore, it objectively represents a task for this reaction in the address language. But the author of t would not be able to set any task for the reaction if he had not a slightest a priori idea of what he was expecting back, i.e. a description of the desired reaction. A certain "reaction language" can help to describe desired reactions; we shall consider it in Chapter 12. We designate a desired reaction description in this language as r. R_G stands for the set of all descriptions which S_G can use for expected reactions; R_A designates the same set of S_A.

As for S_A's reactions to S_G's addresses, S_A has to use an algorithmic module to produce a reaction. Just as a whole algorithm $f_k(a^{(n)})$, this module is given as its module body and a vector of its arguments. We shall refer to the module body as the *body of the reaction r*. A fixed module can be defined just as it was done for a whole algorithm above. Let us assume that all modules of an algorithm are fixed if the algorithm is fixed itself.

Let's consider the mapping

$$T_G \mapsto R_G \,. \tag{7.1}$$

We shall call S_G's address language *uniexpressive*[†] if the mapping Eq. (7.1) is univalent, i.e. if any address $\forall t \in T_G$ can be caused by *the only* desired reaction $r \in R_G$. The body of r, described in the reaction language, will be called "the meaning that S_G ascribes to his address t" or, briefly, *the meaning of the address t*. From this definition it follows that two reactions of the same body ascribe *the same meaning* to the address t.

We shall call S_G's address language *simply non-uniexpressive* if $\exists\{\hat{t}\} \subset T_G$, $\{\hat{t}\} \neq \emptyset$ such that each address $t \in \{\hat{t}\}$ is mapped by Eq. (7.1) onto *more than one* descriptions of different bodies of reactions from R_G. It means that each address from $\{\hat{t}\}$ has more than one meaning and a finite probability $\hat{P}$ exists:

$$\hat{P}(\forall i:\ t_i \in \{\hat{t}\}\,) > 0 \,.$$

Finally, we shall call S_G's address language *absolutely non-uniexpressive* if *each* address from T_G has more than one meaning. It is easy to write appropriate definitions for S_A's address language too.

In the following sections the introduced notions will help us to reveal a few facts concerning the man-to-computer NL dialogue.

[†]This clumsy term calls for an explanation. The Russian word "однозначный" (*odnoznachnyj*) can be translated in many ways: "univalent", "unique", "one-valued", "monosemantic", "unambigous", etc. The main concern was to underline the linguistic aspect of the term but to follow the mathematical context. Our attempt resulted in the word "uniexpressive" that actually means "having one meaning".

7.2 Theorem on the absolute non-uniexpressiveness of NL addresses

In this section we shall prove that free and easy NL is the worst possible address language, because it displays the worst properties in terms of uniexpressiveness. Namely, we shall prove that NL is an absolutely non-uniexpressive language.

Let us start with two rather obvious postulates P7.1 and P7.2.
We shall use the symbol $\{\mu\}^*$ for a set of environments which comprises more than one environment. The symbol μ_m will designate a separate environment considered as the m-th element of the set $\{\mu\}^*$. As for the address t in the case of NL, it can be nothing other than a separate sentence or a sequence of several successive sentences. For our purposes it is enough to consider it as an arbitrary NL sentence of more than one significant word.

So, let us take an NL sentence t. The subset of all environments that contain t in their NL common use will be called "the environment bundle for the sentence t" and designated as $\{\mu^{(t)}\}$.

With reference to the environment bundle, the following postulate can be suggested:

Postulate P7.1 *For any t of more than one significant word, the bundle $\{\mu^{(t)}\}$ contains more than one environment.*

This phenomenon has many reasons. In particular, one of them is the difference between groups of antecedents for the same parts of a sentence in different environments. For example, the phrase "About 200 cisterns were dispatched yesterday" can occur either in the environment of a railway vehicle factory, or in the environment of a dairy farm, or in the environment "resolving a traffic jam", or even in the environment of a school lesson when a mathematical problem is being solved. The second reason for the phenomenon in question is the logical stress mobility, the third one is the homonimy and the polysemy and so on.

Let us now consider the meaning ascribed by S_G to an NL address t. We have to remind that within the framework of our conceptions this meaning is understood as a description of the expected reaction in the reaction language of a given environment. It is clear that any reaction description can be nothing but a structure made up of elements from some bounded totality. Those elements are symbols of the reaction language alphabet of the given environment. Any letter of this alphabet can take on one of at least two values: "Yes" or "No" (1 or 0) in dependence of whether it is used in the reaction description or not. Of course, elements of the alphabet can have continuous or discrete multi-value scales.

Let us consider the environment bundle $\{\mu^{(t)}\}$ of some sentence t and the meanings that S_G can ascribe to the sentence in all the environments of the bundle. $\{\sigma^{(t)}\}$ will designate the union of the reaction language alphabets of all the environments. Let us arrange this set in some way and denote its u-th element as σ_u. If the element σ_u has several gradations, we shall designate its l-th gradation as σ_{ul}. It would be natural to call the object σ_{ul} something like "the l-th modification of the u-th element". However, for the sake of brevity, we shall transfer onto this object just the name "element", considering the set $\{\sigma^{(t)}\}$ as made up of such elements.

Let $\{\sigma_{ul}^{(t)}\}_m$ denote the set of all the elements σ_{ul} that form the meaning ascribed to the sentence t by an average language speaker in the environment $\mu_m \in \{\mu^{(t)}\}$. Our consideration will not be hurt if we assume that there is a one-to-one correspondence between this meaning and the set $\{\sigma_{ul}^{(t)}\}_m$. If the sets $\{\sigma_{ul}^{(t)}\}_m$ and $\{\sigma_{ul}^{(t')}\}_m$ match, this idealization suggests thinking of the meanings ascribed to the sentences t and t' as equal. On the contrary, a mismatch of the said sets will be interpreted as a mismatch of meanings.

Now the introduced designations will help us to give definitions for identical, different and synonymous sentences.

We shall call sentences t and t' *identical* ($t = t'$) if they have the same meaning in the NL use of any environment from the bundle, that is

$$\forall\, \mu_m \in \{\mu^{(t)}\}: \quad \{\sigma_{ul}^{(t)}\}_m \;=\; \{\sigma_{ul}^{(t')}\}_m\,.$$

Strictly speaking, the present interpretation requires identical sentences to match completely. Usually sentences can be considered practically identical if they can be converted to each other via a transformation from some class of syntactical transformations (the so called identity transformations). As a rough approximation, the following sentences are identical: "Walking along the street he did not turn back" and "He did not turn back, walking along the street".

We shall call sentences t and t' *different* ($t \neq t'$) if in the bundle there is at least one environment, where these sentences have different meanings, that is

$$\exists\, \mu_m \in \{\mu^{(t)}\}: \quad \{\sigma_{ul}^{(t)}\}_m \;\neq\; \{\sigma_{ul}^{(t')}\}_m\,.$$

If sentences t and t' in an environment μ_m comply with

$$\{\sigma_{ul}^{(t)}\}_m \neq \{\sigma_{ul}^{(t')}\}_m\,,$$

they are called *non-synonymous* in the environment μ_m ($t \not\sim t'$). Since the non-synonymy is defined here as a mismatch of the sets of the meaning elements of the sentences t and t', we can generalize that definition for the case when the sentences t and t' are considered in different environments:

$$\{\sigma_{ul}^{(t)}\}_m \;\neq\; \{\sigma_{ul}^{(t')}\}_{m'}\,. \tag{7.2}$$

It only requires a new, possibly non-stationary environment $\mu_{mm'} = \mu_m \cup \mu_{m'}$.

Unlike the non-synonymy, the synonymy of sentences t and t' can be considered only within the same environment.

Namely, we shall call sentences t and t' *synonymous in an environment* ($t \sim t'$) if they have identical meanings in the NL use of this environment, and in the bundle there is at least one environment where t and t' are non-synonymous (i.e. the notion of synonymy concerns only different sentences):

$$\exists\, \mu_m, \mu_{m'} \in \{\mu^{(t)}\} : \quad \left\{ \begin{array}{lcl} \{\sigma_{ul}^{(t)}\}_m & = & \{\sigma_{ul}^{(t')}\}_m \\ \{\sigma_{ul}^{(t)}\}_{m'} & \neq & \{\sigma_{ul}^{(t')}\}_{m'} \end{array} \right. .$$

The notion of synonymy/non-synonymy allows us to formulate postulate P7.2, which can hardly evoke any doubts, because it is corroborated by everyone's language experience.

Postulate P7.2 *Any sentence t used in some environment has in this environment no less than one sentence synonymous to t and no less than one sentence non-synonymous to t.*

Now we can formulate the following statement:

Theorem 7.1 *Free and easy NL as S_G's address language is* absolutely non-uniexpressive.

Proof: Let us take an NL sentence t and its environment bundle $\{\mu^{(t)}\}$ and an environment $\mu_m \in \{\mu^{(t)}\}$. Let the meaning of t in the environment μ_m be $\{\sigma_{ul}^{(t)}\}_m$.

First we are going to prove that the relation between $\{\sigma_{ul}^{(t)}\}_m$ and $\{\sigma^{(t)}\}$ is a strict inclusion. In fact, due to P7.2, $t' \not\sim t$ can be found in μ_m, and it means that $\{\sigma_{ul}^{(t')}\}_m \neq \{\sigma_{ul}^{(t)}\}_m$. Then in the union $\{\sigma_{ul}^{(t')}\}_m \cup \{\sigma_{ul}^{(t)}\}_m$ there is at least one element σ_{ul}, that does not belong to *either* $\{\sigma_{ul}^{(t')}\}_m$ *or* $\{\sigma_{ul}^{(t)}\}_m$. For definiteness sake, suppose

$$\sigma_{ul} \notin \{\sigma_{ul}^{(t)}\}_m \,. \tag{7.3}$$

At the same time, by the definition of $\{\sigma^{(t)}\}$,

$$\sigma_{ul} \;\in\; \{\sigma^{(t)}\}\,, \tag{7.4}$$

$$\{\sigma_{ul}^{(t)}\}_m \;\subseteq\; \{\sigma^{(t)}\}\,. \tag{7.5}$$

Comparing Eqs. (7.3), (7.4) and (7.5) we obtain that

$$\{\sigma_{ul}^{(t)}\}_m \subset \{\sigma^{(t)}\}\,, \tag{7.6}$$

which is just what was to be proved on this stage.

And now the main statement of Theorem 7.1. We shall form a difference set designated as $\{\sigma_{ul}^{(t)}\}_{-m}$:

$$\{\sigma_{ul}^{(t)}\}_{-m} = \{\sigma^{(t)}\} \setminus \{\sigma_{ul}^{(t)}\}_m \,. \tag{7.7}$$

According to Eqs. (7.6) and (7.7), $\{\sigma_{ul}^{(t)}\}_{-m} \neq \emptyset$. Let us take an element $\sigma_{ul} \in \{\sigma_{ul}^{(t)}\}_{-m}$ and search the bundle $\{\mu^{(t)}\}$ for an environment μ_q such that

$\sigma_{ul} \in \{\sigma_{ul}^{(t)}\}_q$. This environment μ_q exists by virtue of P7.1 and because Eq. (7.7) makes $\{\sigma_{ul}^{(t)}\}_{-m}$ a part of $\{\sigma^{(t)}\}$, which is the union of the sets $\{\sigma_{ul}^{(t)}\}_m$ for all m of the bundle.

According to postulate P7.2, from $\mu_q \in \{\mu^{(t)}\}$ it follows that in the environment μ_q there is a sentence t'' synonymous to t. From the synonymy of t'' and t it follows by definition that

$$\{\sigma_{ul}^{(t'')}\}_q = \{\sigma_{ul}^{(t)}\}_q$$

and hence

$$\sigma_{ul} \in \{\sigma_{ul}^{(t'')}\}_q \,. \tag{7.8}$$

Now let us find in the environment μ_m a sentence t''' synonymous to t (such a sentence exists by virtue of postulate P7.2). From $t''' \sim t$ it follows, that $\{\sigma_{ul}^{(t''')}\}_m = \{\sigma_{ul}^{(t)}\}_m$, and

$$\sigma_{ul} \notin \{\sigma_{ul}^{(t''')}\}_m \,, \tag{7.9}$$

according to Eq. (7.3). Comparing Eqs. (7.8) and (7.9), see that

$$\{\sigma_{ul}^{(t'')}\}_q \neq \{\sigma_{ul}^{(t''')}\}_m \,. \tag{7.10}$$

After Eq. (7.2) it means that

$$t'' \not\sim t''' \,. \tag{7.11}$$

At the same time, we see

$$t \sim t''' \tag{7.12}$$

in μ_m, and

$$t \sim t'' \tag{7.13}$$

in μ_q (since t'' and t''' are taken so).

A comparison of Eqs. (7.11), (7.12) and (7.13) proves that the same sentence t has *different* meanings in the environments μ_m and μ_q, Q.E.D.

Let us see how the absolute non-uniexpressiveness of NL as the address language affects its utility for the man-to-computer dialogue.

7.3 Theorem on the necessary uniexpressiveness of addresses in a non-stationary environment

In this and following sections of the present chapter we shall prove and comment the following statement:

Theorem 7.2 *In a* non-stationary environment *the following condition C7.1 is necessary for the couple S_G—S_A to solve a problem $\forall z_n \in Z$ successfully:*

Condition C7.1 *S_G's address language must be not absolutely non-uniexpressive.*

This condition does not work in a K-stationary environment.

Proof: Before starting to prove the theorem, we have to specify what we mean by "solve a problem z_n successfully". For the sake of simplicity, let us assume that S_G proposes a correct solution method for every received problem z_n, and S_A can completely realize this method. According to Eq. (7.1), any dialogue address of either interlocutor corresponds to a reaction he is expecting from the other. Hence, for them to "solve z_n successfully", it is obviously sufficient for the author and the addressee to ascribe the same meaning to any address. We consider the fulfilment of this condition as equivalent to the successful solution of the problem z_n.

Now let us start proving Theorem 7.2. First we shall prove the necessity of condition C7.1. Let S_G's address language be absolutely non-uniexpressive. By virtue of Eq. (4.5), in a non-stationary environment any problem z_n is a priori considered new for S_A, i.e. of a type never met before. Let the dialogue have taken S_G a sequence $\{t\}_{Gn}$ of I addresses to solve z_n:

$$\{t\}_{Gn} = t_1, \ldots, t_i, \ldots, t_I$$

and it is known that in practical algorithms always

$$I \gg 1 . \tag{7.14}$$

From the absolute non-uniexpressiveness of the language it follows that every address from the sequence $\{t\}_{Gn}$ has more than one meaning. Let s_{ij} designate the j-th possible meaning of the i-th address.

Suppose that S_G can associate the address t_i with a (bounded) set B_{Gi} of b_{Gi} meanings: $b_{Gi} > 1$. Suppose also that, for the same address t_i, S_A can reconstruct a (bounded) set B_{Ai} of b_{Ai} meanings: $b_{Ai} > 1$. We shall designate by B_i the union

$$B_i = B_{Gi} \cup B_{Ai} .$$

Let us also consider the intersection

$$B_{GAi} = B_{Gi} \cap B_{Ai}$$

where B_{GAi} consists of b_{GAi} meanings. It is clear that $b_{GAi} \leq b_{Gi}$.

$P_{ij}^{(G)}$ stands for a probability of the following event: S_G means the j-th meaning of his i-th address. We denote as $P_{ij}^{(A)}$ the probability of S_A's selecting the j-th meaning of the i-th address on receiving it. This probability is considered existing and known.

As for S_G, we should think that if $\forall\, s_{ij} \in B_i \setminus B_{Gi}$, then

$$P_{ij}^{(G)} = 0 . \tag{7.15}$$

At the same time, in case of

$$\forall\, s_{ij} \in B_{Gi} ,$$

the probabilities $P_{i1}^{(G)}, \ldots, P_{ij}^{(G)}, \ldots$ exist, but S_A does not know them because he can not foreknow possible addresses of S_G for a new problem. Hence, regarding S_A in case

$$\forall\, s_{ij} \in B_{Ai}\,,$$

it is natural and usual to assume all those meanings to be equiprobable, that is

$$P_{ij}^{(A)} = \frac{1}{b_{Ai}}\,. \tag{7.16}$$

At the same time, in case $\forall\, s_{ij} \in B_i \setminus B_{Ai}$,

$$P_{ij}^{(A)} = 0\,. \tag{7.17}$$

Let us make a few natural simplifying assumptions.

Postulate P7.3 *S_G's expressing a meaning with his i-th address and S_A's ascribing the same or another meaning to this address are independent events.*

Postulate P7.4 *If a single address from $\{t\}_{Gn}$ gets a wrong meaning, then the problem z_n will not be solved successfully because this address will mislead the process of constructing the algorithm.*

Postulate P7.5 *Successes and failures in ascribing meanings to i-th and i′-th addresses are independent events, $i \neq i'$, $\quad i, i' \in \overline{1, I}$.*

Let us estimate the probability of success in the computer S_A's interpreting S_G's i-th address. We shall designate this probability by P_i. We have already noted that an address interpretation is considered successful if S_G and S_A have ascribed the same meaning to the address.

We shall prove the following lemma to estimate the probability P_i.

Lemma 7.1 *Under assumption P7.3 and condition $b_{Ai} > 1$ for $\forall\, i \in \overline{1, I}$, the following statement is correct:*

$$P_i \leq \frac{1}{2}\,.$$

Proof of Lemma 7.1: As we noted, the condition for an address t_i successful interpretation is the subscript j matching for the meanings ascribed to t_i by both parties. Thus the success probability P_i must be computed by the full-probability formula:

$$P_i = \sum_{s_{ij} \in B_i} P_{ij}^{(G)} \cdot P_{ij}^{(A)}(j)\,,$$

where $P_{ij}^{(A)}(j)$ is a conditional probability of S_A's selecting the meaning s_{ij} under the condition that S_G has meant the same. And according to assumption P7.3, we obtain

$$P_{ij}^{(A)}(j) = P_{ij}^{(A)}\,,$$

and thence

$$P_i = \sum_{s_{ij} \in B_i} P_{ij}^{(G)} \cdot P_{ij}^{(A)} . \tag{7.18}$$

Let us split the sum Eq. (7.18) into three items:

$$P_i = \sum_{s_{ij} \in B_i \setminus B_{Gi}} P_{ij}^{(G)} \cdot P_{ij}^{(A)} + \sum_{s_{ij} \in B_{GAi}} P_{ij}^{(G)} \cdot P_{ij}^{(A)} + \sum_{s_{ij} \in B_i \setminus B_{Ai}} P_{ij}^{(G)} \cdot P_{ij}^{(A)} .$$

It is obvious that the first item of the sum is 0: according to Eq. (7.15), each $P_{ij}^{(G)}$ equals 0. The third item is 0 because each $P_{ij}^{(A)}$ equals 0 according to Eq. (7.17). As for the second item, from Eq. (7.16) it follows that

$$\forall\, P_{ij}^{(A)} : \quad P_{ij}^{(A)} = \frac{1}{b_{Ai}} ,$$

and then

$$P_i = \frac{1}{b_{Ai}} \cdot \sum_{s_{ij} \in B_{GAi}} P_{ij}^{(G)} .$$

b_{Ai} is an integer greater than 1. Consequently, $1/b_{Ai} \leq 0.5$, and this fact together with $b_{GAi} \leq b_{Gi}$ gives

$$\sum_{s_{ij} \in B_{GAi}} P_{ij}^{(G)} \leq 1 ,$$

because only all the b_{Gi} meanings of s_{ij} altogether form a full event system with a total probability of 1. And it means that for $\forall\, i$

$$P_i \leq \frac{1}{2} , \tag{7.19}$$

which is just what was to be proved in Lemma 7.1.

Let us continue proving Theorem 7.2. $P_n(I)$ will designate a probability of S_A's interpreting all I addresses of S_G successfully. According to assumption P7.5, a value of $P_n(I)$ must be computed as a probability of coinciding independent events, that is by the formula of the product of probabilities

$$P_n(I) = \prod_{i=1}^{I} P_i .$$

Then from Eq. (7.19) it follows that

$$P_n(I) \leq \frac{1}{2^I} . \tag{7.20}$$

Let $\neg P_n$ stand for the probability of a problem z_n solution *failure*. Postulate P7.4 says it is the probability of S_A's misinterpreting at least one S_G's address from $\{t\}_{Gn}$. It means that

$$\neg P_n = 1 - P_n(I) = 1 - \frac{1}{2^I} .$$

In accordance with Eq. (7.14), one can write down:

$$\neg P_n \approx 1 \,. \tag{7.21}$$

This means that with the aforesaid assumptions an absolute non-uniexpressiveness of S_G's address language is necessarily followed by a problem z_n solution failure in an non-stationary environment. This fact completes the proof of the condition C7.1 necessity and of the first part of Theorem 7.2.

It is easy to see that qualitatively the same unconsoling conclusion has to be inferred in the case of not an absolute but simple non-uniexpressiveness of the address language. Really, this non-uniexpressiveness manifests itself in a positive probability $\widehat{P}$ (by the definition of the subset $\{\widehat{t}\}$, see Section 7.1) of addresses from the subset existing within $\{t\}_{Gn}$. Having taken into account Eq. (7.14), we can assert that the product $\widehat{I} = \widehat{P}{\cdot}I$ can exceed a certain integer, which is considerably greater than 1. It is also easy to see that Eq. (7.20), with I replaced by $\widehat{I}$, leads to Eq. (7.21) just as it was in the case of an absolute non-uniexpressiveness. Thus, if a dialogue is long enough, the address language simple non-uniexpressiveness leads to a z_n solution failure with a probability close to 1. The only difference is such a failure takes more time to reach it.

The said facts suggest statement S7.1 which is very important to the man-to-computer dialogue:

Statement S7.1 *In order for problems in a* non-stationary environment *to be solved successfully, the S_G—S_A dialogue should use a uniexpressive address language.*

Note that all programming languages, operating system interfaces and computer addressing formats keep to this rule. In fact, if a computer is universal, it corresponds to a non-stationary environment.

In the next section we shall prove the second part of Theorem 7.2.

7.4 Solving problem z_n in a K-stationary environment

Let us make another assumption. It concerns the cooperativeness of S_G's behavior in the S_G—S_A dialogue. More specifically, we are interested here in how S_G formulates his addresses to S_A. We shall think that S_G always seeks to form his addresses so as to help his interlocutor understand him correctly (it must be emphasized because the inverse goal is also possible. This is to mislead the interlocutor, but here we are not interested in that). In the discussed situation, "to be understood correctly" means that S_G wants S_A to ascribe a certain meaning $s_{ij'}$ to his i-th address. Therefore, he forms this address for the set B_{Gi} of its possible meanings to contain $s_{ij'}$. In terms of the formalism we have developed, this assumption can be presented as the following postulate:

Postulate P7.6 $\forall i \in \overline{1,I}$: $s_{ij'} \in B_{Gi}$, *where $s_{ij'}$ is the meaning that S_G wants S_A to ascribe to his i-th address.*

So, let us come down to the second part of Theorem 7.2.

We would like to remind that in a K-stationary environment (say μ_m) the set A_m of K_m fixed algorithms is in use. Let us also remind that an algorithm is fixed (i.e. invariable) if all its modules have fixed bodies, among them the i-th module that executes a reaction to the i-th address by S_G.

In its turn, the i-th module body being fixed means by definition that the body of the reaction to S_G's i-th address and the meaning ascribed to it S_A are invariable. Say it is a meaning $s_{ij'}$. The invariance of $s_{ij'}$ means that, whatever the i-th address of S_G, S_A will always ascribe to it the only meaning $s_{ij'}$. Hence

$$P_{ij}^{(A)} = \begin{cases} 1 & \text{if } j = j' \\ 0 & \text{if } j \neq j' \end{cases} . \tag{7.22}$$

From postulate P7.6 it follows that S_G's knowing that the proper meaning of the address is $s_{ij'}$ gives

$$P_{ij'}^{(G)} = 1 . \tag{7.23}$$

Recall that here $P_{ij}^{(G)}$ is the probability of S_G's ascribing the j-th meaning to the i-th address. Taking into account Eqs. (7.22) and (7.23), we obtain for Eq. (7.18):

$$\forall i : \quad P_i = \sum_{s_{ij} \in B_i} P_{ij}^{(G)} \cdot P_{ij}^{(A)} = 1$$

independently of what b_{Gi} and b_{Ai} are. And from this it follows that

$$P_n(I) = \prod_{i=1}^{I} P_i = 1 ,$$

which just means that the address language non-uniexpressiveness, including its absolute non-uniexpressiveness, does not hamper a problem z_n solution success in a K-stationary environment. Therefore, condition C7.1 of Theorem 7.2 *becomes unnecessary in a K-stationary environment*, Q.E.D.

It is easy to see that the result of the theorem is still correct for a computer dealing with several K-stationary environments at once. In fact, even in case Eq. (4.3) with M and all K_m's finite, the sum

$$K = \sum_{m=1}^{M} K_m$$

is also finite, and we obtain a K-stationary environment again. With a certain reserve, Theorem 7.2 works in case of stationary environments with another stationarity strength than considered, for example, in case of Ξ-stationary environments (see Section 5.3). However, later we shall have in mind only K-stationary environments for the sake of definiteness .

So, a joint consideration of Theorem 7.1 and statement S7.1 (resulting from Theorem 7.2) brings us to the following *fundamental facts*:

Statement S7.2 *It is* impossible *to use free and easy NL as a man-to-computer dialogue address language in a* non-stationary *environment.*

Statement S7.3 *The environment* K-stationarity *is a necessary condition for the man-to-computer NL dialogue to become possible.*

Thus, in our further investigation we shall consider only K-stationary environments. In the next chapter we are starting a discussion about the linguistic support for man-to-computer NL dialogues in a K-stationary environment.

Chapter 8
CONVENTIONAL LINGUISTICS IN INVESTIGATIONS OF LANGUAGE AND IN COMPUTER UNDERSTANDING OF NL TEXTS

8.1 Possible approaches to the problem of computer NL understanding. Orientated linguistics

The results of the previous chapter allow us to estimate how adequate different linguistic views are to the problem of computer understanding of NL addresses in the man-to-computer dialogue. It is natural to start with conventional linguistics.

Quite an obvious reason for conventional linguistics being inadequate to the problem of man-to-computer NL interaction is connected with the set of texts involved in the interaction. In Section 6.2 we noted that in our model that generated a very general concept of activity, all texts addressed by S_G to S_A, i.e. texts to be understood by S_A, were no other than *formulations of tasks* to execute an upper OPT. And it does not matter how free those texts are in terms of NL and what kind of activity they concern. Thus, we can assert that if the text addressee is a computer, i.e. in the course of man-to-computer communication, the computer must understand not all free and easy NL texts but only texts which express tasks and, furthermore, tasks from the K-stationary environment where the computer is working at the current moment.

The intuition suggests that the subset of those texts must be an extraordinarily small part of the entire language. Similarly, it is intuitively clear that there must be something resembling the physical laws of conservation, which allows "exchanging" a low cardinality of the understandable language subset for a high performance of understanding procedures.

It would not be true to say that the possibilities offered by the narrowing of subject and problem domains went unnoticed. Almost every work attempts to use this narrowing in some way. The trouble is that the means of conventional linguistics (morphological, superficial syntactical, deep syntactical text analyses, etc.) *will never ever extract the sought-for language subset*, because they are initially aimed at the entire language! Those means can distinguish between simple and complex sentences, active and passive forms, etc. but they are not able either to recognize which of two grammatically (i.e. morphologically, syntactically, semantically) identical texts contains a task, or to interpret this task. That is why the scientists who try to take into account professional and topical specifics of NL texts but follow conventional linguistics practically never achieve more than a specialized dictionary.

Thus, conventional linguistics is inadequate to the considered problem because it does not have any mechanism of extracting the subset of texts possible in the given K-stationary environment out of the set of all NL texts.

As a matter of fact, now the root of this inadequacy can be indicated: it becomes evident in the light of statements S7.2 and S7.3. Here it is: free and easy NL as a universal means of people's communication and seemingly the same free and easy NL as a man-to-computer dialogue addresses language appear to be *qualitatively different objects* with essentially different properties.

In fact, if an environment covers all kinds of people's activity, it must be qualified non-stationary. As "the entire NL" generally provides communication in all those kinds of activity, we may conclude that NL as a *universal language of man-to-man communication* is adequate to a non-stationary environment. Therefore, conventional linguistics, intended for studying "the entire language", is adequate to studying and describing it in this role. So we can speak of conventional linguistics as the "linguistics of non-stationary environments" (It is quite a different thing whether this linguistics satisfies even "its own" non-stationary environments, and we shall touch on this matter in Section 9.3).

However, things stand quite differently if NL works as an address language in the process of man-to-computer interaction. According to statement S7.2, this interaction is impossible in a non-stationary environment, and according to S7.3, the necessary condition for its being possible and successful is the environment K-stationarity. But conventional linguistics, i.e. "the linguistics of non-stationary environments", does not (and cannot) involve the idea of K-stationarity at all, either in direct or in indirect form. Here comes an evident paradox: as conventional linguistics is the only NL processing tool, we are forced to apply the linguistics of non-stationary environments to the problem that turns out to be unsolvable in environments of this type, as it follows from S7.2.

In order to illustrate what was said above, we would like to make the following remark. Real, though poor work of conventional linguistic NL understanding systems can be explained by their actual functioning in K-stationary environments, no matter whether the designers realize that or not. The lack of operational quality in those systems can be explained by the fact the linguistics of non-stationary environments is applied to dialogues from K-stationary environments.

From this it follows that the man-to-computer NL dialogue, at least within the framework of our model of activity, calls for a new conception of computer understanding of NL dialogue addresses. It should rely upon the *environment K-stationarity*, whereas its text analysis principles must be directly orientated to *detect texts with tasks* in a current subject domain and then to *interpret them as tasks*, i.e. in terms of possible tasks and their components. In other words, along with conventional linguistics of "all-topical" man-to-man interaction, there should be another, alternative linguistics aimed at the computer understanding of NL addresses in K-stationary environments and at the interpretation of tasks. For brevity sake, we shall refer to this hypothetical alternative linguistics as *Orientated Linguistics.*

This new linguistics is actually a new scientific trend. Creating it, we would hate to reproduce the flaws of conventional linguistics in its application to man-to-computer dialogue addresses. So, we have to consider these flaws thoroughly to reveal their deep roots. Chapters 8, 9, and partly 10 are devoted to the analysis and study of their practical manifestations.

8.2 Why it is necessary to distinguish orientated linguistics from conventional linguistics in methodological aspect

Let us begin with the following terminological refinement. In common use the term "linguistics" covers a wide and rather fussy range of questions, which includes not only understanding of NL texts but their production, translation, styles, etc. as well. In that connection we must make a reservation: hereafter we shall apply the terms "conventional linguistics" and "orientated linguistics" to the only line of NL study that is the NL texts understanding problem. Having this settled, we can pass on to the question of two kinds of linguistics that we are interested in.

The main difference between the philosophies of conventional and proposed orientated linguistics will manifest itself in the role of NL in each of them.

Let us take conventional linguistics first. Here the role of NL resides in being the central and sole object of research. Accordingly, the goal of all researches is to reveal the structures of NL texts at different language levels, from lexics to deep semantics and pragmatics, and to extract and formulate the regularities supporting those structures. Passing now from the goals to the means of research we can see there the linguist's language knowledge and intuition, elements of some mathematical disciplines, as well as some branches of computer technology and algorithms. In this way, the *goal* and the object of research in conventional linguistics is *natural language* itself; as for computer algorithms, they are just *means* of reaching the goal.

Let us now come down to what we are going to construct as orientated linguistics. Suppose that we conduct a computer-aided activity of an absolutely non-linguistic nature in the dialogue mode. Remember that we are considering only cooperative dialogues, in which the active party seeks to be understood (and not to mislead the interlocutor) and the passive one wants to understand correctly what is said. As it has already been mentioned, in a dialogue we can use many types of man-to-computer interface; in particular it can be a natural language interface. In this case we run into NL again, but in comparison with conventional linguistics it plays here quite a different role. Really, the *goal* and

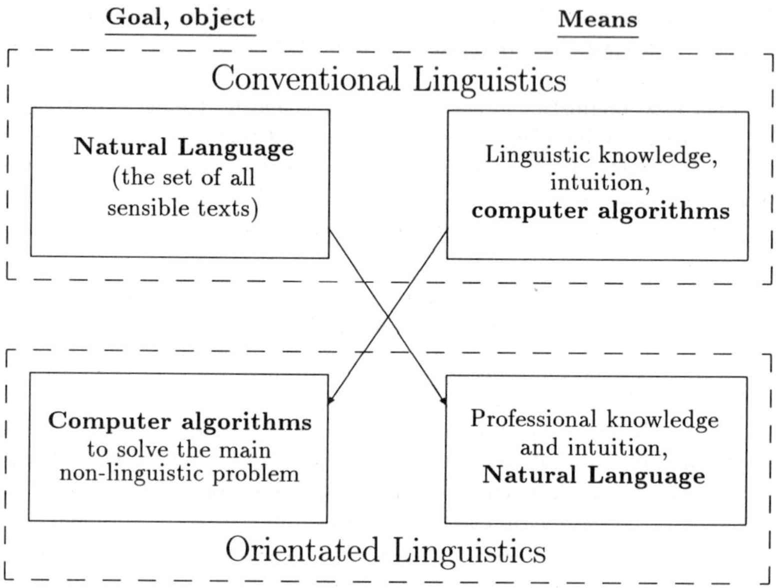

Figure 8.1

object of activity in this case is to construct or adjust *computer algorithms* to solve the main, non-linguistic problem, whereas *natural language* is just one of the *means* of reaching the goal.

So, as far as NL is concerned, orientated linguistics in comparison with conventional one, swaps places of the goal and the means, as it is shown in Fig. 8.1. This fact is of primary importance: swapping places of categories of such a high philosophical level as the goal and the means cannot help affecting dramatically all subordinate levels: conceptual, theoretical, algorithmic, etc. Our next problem is to make clear what will be changed in practice after swapping places of the pointed categories.

8.3 The role of the text and its analysis in conventional and orientated linguistics

When conventional linguistics gives way to orientated one, there happens a radical change of the *text analysis goal and direction.*

Intuitively speculating, we can say that conventional linguistics treats the computer NL text understanding problem as follows: the computer system receives a text at the input, and returns the sense of the text at the output. Correspondingly, the *text analysis* in the system is aimed at *revealing sense* and elucidating all its numerous components, nuances, aspects. The *role of the text* here is to *contain the sense.*

This conception seems inadequate in orientated linguistics which proceeds from an auxiliary function of NL in the process of an activity. In real applications the hearer's grasping the sense of what the speaker has said never represents his ultimate goal: people speak or write only when they want the addressee (a particular person, an anonymous reader, the mass listener, a computer) to accomplish some desired *reaction* which can be either physical or mental, or both. This becomes especially obvious when the NL text addressee S_A is a computer or computer system. We have already seen that whatever an address to the system consists of, whatever language (natural, formal, pictorial, etc.) it is presented in, and whatever kind of activity it concerns, it is always a *task*; the system's reaction should be to carry out this task.

From that point of view it is absolutely immaterial whether the computer understands the sense and what it understands by "sense". We only want it to fulfill correctly and completely the task that the text contains.

From the said it follows that the *text analysis* in an applied computer system must be aimed not so much at revealing the text sense (whatever this means) as at revealing *information about the task.* Thus the *role of the text* here is to *contain the information about the task.*

Now we have two fundamentally different views on the essence of the problem "NL text understanding":

1) understanding is converting a text into the text sense;

2) understanding is converting a text into information about the task hidden in the text.

Since there are two very different approaches to the same problem, the primary task is to compare them in order to clear up their prospects of serving for the man-to-computer business dialogue.

The said comparison should involve the following *two stages*:

1. For each of the two approaches the sought-for object must be exactly defined: the "text sense" in conventional and the "information about the task" in orientated linguistics.

   Without that neither the statement nor the solution of the understanding problem can be discussed in scientific terms.

2. For each of the two approaches it must be analyzed how an input text is processed to get the sought-for object.

   That is necessary to expose the true essence of the text processing result and to estimate its correspondence to the declared one.

In the next section of this chapter and in the two following chapters we shall consider the questions of these stages as they are seen in conventional linguistics. Then we shall clear up these questions from the standpoint of orientated linguistics.

So, we are beginning from conventional linguistics.

8.4 On the sense of the notion "sense"

Let us consider the question of the first stage, which is to give an exact definition for the "text sense" as the sought-for result of the NL understanding process in conventional linguistics.

At this point we meet rather a strange phenomenon. Looking through the literature on NL (linguistic, psychological, on computer understanding, computer-aided translation, etc.) one can find *no* satisfactory definition for the notion "text sense" or for the relative notion "understanding", neither descriptive nor procedural. And this means that all the investigations of the computer NL understanding aimed at extraction of sense from a text make attempts to solve a problem which cannot be even stated accurately! Here appears quite a fairytale-like situation: "Go I know not where and fetch I know not what".

This funny situation calls for an explanation. The following reasoning proposes one.

In conventional linguistics the word combination "text sense" implies that a text, i.e. a finite one-dimensional symbol chain, can contain and convey a sense. Let us test whether this premise is correct.

As it has already been mentioned, the final goal of any sensible text is to make the interlocutor react in the way the author of the text wants. We mean not a purely behavioristic act that is an observable movement or another physical action. The desired reaction may be for the most part mental, like these:

- memorizing some data;
- switching on one's spatial imagination, for example, after reading the phrase "Consider a plane sectioning the sphere";
- assuming a certain emotional state, for instance, in response to tender addresses like "Oh, my darling";
- creating a pleasant communicative situation (that is why jokes and polite expressions like "please", "would you be so kind", etc. are inserted into texts);
- getting aesthetic satisfaction, for example, from music of the verse, sometimes even in an unknown language;
- exiting the sense of humor;

- making a plausible reasoning or logical inference;

- and so on and so forth.

Moreover, practically always many of these components are combined and mixed, sometimes involving physical actions. Now we may say that the man's reaction to a text is *compound.*

Thus, a text recipient constructs *in his brain* a huge complex to implement such a complicated, delicate and versatile reaction with all its business, emotional, logical and many other components. It is this intricate structure that can be associated with our intuitive understanding of the *sense evoked by a text* (but certainly not "contained in the text" as it is usually supposed).

For example, asking a resort girlfriend the question "Do you remember last June?" certainly means not to remind her that the last year had June between May and July, but to make her form in her brain a very intricate complex made up of sea and moon visual images, and of acoustic and smell associations, and of a certain mood, and of her attitude to the speaker, etc. Certainly, the phrase "Do you remember June?" does not contain all these things. Apparently, it is simply a *code* which triggers the mechanism forming the mentioned complex in the listener's brain. In its turn, when the author gets the text "Yes" or "No" as an answer it raises in his brain a lot of images and feelings, jolly or gloomy respectively, and that is what the text was intended for. Of course, the sense evoked by the text "Yes" in this situation has nothing to do with the sense evoked by the same text when a person is letting another person know whether his breakfast is ready. Continuing with examples, we could mention the phrase "John threw the book to Mary by his foot" which was said probably to make a reader create a complex of ideas about John's scorn of Mary, about his despising her feelings and so on, and not to inform the reader that it was just the book that took part in the action and changed its owner in this way, as it is stated in [8].

From our standpoint, an attempt to describe the notion "sense" in formal terms (here it is, of course, "sense in brain" instead of "text sense") comes inevitably to the idea of a multidimensional and multi-level structure made out of a great number of elements: objects, relations, speaker's attitude to those objects and relations, sensations, etc. On top of this, there are uncountable vertical and horizontal inner links (like associations, logical implications and so on).

As it is known, structures of this kind can not be simulated as a visible and closed mathematical system. They admit (theoretically) of only a naturalistic, physical simulation. Suffice to recall the attempts of mathematical simulation of large neuron-like nets.

Speaking in a more specific manner, even if some "sense" seems to be isolated and limited, its structure involves such an enormous multitude of elements and links concerning different components of the prepared reaction, that any complete *deterministic* presentation of this structure becomes boundless (not to mention the poor formal representability of the elements themselves).

Just the same, *stochastic* ideas are out of the question as well, in particular because the structure elements appear to be qualitatively heterogeneous and mutually dependent due to the mentioned global inner links.

Thus, there are no way of constructing a satisfactory mathematical model of sense by the existing mathematical means. This *fundamental* fact is the reason for *the absence and*, more than that, *impossibility of any formal definition of "sense"*.

One has to consider sense to be an immanent, inseparable and therefore unobservable property of brain. Then one cannot treat a text either as a container or as a conveyer of sense. It just plays the role of some code (like genetic), causing the addressee's brain to erect a very intricate structure. This is the sense the author has desired in order to get some desired complex reaction.

As for the latter, the aforesaid suggests that non-formalized components (aesthetic, emotional, etc.) always take part in any human reaction to a text, and this part can be considerably greater than that of business, formalized components. Therefore, practical success of an NL understanding computer system, no matter what linguistics it is based on, depends on whether particular applications can do only with business components of reactions or non-formalized components are also important. The modern applications of those systems in capacity of linguistical processors for MIS's, DBMS's, expert systems seem to be of the first kind. As for the applications like computer translation of fiction (and even educational and scientific literature) from one NL to another, the rightfulness of ignoring non-formalized reaction components is not evident at all. That is what makes us look closer at another aspect of computer understanding, mentioned at the end of the previous part. This aspect was involved in the discussion by the question of whether an NL text was created for computer or human understanding. It was found out that a man always (though sometimes unconsciously) relies only on formalized reaction components, when consciously addressing a computer. Words and word-combinations of no concern to those components can get into texts due to the inertia of man-to-man communication exclusively and are a sort of "noise" with respect to business reaction components. Quite the opposite situation takes place if a text is addressed to another man: just what concerns non-formalized components of the expected reaction often can be of the highest and even absolute importance, as it was mentioned above. These observations can serve as another illustration of the already discussed phenomenon: the same free and easy NL as a man-to-man communication language is adequate to a non-stationary environment and belongs to it, but when it is used as a man-to-computer communication address language it is opposed to this type of environments. However, a more profound and less empirical explanation of that phenomenon is what we intend to present below.

From the fundamental impossibility of any formal definition for the notion "sense" it follows that whatever the result of a computer (and therefore formal) text analysis could be, *it will never represent the text sense.* For conventional linguistics, this conclusion answers the question of the first stage among the two drawn out at the end of Section 8.3.

In the next section we shall suggest one explanation for this result and shall discuss how it affects the prospects of using the conventional linguistic (simply "conventional", briefly) text analysis in man-to-computer NL dialogues.

8.5 On incorrectness of the NL understanding problem in conventional linguistics

So, a formal analysis of NL texts, be it conventional or whatever, *cannot produce an NL text sense* when it is comprehended as we described above.

Nevertheless, this fact, though very painful for those who believe in the "text sense" and its technical extractability, does not mean that it is impossible to use the conventional analysis in applications. In fact, this analysis still extracts *something* from a text, be it not sense, and that "something" still can contain some task information: otherwise conventional man-to-computer NL interaction systems would not function at all.

Of course, we are aware that conventional analysis aimed initially and basically at the text sense extraction cannot help being extremely complicated: this is a natural tribute for the utopianism of the aim. As a result, using a "heavy cannon" of conventional analysis to extract from a text the information on the expected reaction looks like using a sledge-hammer to crack a nut.

We are interested not only in stating this fact, but also in where and why the mentioned intricacy arises in the understanding procedure.

We shall see the reason: it is that the NL understanding problem in the course of man-to-man communication is one of the so-called incorrect problems.

To find out where this incorrectness comes from and how it affects the results of conventional computer "understanding", we shall have to investigate how the conventional analysis processes a text. This investigation was proclaimed by the second stage drawn out at the end of Section 8.3.

In the next chapter we shall start our consideration of the second stage for conventional linguistics with a discussion of the incorrectness of the NL understanding problem in this kind of linguistics.

Chapter 9
INCORRECTNESS OF THE UNDERSTANDING PROBLEM IN THE CONVENTIONAL INTERPRETATION

9.1 "Understanding" in conventional linguistics as an inverse problem

In Section 8.5 we said that the inadequateness of conventional linguistics to the NL understanding problem rooted in the incorrectness of this problem. And this incorrectness is a consequence of its being an *inverse* problem.

The physical nature of the NL communication channel permits an interaction initiator to communicate with his interlocutor only by means of a finite one-dimensional character chain which is an NL text. The author of a text maps some image (sense, message) occurred in his brain onto that character chain thus solving a *direct* problem. This mapping turns out to be degenerated, connected with a colossal loss of information.

The character chain being received, a human recipient, in his turn, uses it to restore the sense (a human being is able to do that!) as close as possible to what the author has meant. In so doing, the recipient solves an *inverse* problem and comes across a likely colossal *information deficiency.* Fig. 9.1 sketches the situation. This information deficiency can explain all the difficulties connected with NL understanding, in particular with computer NL understanding. First of all, the radical difference between the conventional and orientated approaches to understanding, reported in Section 8.2, shows itself in their methods of reacting to the mentioned deficiency. Since in this chapter we are interested in the conventional approach, we are considering here the deficiency reacting method

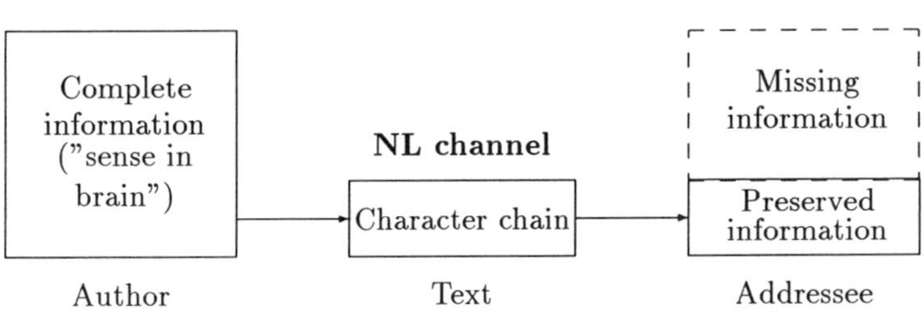

Figure 9.1

peculiar to this approach.

The conventional linguistic approach seeks to imitate the man's NL understanding mechanism, i.e. to restore the sense that has generated a given text. Therefore we must first clear up how the mentioned deficiency prevents the sense from being restored.

In so doing we may lean, at least in the conceptual aspect, upon the evident closeness (actually belonging) of the text understanding problem to the huge class of problems (commonly inverse too) studied in the incorrect problem theory: both cases are characterized by a radical information deficiency in the problem premises. Although the mathematical theory of incorrect problems was created for continuous objects, and our NL texts look rather like discrete objects, the basic methodological ideas of this theory can be successfully projected onto the conventional linguistic NL understanding problem. In the next section we shall consider some facts of the incorrect problem theory when applied to the discussed problem.

9.2 Properties of incorrect problem solutions

If a problem is characterized by a considerable incompleteness of initial premises, it is usually called ill-defined or incorrect. It is known from the incorrect problem theory [9, 10] that solving those problems is connected with two fundamental difficulties.

1. *Plurality* of possible solutions: more than one solution satisfy the problem premises. Usually the premises do not allow choosing the only correct solution among them and forbid even setting this task.

2. *Instability* of solutions: it manifests itself in that even a low "noise-like" disturbance can push a solution to another domain of the solution space, maybe very far from the "true" one.

Because of the noted similarity between a classical incorrect problem and the NL understanding problem, both of the pointed difficulties must be peculiar to the latter.

In fact, we already revealed the plurality of possible solutions when in Chapter 7 we proved the absolute non-uniexpressiveness of NL as an address language. We would like to add that the phenomenon of non-uniexpressiveness is considered by conventional linguistics as well, where it is known as the "text polysemy". However, if one becomes familiar with the literature and practical projects, he can see that they always produce a single construction ("the text sense") in response to a text and treat the polysemy as a headache which occurs sometimes (but more frequently than they want) to obscure linguistic constructions. At the same time, we have proved that it is actually a natural property, inherent in any address and, particularly in any sentence.

As for the second difficulty (the instability of solutions), its existence may be proved just by an example; this is a common way to prove existence theorems. Our proof will be convincing if we admit the following postulate:

Postulate P9.1 *If a word of a sentence is changed for another word, whose spectrum of meanings does not intersect that of the first word, this substitution affects the meanings provoked by the sentence.*

Note that we still lack any formal definition of sense, thus staying on the intuitive level.

Here the "noise-like" disturbance appears as an occasional deletion, insertion, transposition or substitution (a result of a misspelling, misprint, channel disturbance and so on) of one or more letters or punctuation marks; the latter can lead to syntactical errors. It is enough for us to demonstrate examples of letter substitutions.

The common way of studying the influence of disturbances is to form a space with garbleable objects (words here) represented as points and with a certain proximity measure established. If an input word does not match any dictionary word, it is associated with the word that is nearest in terms of the adopted proximity measure. A substitution occurs if some interferences distort a word so that it is closer to a wrong dictionary prototype rather than to "its own" one.

Thus a "noise"-caused change of one word for another does not require an exact match of the garbled word with some other dictionary prototype, as one could suppose and as it happens in the example "The bear knocked him down" → "The beer knocked him down", where "a" is changed for "e" in the word "bear". With "b" in "bear" changed for "p" and "r" changed for "v", the resulting word "peav" will be interpreted as "peak" or "peal" or "pear" by different proximity measures. In addition to the said, our experimental data prove rather a high probability of a sensible phrase resulting from changes like these. It can be easily explained by the evident prevalence of metaphorical situations over simple subjective ones in the modern language: a person is always ready to meet a metaphorical text and to interpret it. For instance, it is not so difficult to imagine problem domains where the blank in the text "The ... knocked him down" can be quite naturally filled in not only by the word "beer" (which already makes a metaphor) but also by the words "wear" (to describe the feelings of an old car owner), "peak" (in a story about a mountaineer), and even "tear" (meaning a tear on a beloved woman's cheek), not to mention the material nouns "pear" or "beak". Moreover, a reader is often supposed to interpret a text metaphorically thus following the author's idea in a poetic work.

The said suggests concluding that the NL understanding problem incorrectness can bewilder even a human being, though the latter evidently possesses powerful means of minimizing the effect of this incorrectness together with the understanding unambiguity and instability. Certainly, those means are based on the outstanding power of human intellect as well as on both conscious and unconscious components of human knowledge. It is clear that this knowledge is an external (with respect to the text) source providing additional information to make up for at least a part of the text information deficiency.

The incorrect problem theory says additional external information is necessary to regularize a problem. The process of its use is referred to as the regularization of an incorrect problem. We think it convenient to use those terms in the following sections though we cannot directly connect them with mathematical tools of the pointed theory because this theory actually concerns continuous objects, as we have mentioned in Section 8.1. When considering the regularization of problems, it will be interesting to compare its implementations in human and computer understanding. Let us start from the human regularization.

9.3 Human regularization of the NL text understanding problem

As it is said above, an incorrect problem regularization is an exact or hypothetical restoration of as much of the lost data as possible, which is followed by adding this regularizing information to the solution.

In so doing the man faces a serious problem because he never knows what particular additional information is necessary to interpret a sentence, until he analyzes the sentence completely. It means that at any instant the fund of available information must cover (in line of conventional linguistics) *all known language rules and regularities* to provide exposed grammar structures with semantic knowledge items, and *all known facts and regularities of the world* to base those semantic knowledge items on the world realities and to give them the unambiguity and the stability thereby.

From this the following conclusion derives.

There are two conditions for the conventional analysis to interpret a sentence unambiguously, stably and, in addition to these, correctly. Firstly, all its levels should be supplied with *all existing knowledge about the language and the world.* Secondly, there should be a *convergent algorithm to select* the set of currently necessary knowledge elements among their general collection. These capabilities of human brain allow the man to form in his brain the sense provoked by the text. In most cases (not always) he does it unambiguously, stably and correctly, just like it is required.

The man comes to this via a complicated iterative process including data verification loops, where additional information of the intermediate levels is tested for the resulting text interpretation non-discrepancy, unambiguity and verisimilitude. It should be emphasized that within a single level one can fail to reach the regularization correctness and unambiguity, even on the lower linguistic analysis levels, despite those levels are commonly considered as relatively simple. This happens to matching case forms or to sequences of words, which may be homogeneous parts of the sentence not always. It would not be an exaggeration to think that the volume and organization of necessary knowledge about the language and the world altogether with needed wits, professional skills, etc. are close to *the entire human consciousness.*

Here is another remark. If some situation prevents a man from using the whole variety of conscious and unconscious components of his intellect, then the mentioned effects, i.e. the text sense ambiguity and instability, can be observed in his understanding of man-to-man dialogue addresses. It can happen to a person who is reacting to short addresses without deepening into the environment, the object and problem domains, the context, where those addresses come from. Cases like this often produce a text ambiguity, i.e. different people extract different senses from the same text and, therefore, react differently. An illustrative example is that a joke causes different people in different situations and moods to react in different ways. The human text-to-sense reconstruction instability can be illustrated by funny incidents with telephone and telegraph information transmission.

Thus we have discussed the peculiarities of the human regularization. Now let us consider what opportunities exist in computer NL text understanding within the boundaries of conventional linguistics.

9.4 "Computer" regularization when aimed at sense extraction

In considering the "computer" regularization of the understanding problem, it would be natural to carry out a strict reasoning. But staying within conventional linguistics, we still come across the lack of exact definitions for some notions. Therefore, in the current and following sections of this chapter, our fixing necessary facts still will be based on just common sense.

We shall proceed from the reasonable presumption that one can hardly expect computers to imitate the human consciousness more or less closely in the near future. In Chapter 8 we already observed one consequence from this fact: it was impossible to equip a computer with an intellectual power necessary for the comprehensive text sense reconstruction, at least in our interpretation of the sense.

Theoretically speaking, we could suppose that this grievous fact has the reverse side, and this side is good. In fact, though the intellectual power goes down to the computer feasible level, and not sense but something more trivial results from the computer action, we can expect the triviality of this "not sense" (we shall call it "pseudo-sense" below) to reduce the ambiguity and instability.

Unfortunately, the available data do not corroborate this supposition. Suffice it to mention the permanently appearing and often irremovable ambiguity and instability of syntactic analysis trees and transformation procedures [11, 7] or the ambiguity of deep semantic cases [8, 12]. Thus, a forced replacement of the sense by the "pseudo-sense" does not ensure the unambiguity, stability and correctness of conventional linguistic system functioning either.

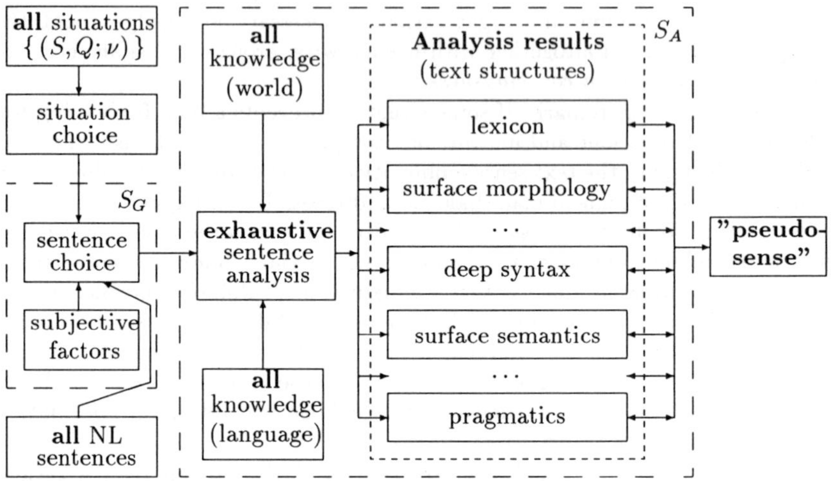

Figure 9.2

Yet there is a room for another supposition: it makes sense to seek a reason for the regularization failures in the very aiming of the conventional linguistic approach at the sense extraction. Will an initial replacement of that aim by a less pretentious extraction of only data on expected reaction formalizable components (here by means of conventional linguistics) allow us to obtain always a unambiguous, stable and correct result?

Answering this question we can not lean upon publications any more because in conventional linguistics there are no works aimed at extraction of data on the expected reaction, not the sense. That is why we have to probe into the conventional text analysis technology. We shall do it in the next section.

9.5 "Computer" regularization when aimed at extraction of reaction components

Let us consider a typical conventional-linguistic NL sentence processing procedure shown schematically in Fig. 9.2. The scheme reflects the following events. A spontaneous or purposeful transition creates some situation $(S, Q; \nu)$ at a moment ν. As conventional linguistics lacks formal and therefore programmable means of extracting object domains (OD, Section 3.4) and finite problem domains (FPD, Section 4.2), the situation $(S, Q; \nu)$ must be considered as an element of the set $\{(S, Q; \nu)\}$ of *all* possible situations. We should note that there are no grounds to consider the set $\{(S, Q; \nu)\}$ as bounded and its structure as observable. Hence, S_G finds himself in an extreme predicament: from nothing it follows that in the process of his informational activity his available means of analyzing the situation

$(S, Q; \nu)$ will be sufficient to interpret the situation correctly. Nevertheless, S_G is obliged to figure out whether the situation is requiring him to react and to send a proper NL address to S_A. If S_G thinks the address necessary, he chooses a text for it. Here S_G finds himself in a predicament again: the choice is to be made among the set of *all* sensible NL sentences, because (as we have already noticed) conventional linguistics does not possess any formal means of sorting texts according to their belonging or not belonging to the given OD—FPD. As Fig. 9.2 shows, the text choice is affected not only by how S_G interprets the situation $(S, Q; \nu)$ and how rich his language repertory is, but also by various subjective factors (his elocution, sense of humor, fatigue and so on).

When received by S_A, the NL sentence goes through a multilevel linguistic analysis at all grammatical levels: lexics, surface morphology, deep morphology, surface semantics and so on. Since the text has been selected among the set of all possible sentences, the linguistic analysis should be maximally complete and deep, as well as supported by all available NL knowledge, as it is shown in Fig. 9.2. If the computer text processing is concerned, we have to put up with the fact that it is purely formal knowledge. The linguistic analysis results are verified at the pragmatics level which leans upon a "world model". As the situation $(S, Q; \nu)$ is taken from the set of all possible situations, the "world model" should contain all available knowledge about Q. But in case of computer processing it can be purely formal knowledge with its completeness unknown.

Note that the unboundedness of the set of all sensible sentences and the forced truncation of informal knowledge make S_A's activity within the framework of conventional linguistics as difficult as that of S_G: it can be an intricate not to say unsolvable problem to derive the desired adequate reaction to a text from its analysis.

As it has been said, the conventional text analysis is multilevel. At each grammatical level the text structure is represented in the level-appropriate form. Although not always proclaimed, the main goal of the analysis at any level is to charge words (or word combinations) of the sentence with some level-peculiar *roles* and to formulate hypotheses about relations between those bearing the roles.

For example, even at the lexical level the test for a word being a noun or a verb can narrow the range of the word probable semantic roles; at the morphological and surface-syntactical levels the test for the sentence parts homogeneity helps to establish the equality of their roles; at the deep-syntactical level there appears a hypothesis about the control channels between the bearers of the roles and so on.

We should admit that the role-aimed analysis seems natural and logical independently on whether its result is a sense or "pseudo-sense" or whatever. In particular, it is easy to warrant the statement that in conventional linguistics the extraction of the expected reaction components should be executed by means of the very same data about the roles.

But the matter is that all the data about semantic roles and their relations *are not given explicitly* in the text of a sentence; they *come from outside* as hypotheses which are generated in accordance with the sentence analysis results and on the basis of two knowledge complexes of the same nature as the ones for the human understanding. They are the available formal knowledge about the language and the available formal knowledge about the world. And it follows from nothing that the necessary degree of that knowledge complexity and refining will be lower than that necessary for the sense ("pseudo-sense") extraction. But adding external information is just a problem regularization tool and it therefore follows from nothing either that the regularization of extracting reaction components will be more efficient than that of the sense extraction in terms of the conventional analysis unambiguity, stability and correctness.

Let us illustrate the said by a user's address to an oil-products distributing computer system. The address was recorded in actual practice. The user was interested in two kinds of products at once, but remembered his intention only when he was finishing the query. Not wishing to repeat the query from the very beginning, he simply added the name of the forgotten product at the end of his text. As a result, the address was formed as the following (translated from Russian):

(a) "When did they send the winter black oil from the base to the store and kerosene?"

Though the construction sounds clumsy, a human being is sure to interpret it with no difficulty. At the same time, its formal linguistic analysis runs into serious obstacles. In effect, the morphological and surface-syntactical levels would put forward (and quite rightfully, by the way) the hypothesis that "store" and "kerosene" are homogeneous parts of the sentence. Of course, the pragmatics level could object, but it needs more than a world model reflecting the oil-products distribution OD completely. In fact, the same object domain can offer an FPD where "store" and "kerosene" are homogeneous parts for real. For example, this FPD may include the following text:

(b) "Display me the information about the store and kerosene".

But conventional linguistics lacks any notion of FPD! Therefore, the process of revealing roles in text (a), as the conventional analysis implements it, can lead to an ambiguous, unstable and incorrect result. The repercussions of this for either the "pseudo-sense" or the sought-for data about the expected reaction are obvious.

The described effect is fundamental for conventional linguistics and can not be eliminated within its framework. One may try to reduce its occurrence probability by completing and arranging the language and world knowledge as well as by improving the linguistic analysis. But free NL communication in any OD can use texts of any grammatical complexity and senses of any semantic and pragmatic intricacy. Thus, for a conventional linguistic system to minimize the probability of an ambiguous, unstable and incorrect result, it must be equipped with the mentioned capabilities of performing a maximally exhaustive linguistic analysis and exploiting all available language and world knowledge, as it is shown in Fig. 9.2.

Everybody knows that computer implementable knowledge about the language and the world is *imperfect in principle* because those knowledge complexes are informal systems. Therefore a formal model cannot be complete with respect to them, whereas the computer can accept only a formal model. It means that regularizing information for the considered problem will never be exhaustive in principle.

The said suggests the following summary of the reasoning conducted in the current and previous sections. Whatever type of result the conventional-linguistic sentence processing is aimed at, be it the sense, pseudo-sense or the expected reaction data, its *unambiguity, stability and correctness can not be guaranteed for any sentence* in general.

At the same time, the necessity of maximally complete analysis and knowledge leads to an unlimited intricacy of the system which is partially displayed in Fig. 9.2 by the vertical channels of interlevel data support and verification and by the remarks about the analysis and all formal knowledge completeness.

So, within the framework of conventional linguistics both possible aims (the "sense provoked by the text" and the expected reaction data extraction) gravitate to practically the same intricate text analysis structure generalized in Fig. 9.2. Thus, conventional linguistics gets an answer to the question of the second stage pointed at the end of Section 8.3.

In the next section we shall sum up the second part of the book by forming our standpoint for the question of our primary interest: whether it is expedient to lean upon the conceptions and methods of conventional linguistics in developing "business" computer systems which could understand free and easy NL texts from the common use of FPD's of K-stationary environments.

9.6 Non-adequateness of the conventional-linguistic approach to the problem of computer understanding in FPD

So, for the computer to regularize the understanding problem in conventional linguistics, it must process each text by means of an exhaustive grammatical analysis (at all levels) and all available knowledge about the language and the world. But unlike the classical regularization of many continuous problems, it does not guarantee a unambiguous, stable and correct interpretation of any text *by principle.*

On top of this, the knowledge and analysis involved are extremely huge and complicated. Famous Russian generalissimo Suvorov used to say: "Hard in training, easy in fighting". The conventional linguistic NL text "understanding" can be characterized by another saying: "Hard in training, hard in fighting as well".

"Training" means here the accumulation and formalization of language regularities; establishing, structuring and filling a store of NL knowledge and knowledge about the world — though they cannot be complete by principle. "Fighting" means the very process of text analysis when every text puts to work the *entire* store of the knowledge: anything of concern to the text (and nothing more) is being sought there.

Things would stand better if real applications used not all texts of any grammatical complexity, but only some subset of grammatically simpler texts. Although any FPD selects usually a tiny subset of texts for the use, the selection criteria have nothing to do with the language grammar. Hence, whatever application, in general there may occur texts of any grammatical (including semantic, in conventional linguistics) complexity. Therefore a text may require any known language rules and regularities, among them the most complicated ones, to be included into regularizing information. In other words, even if a conventional text analyzer is designed for application purposes, it will not be simpler than an analyzer designed for arbitrary texts of the "entire language" because in both cases it is necessary to be "on the alert" and know how to use all updated knowledge about the language and the world.

No doubt, such an expensive result of text processing, which is a complicated multilevel structure (treated commonly as the "text sense"), contains data about the task, i.e. the only thing orientated linguistics is interested in. Yet in terms of volume and complexity, those data make an insignificant part of the mentioned structure. In fact, a variety of texts, occurring in business dialogues within a particular FPD of a K-stationary environment, is just a small part of the set of all NL texts. But a procedure of extracting only the required business reaction data in this FPD is deliberately less complicated than a maximal semantic complexity (in the conventional-linguistic meaning of this term) which can be found in texts of the entire NL.

It is these principal difficulties that are responsible for the mentioned market lack of conventional-linguistic computer NL understanding systems with rather a free address form, a human-like understanding probability and not so high a computer performance consumption.

And what is the reason for permanent failures of conventional linguistics in everything about computers? We think it is an incomplete comprehension of what the term "Natural Language" means.

The matter is the following. When applied to the field of man-to-man interaction, this term means not simply a lexicon with linguistic (that is morphological, syntactical, etc.) knowledge, but an *indivisible integral* complex of these together with the *consciousness* perceiving an NL text and relating it with the conscious and the unconscious and the intuition and the emotions and so on and so forth. The pure linguistic part of this complex is observed rather as an iceberg top, whereas the consciousness elements lie under water. It is the integrated and systematic functioning of this complex that helps to avoid ambiguity and instability in real man-to-man NL interaction. The natural language ambiguity, "fuzziness" and "indistinctness", which create obstacles for linguistics, actually manifest one side of a grand *compromise* embodied in the language. They are a sort of tribute for the other side of that compromise, namely for the incredible and unrealizable ability of the language (if this term includes the consciousness as we have noticed) to express the most delicate, metaphorical and abstract thoughts, the slightest nuances, the most distant associations and allusions, the most hidden displays of humor, sadness and so on. By the way, the current, rather indistinct reasoning is possible only due to this ability of the language. The word "unrealizable" is used above quite literally: all the said in Section 8.4 about the "sense in brain" stays behind it.

But going into the problem of computer NL understanding we can take only the iceberg top with us! All nonformalizable matters, i.e. the main part of the human consciousness, cannot be embedded into the computer. Thus in case of man-to-computer NL interaction the word-combination "Natural Language" terms *quite another* object than in case of man-to-man communication, and this object has quite different properties; in particular it is differently uniexpressive and differently stable. Natural language itself made a laughing-stock of linguists when its mentioned fuzziness allowed them to apply the term "natural language" to both the lively language which was the whole iceberg and the subject of linguistic investigations which was the iceberg top. The latter is quite legal but should have another name. By the way, it was this circumstance that forced us to introduce our clumsy term "address language" as there was no saying better. As for man-to-man communication, the consciousness saturated everything connected with NL but remained invisible like a common multiplier taken out the brackets of the NL concepts. Just the same, we do not notice the Earth gravitation and the air oxygen though our life is full of them (or owing to that).

Thus we should not be astonished by a paradoxical difference in the properties of seemingly the same free and easy NL as a means of man-to-man communication and as an address language for man-to-computer communication. The matter is that there are two different objects and this fact is a part of the nature which must be considered as the starting point of any reasoning.

As we see, in the philosophy of the conventional linguistic approach to NL understanding there are fundamental facts that make this approach inadequate to the computer NL understanding problem.

From the said it follows that the problem of purely computer NL understanding in its conventional linguistic formulation would be considered an abstract theoretical pretense if it were not for the mentioned problem of computer translation from one NL to another. This problem is of great practical importance, and one has to accept the translation systems bulkiness and complexity [13]–[15], as well as the inevitable "human" post-editing, which is connected with the incompleteness mentioned above. As we shall see in Section 15.3, the translation adequacy cannot be guaranteed without the post-editing, because esthetic, emotional, intuitive, in brief informal aspects of the text sense can be lost otherwise.

As for the computer NL understanding in business, non-linguistic applications, conventional linguistics does not suggest any satisfactory prospects. Thus we have grounds to consider orientated linguistics and to estimate it in terms of the two stages projected at the end of Section 8.3. We shall be dealing with orientated linguistics in the third part of the book.

Part III

ORIENTATED LINGUISTICS OF MAN-TO-COMPUTER COMMUNICATION

Chapter 10
NARROWING OF THE S_G — S_A DIALOGUE BOUNDARIES IN ORIENTATED LINGUISTICS

10.1 Introductory notes: man-to-computer and man-to-man NL communication

Now we are starting to develop foundations of orientated linguistics. Right here we would like to make a refinement. The necessity of this linguistics was grounded in Chapters 8 and 9 by a specific role of NL as a natural means of transmitting tasks from the author to the executor. If the executor is a computer system, formal and deterministic, this fact is sure to impart a certain formal structure to tasks. In its turn, this will bring definiteness and lucidity to the set of possible NL texts, as well as to the manner and mechanism of their interpretation as tasks. Thus we can expect orientated linguistics to be very helpful in the case of computer executors. Therefore, the basic task of this part of the book is to consider orientated linguistics in its application to man-to-computer communication.

And from nothing it follows that orientated linguistics is useless in man-to-man communication. In fact, it was mentioned in Section 8.3 that any address to any interlocutor pursued a goal. This goal was to get the interlocutor's reaction of some desired type, and the NL text of the address was just a description of the task. Now it is important for us to emphasize that this assertion concerns not only man-to-computer but *man-to-man* communication as well (Section 8.4). The only difference is that not all man-available reaction components can be implemented on the computer. From nothing it follows either that this difference changes the task text organization and structure principles. For example, the texts "This nail is in your pocket" and "This man is in your pocket" are structured and formulated identically though the former calls for a more or less behavioristic reaction and the latter demands a powerful intellectual effort.

Now it is clear that the peculiarities of man-to-computer NL communication expose themselves not in a special text organization of computer-addressed tasks, but in those tasks intentionally or unconsciously including only formalizable reaction components and only computer available operations.

Thus orientated linguistics with its knowledge of the man-to-computer interaction NL task text structure can be (at least partially) applied to tasks conveyed by man-to-man communication discourses.

That is why this part of the book is followed by Part IV where orientated linguistics is tried in the computer processing of NL texts *addressed originally to the man* and not connected with any computer activity. And here we are going to discuss orientated linguistics with respect to NL texts *addressed consciously to the computer.*

So, let us start considering the foundations of orientated linguistics.

10.2 Selected set of texts. OD–FPD and SST filters

It is an important fact that possible contents (see Chapter 6) of the S_G—S_A dialogue appear to be quite definite in the considered model.

First of all, the environment K-stationarity permits us to assert that a new situation $(S, Q; \nu)$, making S_G initiate a dialogue with S_A, comes not from the set $\{(S, Q; \nu)\}$ of all possible situations (as it was in the case of conventional linguistics with no OD and FPD formalisms developed) but from a subset of situations which is possible in the given OD–FPD couple. As we remember, orientated linguistics possesses the appropriate formalisms: in Sections 3.4 and 4.2 the formal objects corresponding to OD and FPD were designated as Σ_M and A respectively. Selecting the subset of situations for Σ_M and A from the set $\{(S, Q; \nu)\}$ is a function of some *OD–FPD filter*, symbolized by "Σ_M & A filter". As we shall see below, it is not the only filter in the considered type of communication.

The dialogue contents will get more definiteness if we remember that there are three kinds of the subject's activity. Therefore, S_G's task for S_A within a given couple OD–FPD can be one or a combination of the following:

1. Operative activity. Q is carried to some new state by means of an algorithm represented by its tail (or tails if the transition is not an OPT).

2. Selective activity. The desired goal state of Q is selected from some bounded set of goal states, possible in a given initial state. Here S_A may use a multioptional multicriteria choice algorithm.

3. Informational activity. A totality of data about the current and/or goal states is formed to determine a would-be expediency, feasibility and direction of the object Q transition.

We have already mentioned that all the three kinds of activity reach their goals by means of appropriate algorithms made up of more than one operation. Therefore, we shall consider only operative activity, as we did before.

With this kind of activity, S_G's task for S_A is either a change of the object Q (an active operation) or a request for data about the current state of Q (a test operation).

As for active operations, S_G's addressing S_A can be nothing but S_G's informing S_A of his idea of how Q is to be changed. Then S_A must interpret it as a task for this change. We have already seen that this idea can be realized only as a goal operation from the set $\{\alpha^*\}$ of a given polytrapezium. Then it belongs to one of K classes of the set A, with the number K of classes and the number of the polytrapezium operations bounded in any of those classes. If S_G is still interested in his tasks to be correctly interpreted and therefore does not vary task texts in an exotic manner, the number of finite texts, which represent tasks for an operation with an occurrence probability greater than some low threshold, can be considered limited. And the set of all possible NL texts connected with active operations can also be considered *limited* if S_G and S_A are cooperating.

As for test operations, one should also consider the cardinality of the set of the object Q characteristics S_G may be interested in. As we suppose the set X to be bounded, there come abovelike reasons for thinking a set of texts connected with test operations *bounded* as well. All the said helps to understand how small the set of task texts for active and test operations in some FPD is in comparison with the set of all sensible NL texts which is usually considered as denumerable.

The mentioned set of all NL texts, which are able to convey tasks for active and test operations in some FPD, will be designated by T and referred to as *selected set of texts* (SST). Intentionally or unconsciously selecting only texts of the set T from the boundless set of all sensible texts, one who sets tasks provides another filter: it has the set of all texts at the input and lets through only texts from T. We call this filter *SST filter* and symbolize it by "filter T". Note that the OD–FPD filter is realized by a K-stationary environment itself (be it industrial, administrative, etc.) because this environment raises problems from only K certain classes, whereas the SST filter is realized by the "sub-subject" S_G, plunged into this environment.

10.3 Narrow problem domains

For the sake of brevity, we shall refer to one who sets tasks as generator. Similarly, the one who executes those tasks will be called executor.

It follows from nothing that the generator and the executor are the same person; from nothing it follows either that a polytrapezium can have the only generator and the only executor. Their possible plurality is of primary interest for us here.

Let there be some number (finite, of course) B of possible task executors, and let the environment and polytrapezium be K- and $\widehat{K}$-stationary respectively. Then from the set $\{\alpha^*\}$ one can select B subsets $\{\alpha_1^*\}, \{\alpha_2^*\}, \ldots, \{\alpha_b^*\}, \ldots, \{\alpha_B^*\}$ so that

$$\bigcup_{b=1}^{B} \{\alpha_b^*\} = \{\alpha^*\} ,$$

and the b-th executor is charged with operations from $\{\alpha_b^*\}$. As $\{\alpha_b^*\}$ is a part of

$\{\alpha^*\}$, in the general case one can expect $\{\alpha_b^*\}$ to comprise operations not from all the K classes of possible goal operations but from a smaller number $K_b < K$ of the classes. Thus the executors can be specialized in some fixed subsets of operation "prototypes", suggesting some benefits.

In the already mentioned example of the car maintenance, the staff is always grouped into metal craftsmen, electricians, painters and so on. Workers' specialization on an assembly line can be another example. A_b will stand for a subset of the set A of classes, which concerns the b-th executor's competence; the cardinality of A_b has been already denoted as K_b. We would like to remind that the sets $\{\alpha_b^*\}$ and A_b can be of different cardinalities. The definition of the set A establishes for each element of the set A_b to contain at least one goal operation, but it does not forbid more operations contained.

A substitution of the set A by the subset A_b gives us an example of the FPD narrowing by means of a *decomposition into subdomains.* Here it is done in accordance with the executors' individual competence. For these narrowed subdomains to be distinguished from the mother FPD, they will be referred to as *narrow problem domains* (NPD), adding a subscript (subscripts) to indicate mnemonically a criterion (or criteria) of the FPD decomposition. In the given example of "executors' competence decomposition" we shall keep the notation $\text{NPD}_{(b)}$. Practice can suggest some other criteria, for instance, the time criterion for periodical activities like the agricultural season technologies. In cases like this the number of subscripts in the indication $\text{NPD}_{(b..)}$ reflects the number of FPD decomposition tree levels whereas their order shows the order of criteria used for the decomposition. The subset of classes of the $\text{NPD}_{(b..)}$ may be denoted as $A_{(b..)}$.

We would like to add that the NL use in NPD's formed by an FPD decomposition is very sensitive to the adequacy of this decomposition. Besides it helps to estimate the naturalness and sufficiency of this decomposition, it even suggests necessary corrections. We shall see an example of this below. The problem of FPD decomposition into a complex of NPD's and some NL phenomena, connected with this problem, will be discussed in the following chapters (the so called pre-recognition).

Now we are ready to consider the structure of a task and its realization as an NL text.

10.4 Environment stationarity degree and the content of a task

The introduced notions of information and work periods of the subject S's activity about Q are well coordinated with the division of functions between the "sub-subjects" S_G and S_A. Namely, during an informative period S_G forms a project (x_a', α) and formulates it as a task. Work periods concern S_A who finds a proper algorithm for the task (if its name is not a part of the task description text) and launches it.

What must a task text contain so that S_A can accomplish the task? It is clear that the answer depends on the environment stationarity and its strength.

First, let us consider the weakest environment stationarity (among those discussed in Section 5.3), which is the NL use stationarity. An environment of this type can generate tasks which S_A does not have ready algorithms for. What is more, for many of them it is usually impossible even to produce modules of a level higher than the linguistic interpretation of NL text fragments. If S_A is able to fulfill tasks only and can not construct necessary algorithms, S_G must supplement a task with a detailed (but, of course, bounded) NL description of its realizing algorithm. Inasmuch as elements of the task and its realizing tools may take turns (for example, "... At first, let's calculate finite differences. Proceed as follows: ... "), we have to think that the executor gets information about the algorithm *from the very text of the task.*

The experience proves it is an exotic situation. We may suppose it emerges when some circumstances force S_G to ask a representative of some object and problem domains to execute an algorithm from another NPD (for example, a female-singer to fix a carburetor). If not in such an emergency, the task text usually contains no information about the algorithm to be launched because this information will never be interpreted uniquely in a weak-stationary environment.

In fact, this type of environments implies an infinite (denumerable) set A of task classes and, correspondingly, of algorithms. Hence, no length-limited algorithm description (including that in NL, of course) can sure a unique choice of the appropriate algorithm: under different circumstances the text will be adequate to different algorithms.

For example, the text "Pete, come here!" will cause a child to react variously (at least in the emotional aspect). It depends upon who is calling him: the mother with a candy or the father with a whip. In the same vein, the text "It will rain tomorrow. Take your umbrella." implies different reacting algorithms in dependence of whether this text is taken from a novel or from a weather forecast. On top of this, even reactions of the same goal can use different algorithms under different circumstances. For instance, a reaction to the text "It's time we had a snack. Jane, cook some coffee." will require different algorithms in a city (where the external circumstances include all the modern conveniences) and on a picnic (a river and a fire). So, information about the algorithm is absolutely useless in a weak-stationary environment.

Let us consider an environment of stronger stationarity now. Namely, it is an environment with a fixed set of high-level modules (we called it Ξ-stationary in Section 5.3). With this type of environments S_G does not have to chew over the contents of the modules in his texts addressed to S_A. The latter must be provided only with necessary data *to select the appropriate module* among a bounded set of them and to determine the values of its arguments. This variant has the following peculiarity. The very OPT modules must be supplemented with the so called communication or syntactical modules implementing all possible links between "basic" modules. Certainly, those linking modules are finite in number;

their arguments must be included in a task. This type of interaction between S_G and S_A was called in [51] and Section 5.3 the programming humanization, if the purpose is to develop programs and the communication tool is NL.

However, we are especially interested in the strongest stationarity, which is K-stationarity, because those environments are wide-spread. Besides, the preceding case of Ξ-stationarity can be treated as K-stationary on the condition that the problem ζ_n of the current module interpretation and execution is considered as a separate problem z_n. In the constructive aspect it is immaterial that the problem is produced by a human being S_G, not by an environment.

But in case of K-stationary environments, S_G's task addressed to S_A allows the latter *to select a ready algorithm* of the problem solution among the K ones and to determine its arguments properly. Within our model of $\widehat{K}$-stationary polytrapezia and K-stationary environments, it means that a task text must enable S_A to recognize the appropriate goal operation (α^*_{am}) in the set $\{\alpha^*\}$ and to determine the $\mathrm{NPD}_{(b..)}$ $A_{(b..)} \ni \alpha^*_{am}$ and to execute the tail α^*_{am}. We shall start the next chapter with a discussion about what data are included in a task text for S_A to do these.

Chapter 11
NL TASK TEXT STRUCTURE IN K-STATIONARY ENVIRONMENT

11.1 Possible sources of information on a task

For S_A to perform the actions mentioned at the end of the preceding chapter, he should possess enough information to identify the goal operation and to assign values to the arguments of its tail.

We dare make another note here. In actual practice the text of a task is not the only source of the information necessary for the task execution. There are two more sources of this information.

The first one is the system knowledge. Some information necessary for the task execution can be a part of this knowledge. Taking this fact into account (consciously or unconsciously), S_G may skip this information in the text. For instance, interpreting the text: "Tell me the current situation of coal in Yaroslavl" the system gets out the value of the argument "time" from its knowledge that "current" means "today's" (within these OD and FPD!). The computer will then substitute the latter by the current date.

The other source is the preceding texts, especially if they come from the same S_G. In this case, S_G usually does not repeat unchanged data values, considering them determined by the preceding text pieces, and S_A restores them by default. This phenomenon, called the ellipsis, is one of the most difficult problems in conventional linguistics [7]. Orientated linguistics resolves this problem in rather a simple way described below in every detail.

Thus in many cases, one can extract information about a task not only from its text. However, linguistics thinks the retrieval of all task information from only the NL representation to be the most general case, and this is why we shall mainly care about this case hereafter.

With this reserve we are starting to discuss the information which makes a task executable.

11.2 Information on the NPD

S_G's task usually concerns not all NPD's but merely some of them or even a single one. The formal indicator of the required NPD is a subscript $(b..)$, whereas its NL indicator is a "subtext", i.e. a word or word-combination functioning as an *NPD name*. An NL text encapsulating a task for a single address to Q is designated t. Its subtext with an NPD name is denoted as $t_{(b..)}$. By its very nature, NL permits an NPD to have various words and word-combinations as its $t_{(b..)}$. One can detect all possible variants, if he explores a representative training set of texts t. We would like to remind that in [51] the NPD identification process was spoken of as the pre-recognition or, more exactly, as one of possible pre-recognition stages.

In fact, a required NPD identification procedure must process an NL text to select words which can belong to subtexts $t_{(b..)}$. Using them, it must identify the present subtext $t_{(b..)}$ and its subscript $(b..)$. In accordance with this scheme, the procedure should be a combination of two blocks:

- a *filter* to process a task text and let through only words of subtexts $t_{(b..)}$,
- a *recognizer* to identify the subtext formed by these words and to determine the concerned NPD together with its $\{\alpha^*\}$.

The mentioned filter can be termed "*NPD filter*". The structure of this filter seems to be quite clear. Its core is a dictionary comprising all the words of subtexts $t_{(b..)}$ from the task texts which used to provoke all the goal operations from $\{\alpha^*\}$ (these words occur in the training set of task texts). Each word or word-combination in the dictionary is associated with the subscripts $(b..)$ of the subtexts $t_{(b..)}$ this word (word-combination) makes a part of.

The NPD recognizer gets clear whether the filtered words and word-combinations form a plausible subtext $t_{(b..)}$ with its subscript combination $(b..)$ allowed. If yes, it outputs this subscript. If no, the author of the text is considered to have used the ellipsis lest he feed the data on all or some of subscripts $(b..)$ he entered earlier: those data are presumed to remain the same (details below).

The pair "NPD filter—recognizer" is designed to cut down S_A's input set $\{\alpha^*\}$ of all possible goal operations to the subset peculiar to the present $\text{NPD}_{(b..)}$. We can denote this subset as $\{\alpha^*_{(b..)}\}$.

It is interesting that a text may include not only the NPD name but some information about the path to the NPD in the FPD decomposition tree as well. One who sets tasks provides this information rather frequently and usually unconsciously, thus simplifying the search. For instance, the text "Go to the electricians, Petrov will adjust the third spark-gap" gives an opportunity of seeking Petrov in a two-level tree, though the inefficient exhaustive search in the set of all workers is still possible.

11.3 Information on the proper algorithm

If a task text contains all the information on the task (it has been agreed above), there must be an indicator of the class $\{\alpha\}_k$ that the sought-for goal operation belongs to. The formal indicator of this class is its subscript k, its NL indicator is a subtext termed the *operation name* and symbolized by t_k. In the just given example, the operation name is represented by the word combination "adjust the third spark-gap". Just like in the case of NPD, an operation (more exactly, $\{\alpha\}_k$ class) may have more than one NL name. Besides "adjust ...", the words "fix ...", "correct ...", "set ..." and others will do. Similarly, our real data base used to be inquired (test operations) in many ways: "Inform me on ...", "What sort of situation do we have in ...", "I need the information on ...", etc.

The operation name is identified by a pair "filter—recognizer" similar to that for the NPD name identification. The filter is termed "operation class filter" or *algorithm name filter*. It lets through only the words and expressions occurred in the subtexts t_k during the training procedure. The operation class recognizer clears up whether these words and expressions form a plausible subtext.

It is obvious that the pair "operation class filter—recognizer" reduces the admissible goal operation set $\{\alpha^*_{(b..)}\}$ endured the previous filtration. Its result is the goal operation subset

$$\{\alpha^*_{(b..)}\} \cap \{\alpha\}_k \, .$$

This subset is denoted as $\{\alpha^*_{(b..)}\}_k$ and called the $(b..)$-th subclass of the k-th goal operation class.

For instance, if the NPD $A_{(b..)}$ concerns an electrician's job, and the operation class $\{\alpha_k\}$ includes the gap adjustment operations, then those for spark-plugs and for breakers will be involved in the subclass $\{\alpha^*_{(b..)}\}_k$, but that for valves will be beyond it.

11.4 Information on the values of the algorithm arguments

Now the task text must help to select a single goal operation among those of the subclass $\{\alpha^*_{(b..)}\}_k$. The experience proves that S_G never (though mostly unconsciously) fails to provide his text with special words and word-combinations for the b-th executor to select the operation that suits S_G's plan (x'_a, α) best of all. These words and word-combinations form a subtext symbolized by t_{am} below. They may be regarded as values of the subclass $\{\alpha^*_{(b..)}\}_k$ "arguments". Varying them, S_G can uniquely define any goal operation. These arguments will be referred to as *individualizing*.

In particular, if the goal operation is declarable (which is the most general case), then an NL text pointing to it contains only individualizing arguments. They allow us to localize the operation in the polytrapezium, thus highlighting it among the set of equivalent operations situated in the polytrapezium arbitrarily. As far as the operation "to adjust the gap of" is concerned, in a car it can be applied to the breaker, each one of the spark-plugs, various relays, valves (the latter is beyond an electrician's NPD, by the way). In the example given in Section 11.1 the words "spark-gap" and "the third" form the subtext t_{am}: they are the values of the individualizing arguments and locate the operation "to adjust ..." in the polytrapezium.

The unique identification of the goal operation was called "final recognition" in [51].

The individualizing arguments are detected by a pair "filter—recognizer" of principally the same nature as the pairs detecting the NPD name and the operation name.

The filter, named here an *individual operation filter*, has the text t at the input and lets through only the words and word-combinations met in subtexts t_{am} during the training procedure. The recognizer clears up whether these words and word-combinations form a plausible subtext.

The pair "individual operation filter—recognizer" terminates the reduction of the whole set of admissible goal operations to a single goal operation α^*_{am}. The result is the subscript am that points to this operation uniquely.

As for executable operations, they have another type of arguments. Those arguments are used in calculations and can be called *working*. Words and word-combinations representing the operation working arguments form a subtext denoted as t_w. The word combination "half a millimeter" in the text "Adjust the third spark-gap. Set half a millimeter" is a working argument of the operation "bending out an electrode". This operation was established to be executable, and therefore it is situated on the tail bottom of the operation "to adjust a gap". The complex of working arguments values will be lettered by w.

Like the other types of subtexts, t_w can be selected and recognized by a pair "filter—recognizer" similar to those mentioned above. In this case the filter could be called *working arguments filter*.

Finishing the discussion about the filters, we would like to note (and it is easy to see) that all the filters in Sections 11.2–11.4 are realized by the executor S_A.

The study of this chapter allows us to infer from our model of activity an exact answer to the question of the first stage among the two raised at the end of Section 8.3. Now we know that the task text conveys information organized as subtexts, and it is these subtexts that orientated linguistics is interested in.

Let us also note that the union of the subtexts $t_{(b..)}$, t_k, t_{am}, t_w may not cover the whole text t, i.e. some words and word-groups in t may have nothing to do with the task information. The totality of these words and word-groups from t will be symbolized by t_{NIL} and represented by the difference

$$t_{NIL} = t \setminus \{t_{(b..)}, t_k, t_{am}, t_w\} .$$

t_{NIL} comprises words and word-combinations irrelevant for the computer, not for a human being. Generally, they appear in a computer-orientated text due to the inertia of man-to-man NL communication. For instance, the word "please" in the text "Please, switch on the first unit" is necessary to induce some desired ethical and emotional components of an interlocutor's reaction, whereas the computer does not demand this word at all. It does not need the article "the" either, because the unit is determined by its exact name "first unit" completely. At the same time, a man cares about the article because skipping it would damage the grammar. Thus, in the above example t_{NIL}={please, the}. Since the subtext t_{NIL} can be simply ignored, it gives orientated linguistics another very powerful source of text analysis simplicity and reliability. We shall comment on this statement in the next chapter, where we shall discuss the orientated-linguistical NL text understanding process based on the recognition of the subtexts $t_{(b..)}$, t_k, t_{am} and t_w in a text t. It will give us an answer to the question of the second mentioned stage.

Chapter 12
NL TEXT ANALYSIS AND UNDERSTANDING IN ORIENTATED LINGUISTICS

12.1 The pattern recognition as the core of NL text understanding in a stationary environment

The above discussed "filter—recognizer" couples produce a four

$$\langle (b..), k, am, w \rangle \, . \tag{12.1}$$

Accordingly, any task text contains the following items (some of them represented indirectly, by means of the ellipsis): the NPD name $t_{(b..)}$, the operation name t_k, the individualizing arguments t_{am}, the working arguments t_w.

Let us illustrate what we have said. We shall consider a real management information system with its NL subsystem based on orientated linguistics. The system works in the OD "Oil-products" and supports several NPD's there. Among these NPD's there is the NPD "Oil-products transportation along Russia". Suppose the following sentence at the input (translated from Russian):

"What did Ufa dispatch yesterday?".

It is easy to see that this text does contain subtexts pointing to the NPD and to the proper reacting algorithm (it is the DBMS's retrieval function) and to the values of the arguments. In fact, the subtext $t_{(b..)}$, represented here by the word "dispatch", indicates that the NPD "transportation" is concerned. The word-combination "What did ... dispatch ...?" forms the subtext t_k being recognized as an indicator of the reacting algorithm "What oil-products were dispatched?" (among the set of $K = 14$ algorithms, including the algorithm "Where was the product delivered from?", for instance). If not only oil-products but, for example, people could also be transported, an individualizing argument *am* would be in need. To provide this argument, S_G who is interested in an adequate system response would insert (unfailingly, though unconsciously) an appropriate subtext t_{am} looking like "What *products* ...". But in the given case no individualizing argument is necessary, and there is no subtext to represent its value in the text above. Lastly, the values of the working arguments "supplier" and "time" are represented by the subtexts "Ufa" and "yesterday". The place of the algorithm argument "consumer" is vacant and the system understands this fact as a command to display all the information on all the consumers supplied by Ufa. If S_G were interested in some particular consumer, he would inevitably reflect it in the text, for example, "What did Ufa dispatch to Nizhny yesterday?".

Apparently, if the computer detects and recognizes such subtexts, extracts the data Eq. (12.1) and executes the proper reaction automatically, it is the computer NL understanding as orientated linguistics views it.

So, we have come to the following *fundamental conclusion*: in Section 5.4 the pattern recognition was discovered to be the core and the essence of any activity in a K-stationary environment; this fact has its NL consequence. Namely,

> *the free NL text understanding problem* in this type of environments is reduced to be a *pattern recognition problem*

or, more particularly, the problem of recognizing subtexts of the four mentioned types. The resemblance of titles between this section and Section 5.4 will underline the obtained result.

The drawn conclusion is extremely important due to some very productive facts of the pattern recognition theory. Those facts will be discussed in Chapter 13, whereas the next section of the current chapter is devoted to the basics of conventional linguistics in comparison with those of orientated linguistics. Then we shall outline the scheme of the NL text understanding process in orientated linguistics.

12.2 The definition of orientated linguistics and its NL text understanding scheme

We would like to remind that here we use the word "linguistics" to term the NL text understanding problem only, just as at the beginning of Section 8.2.

With this refinement, orientated linguistics can be defined in the same way as conventional one. Namely, it is a complex of formally representable knowledge to provide a transition from a symbolic chain (NL text) to some construction, which is considered as the "text understanding result" by agreement.

This definition does not reveal any fundamental difference between the two kinds of linguistics, but the following questions will help to work it out:

1. What ensembles produce NL texts for either linguistics?

2. What is the result of "understanding" in either linguistics?

Now we are ready to answer these questions for both conventional and orientated linguistics. Namely,

1. As for conventional linguistics, texts are taken from the set of all sensible NL texts. In orientated linguistics this role is played by rather a small subset of this set (the SST T).

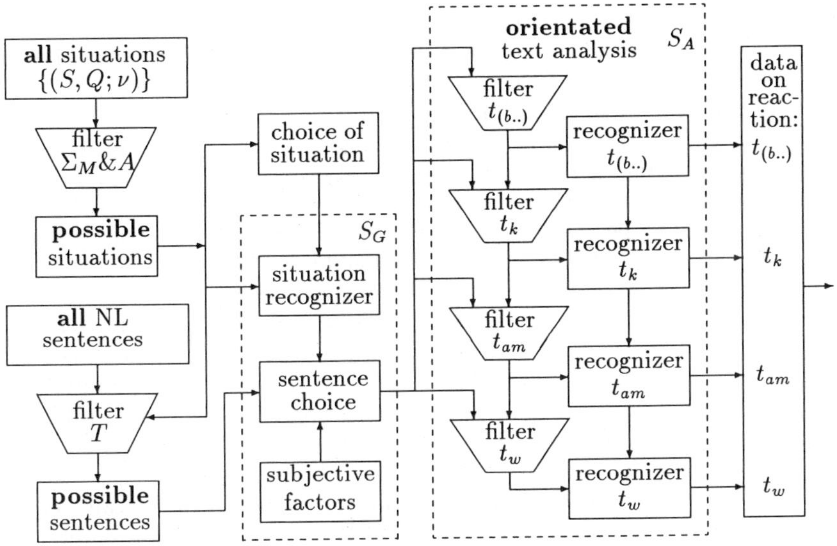

Figure 12.1

2. Conventional linguistics treats the NL "understanding" as a complete reconstruction of the text sense or, at least, of its maximal formalizable part. In orientated linguistics the correct recognition of the required algorithm and its arguments is enough to provide the expected reaction.

All the said above gives the following

Definition 12.1 (Orientated linguistics) *Orientated linguistics is a complex of formally representable knowledge providing a transition from one symbolic chain (the NL text of a task by S_G to S_A) to another symbolic chain. The latter chain represents (in any specified notation) the Eq. (12.1)-type information on the task, under the condition that S_G and S_A activity takes place in a K-stationary environment.*

The text analysis extracting this information will be called *orientated* for brief.

It is clear from the preceding discussion that the knowledge mentioned in the definition of orientated linguistics is that of how the NPD, t_k, t_{am}, and t_w filters and recognizers are constructed and interconnected. A general diagram of these interconnections is given in Fig. 12.1. Let us discuss this diagram. On first thoughts it looks not less intricate than that of conventional linguistics (given in Fig. 9.2), but this impression is wrong, of course. Looking at Fig. 9.2 we felt limits imposed by the amorphous abstractions "all situations", "all sensible texts", "all knowledge about the world", "all knowledge about the language", "total linguistic analysis", "text structures". We used them to denote the informal essences standing behind them, and we understood that their enormous size and poor structuredness would never allow us to specify them any more.

In Fig. 12.1 there is much more certainty.

Though in this research we are interested rather in S_A than in S_G, we should notice that the environment K-stationarity simplifies S_G's activity because he operates with only K types of foreknown situations instead of the unbounded set $\{(S, Q; \nu)\}$. This fact is displayed in Fig 12.1: S_G receives a "coming" situation not from $\{(S, Q; \nu)\}$ but from its subset filtered by Σ_M & A.

What was said is even more true when applied to S_A.

First, as long as S_G stays within his professional field, he generates texts of a very weak probability to be beyond the subset T, though he is able to generate any text from the "entire language" set. As the set T is much less powerful than the "entire language", S_G reduces the amount of possible "language stuff" thus simplifying S_A's text interpretation problem. The subset T is separated by the filter shown in Fig. 12.1 as "filter T".

Secondly, each subtext interpretation level deals with not all possible subtexts but with those let through by the NPD, $t_{(b..)}$, t_k, t_{am} and t_w filters. The supposed environment K-stationarity allows collecting a representable training set (see below) and therefore setting the subtext (and the whole sentence) *correct interpretation probability as close to 1 as desired.*

Let us suppose any text to determine its task uniquely. The basis for that is granted by a thorough statistic research [51], which reported the already mentioned fact: one who is interested in his task to be accurately executed provides the task text with all the data about the task consciously or unconsciously, directly or indirectly (the ellipsis, for instance). We know what these data look like. Thus, the SST maps onto the $\{\alpha^*\}$ set identically, and this mapping determines a division of the SST into a set of classes which is bounded due to the boundedness of $\{\alpha^*\}$. It is clear that then the mentioned high probability of the subtext correct interpretation causes a high probability of the correct reaction to the text. As we remember, the latter is what orientated linguistics considers as the correct result of the text "understanding".

So, the above held discussion and Fig. 12.1 show that the text analysis structure in orientated linguistics appears to be completely determined and uniform. This structure contains only *two types* of blocks: filters and recognizers.

Simply speaking, the filters exist in the form of subdictionaries with the following peculiarities:

1) their volume is very small by the virtue of their functional boundedness;

2) they can comprise both words and word-combinations of subtexts.

As for the recognizers, they basically stay within the framework of the pattern recognition theory: their practical peculiarities will be discussed in the next chapter.

A higher (in Fig. 12.1) level subtext being recognized, the parameters of the next lower filter become definite: this dependence is shown in Fig. 12.1 by the arrows downwards of the three upper "recognizers". For instance, after the system works out that the current text belongs to the oil-products transportations NPD, it will activate the subdictionary of only this NPD algorithm names. One of those algorithms being recognized in its turn, it will determine the possible set of its arguments and, consequently, the appropriate subdictionaries where the names of these very arguments are stored. Besides this descending line, there is an ascending one (not shown in Fig. 12.1) intended for verifying the higher levels by the lower ones in case of predicament. Thus, the set of arguments selected on the level am may confirm or object the selection of the required algorithm subscript k.

When the recognizers produce the data complex Eq. (12.1) it will mean that the text understanding process is finished. Then the data are transferred to form the required reaction of the system.

The natural parametric organization of the "filter—recognizer" couples has an important consequence. This kind of organization provides the simplicity of readjusting the system from one OD–FPD–NPD group to another and even *from one national NL to another*. For instance, the Russian version of the system was given to our Slovakian colleagues. Under Dr. L. Tovarek's (Bratislava) guidance, a single expert readjusted it within a month to three languages: Czech, Slovak and Ukrainian [38]. We dare note that conventional linguistic systems will never allow such a readjustment because of radical differences in morphology, syntax and semantics. It would be like to create the linguistic analysis system anew.

Now we would like to add that the system toggling between languages or between domains can be performed automatically. We shall investigate this possibility later.

Here is another remark to finish this section. We are greatly pleased to notice other scientists lead some ideas close to orientated linguistics. As for computer NL understanding, for instance, a very similar view is proposed by T. Winograd and F. Flores in their marvellous book [39]. The same can be said about the book by Dovgyallo and his colleagues [40].

In the next section we shall discuss whether the conventional grammar concepts can be exploited in the work of the filters and recognizers.

12.3 The conventional grammar elements used in orientated linguistics

It could not pass unnoticed that the previous discussion lacked any mention of the conventional linguistic text analysis levels: morphology, syntax, etc., which are usually subdivided into surface and deep sublevels. We already touched on the root of this effect (e.g. in Section 8.3) when we saw the conventional text analyzing mechanisms processing a text into the information not correlated with the task information. As the latter is the only information of interest in orientated linguistics, any conventional parser as a system just has nothing to do with the NL text understanding problem in orientated linguistics.

However, it does not mean that orientated linguistics necessarily rejects any category of conventional linguistics. Here the following criterion works: grammar categories are identified and taken into account if and only if they can help to detect or identify the subtexts $t_{(b..)}$, t_k, t_{am} and t_w.

In the above mentioned NPD "Oil-products transportations", subtexts with oil-products names play the only role of the proper algorithm "product name" argument, whatever case, number or gender. Then no morphologic data are necessary. Even more, the appropriate subdictionary may include only the word stems thus simplifying and reducing the search. Notice that nothing of the sort is possible beyond the NPD–FPD–OD framework of orientated linguistics. At the same time, the names of cities can play the part of either "the supplier's name" or "the consumer's name" arguments. One of the ways to indicate it in English is to use the propositions "to" (to Moscow) or "from" (from Moscow). So, we have to place these propositions into the subdictionary. With a more inflexional language (Russian, for instance), both propositions and inflectional endings should be placed there, because there appears a curtailed morphologic analysis to recognize cases by means of the endings when the propositions are absent.

As this part of the book deals with man-to-computer (not man-to-man) NL communication, we can point to another important source of simplicity and reliability, which is peculiar to orientated linguistics. It is the possibility of ignoring words and word-combinations of subtexts t_{NIL} (Section 11.4) at all the stages of the analyzing procedure. In fact, these words and word combinations have no effect on the task data. The most evident consequence of this possibility is that t_{NIL} elements may not be placed in any filter subdictionary making the analysis indifferent to errors in them.

We have to notice again that this sort of things is just impossible in conventional linguistics. Even if a word has nothing to do with the task information, it can affect the syntactical or semantic structure of the text. It means that every word must be correctly identified, analyzed and built into the syntactical structure of the phrase. Then the dictionary has to include all words of the language (as many as the available memory allows) together with their variations represented either explicitly or implicitly. A perfect grammar analysis is necessary as well as special facilities to overcome mistakes in all the words, whether or not they affect the proper reaction selection.

In this way the dramatic advantage of skipping t_{NIL} is absolutely clear because it radically reduces the understanding process.

So, the conventional grammar is used in the orientated text analysis as much as it helps to detect and recognize $t_{(b..)}$, t_k, t_{am} and t_w subtexts. The volume and complicity of the grammar knowledge are determined by this purpose only and turn out to be extremely low. With the simplicity and uniformity of the whole orientated analysis structure, it results in very good characteristics of free NL text understanding systems based on orientated linguistics. The following section gives an example.

12.4 An orientated system for industrial purposes

The above used examples in Sections 9.5 and 12.1 are taken from the industrial experience of the orientated NL understanding system, one of its early versions (see Chapter 20 for details). This system supported absolutely free NL database queries. It functioned on minicomputers in real time: the text analysis used to take 1–3 seconds, the typical reaction waiting interval was not longer than 5–7 seconds. The NL understanding system software took under 64 kB of RAM so that almost all computer reserves served for the database management system, i.e. performed their basic duties. For the sake of comparison we would like to note that the most economical contemporary conventional understanding systems took not less than 500 kB of RAM ([16], for example).

During the years of operation the system made not a mistake. Within the oil-products transportation NPD the designers and supervisors failed to produce a humanly sensible and unambiguous text for the computer to interpret incorrectly. Even more, the computer went successfully through incidents like the text of example (a) of Section 9.5 or the text "The Kazakhs to the Kirghizes" which implied a reaction of giving out the information on all the transportations of all the products from Kazakhstan to Kirghizia through all the accounted period. (We wonder how a conventional system would react to this text). Despite the system was not equipped with any error suppression facilities, it used to neglect syntactical errors practically always and was tolerant to a great deal of misspellings. The following examples, translated from Russian, will help to appreciate the stylistic freedom and spelling easiness the system admitted:

"How much furnace fuel was sen**d** from Ufa to Kazakhstan and Altai?"

"T**a**ll me what Khabarovsk delivered to Primorye?"

"And what ab**uo**t Moscow to Petersburg?"

Where d**e**d the diesel fuel go from Byelorussia?"

"What is the tot**l** kerosene provision for the plants of Samara?"

"Give me all the inform**e**tion on the road asphalt deliveries from Perm?"

"Find those goddamned railroad tanks with pet**rp**l from Odessa?"

"Ukrainian deliveries."

"Total deliveries from Moscow."

"How do **t**things stand about diesel oils?"

"And diesel fuels?"

The last sentence gives an example of the ellipsis. We shall discuss this phenomenon in the next section.

12.5 The ellipsis in orientated linguistics

The difficulty of this problem in conventional linguistics derives from the tendency to solve it by the inner linguistic means neglecting what they include in the concept of "extra-linguistic information", i.e. pragmatics.

We think, there are two reasons for this tendency.

The first reason is the good old "conceptional purity" kept up in classical linguistics. This linguistics feels a certain haughtiness and irritation about any infiltration of the life prose, e.g. pragmatics. Suffice it to remember the hard way that the deep semantics walked along to be honored to become a part of linguistics.

The second reason is more objective and less snobbish. Even if conventional linguistics welcomed pragmatics, it would hardly appreciate this knowledge, because this linguistics does not possess any exactly defined object domain concept and has no idea of narrow problem domains. So, there are no means of separating a currently necessary part of the world, narrow enough to be provided with an observable formal model.

We have seen that the concepts of OD, FPD, and NPD are exactly defined in orientated linguistics and make the base for the activity model backing it. The objects behind these concepts are under control, at least, in terms of their narrowness. As a result, in a K-stationary environment it is always possible to separate a narrow OD–NPD "subworld" of things and problems, with all the subscripts $(b..)$, k, am, w running through no more than finite ranges of values. By virtue of this fact, the ellipsis becomes just not a problem in orientated linguistics.

If the ellipsis occurs, the system is guided by a small set of simple rules interpreting defaults. In brief, these rules are as follows.

If a sentence t lacks any $t_{(b..)}$ subtext, t is considered to belong to the previous NPD.

If t does not include any t_k subtext (the reacting algorithm name), it is considered that the author of the text is thinking this information to be known from the preceding sentences. The system reacts to t by the algorithm used for the previous sentence. This operation is transitive. By way of example let us discuss the dialog:

User's query: "How many barrels of oil were sent to Moscow?"

Computer responce: "79 000"

U.: "And to Kursk?"

C.: "21 500"

U.: "And to Perm?"

C.: "33 000"

From the first sentence the system understands that the algorithm "The volume of deliveries to ..." is meant. This algorithm is considered to be proper in the second and third sentences as well.

The interpretation of default arguments depends upon whether a new algorithm or the previous one works in the given sentence (this being cleared up by the above described analysis).

If an algorithm remains the same, the values of its arguments come from the latest sentence. This operation is transitive too. For instance, the arguments "barrels" and "oil" are transferred from the first sentence to the others.

If it turns out that a new algorithm is meant in the given sentence, only its arguments are sought. If their values are named, there are no defaults and the obtained data should be let out to form a reaction. If the sentence lacks values of some arguments of the pointed algorithm, this fact is understood as a command to output the summarized information on these arguments. For instance, none of the sentences in the example above contains a value of the argument "period of time". Depending on the convention, such a default is responded by either a total delivery figure through the whole accounted period or a table of deliveries for each day of this period or both.

Now we can see that the ellipsis problem is also extremely simple in orientated linguistics.

The comparison of the NL text understanding scheme of orientated linguistics with that of the conventional one produces an impression that orientated linguistics has a lot of advantages. The leading role of the recognition procedures (Section 12.1) brings us to the supposition that the orientated analysis inherits those advantages mainly from the pattern recognition. The latter, in its turn, gets its power in the environment K-stationarity. In order to test the correctness of this supposition we shall consider some tenets of the pattern recognition theory essential for our issue. That will be done in the next chapter.

Chapter 13
SOME CONCEPTS OF THE PATTERN RECOGNITION THEORY AS APPLIED TO ORIENTATED LINGUISTICS

13.1 Correctness of the understanding problem in orientated linguistics

It is not a simple coincidence that the title of this section looks counter the title of Chapter 9. Orientated linguistics is based on the pattern recognition, and any pattern recognition problem is always solvable and *correct* if the set of patterns is finite (in our terms it means the environment K-stationarity).

Here is the explanation. To restore an object irrespectively to other objects, one needs an absolute description of this object, i.e. the complete information about it [17]. At the same time, in order to recognize the object among a finite set of classes, a minimal (relative) description of differences between classes is enough. That is why the huge loss of information, caused by the thought-to-text conversion, makes the thought-from-text restoration problem incorrect but does not hurt the problem of recognizing the class of the thought among K known classes.

What strikes is the difference in the mentioned demand for information. For example, only 1 bit of information is necessary to distinguish between moustached and non-moustached faces, while the portrait restoration takes $\approx 3 \cdot 10^6$ bits (TV quality: $\approx 625 \times 700$ pixels and $128 = 2^7$ grades of brightness, i.e. 7 bits per pixel). The greater is the number of classes, the less is the gain, but the basic ratio remains the same. This illustrates the effect of transferring any K-stationary problem (the NL understanding problem included) to the pattern recognition. The wide expansion of K-stationary environments, mentioned in Section 4.3, explains why some elements of the pattern recognition can be found in the great variety of problems.

We would like to highlight the most essential result of orientated linguistics eliminating the incorrectness of the NL understanding problem. In conventional linguistics this incorrectness is followed by the plurality and instability of solutions which properties are of qualitative nature. In orientated linguistics these properties make way for the numeric characteristics such as the misrecognition probability, the "false alarm" probability and the missing probability. Furthermore, the pattern recognition theory offers special tools of minimizing these characteristics.

We shall remind some important concepts of this theory in the ensuing sections of this chapter.

13.2 The problem of likeness. Postulate P13.1

There are two basic ideas in the pattern recognition theory. They are the idea of likeness and the idea of training. We are starting with the former.

As for physical objects, this idea is usually stated as a postulate establishing that the characteristics of objects are alike if these objects belong to the same class. This postulate is founded on the observation that objects of a similar designation and practical use usually have similar physical properties. Postulate P13.1 formulates the inverse dependence that is closer to the point here:

Postulate P13.1 *Likeness of objects' properties means the objects belong to the same class.*

Thus, Postulate P13.1 establishes the likeness of objects in the *implicit* manner. Sometimes this postulate cannot be used and the likeness has to be established *explicitly*, i.e. all similar objects must be listed. It is possible only if the set of objects is finite, which means observable in practical applications. Unfortunately, the implicit approach does not work well for the linguistic objects. Nevertheless, it gives some opportunities discussed below.

Postulate P13.1 is formulated and interpreted in the most natural way if the features of the investigated objects are measured on continuous (usually physical) numeric scales. The space of these features can be provided with some proximity measure as a measure of likeness in terms of the features. Then the essence of Postulate P13.1 can be explained as follows: points representing objects of the same class form a cluster with few points of this class outside the cluster and few points of other classes inside it. In other words, a slight variation of an object's features almost never (except for points near the cluster boundary) pushes the object to another class cluster.

As we see, Postulate P13.1 depends upon whether it is possible to define any natural proximity measure in the feature space. The mentioned simplest case deals with continuous scales. In the case of discrete features it is less convenient but still possible. Here the values of the features must be arranged in some order. The worst situation concerns unorderable discrete, for example, boolean features. In this case it is rather difficult or even impossible to be guided by Postulate P13.1. More information on Postulate P13.1 can be taken from [18, 19].

Now let us clear up whether Postulate P13.1 is applicable to the subtext recognition problem, i.e. the recognition of NL words and word-combinations. These objects are characterized by lexical and grammatical features. Though the latter are correlated with the semantic function of words, this correlation is mediated and indistinct. That is why the grammatical characteristics do not allow going farther than the surface semantic level in conventional linguistics. In fact, even the deep semantic level needs extra-linguistic information.

There are two reasons for this trouble:

1. The grammatical features do not permit ordered scales, thus forbidding any sensible proximity measure. This phenomenon can be named "the grammatical space untopologizability".

2. Besides a lexical object can have different values of the features, it can change the very feature set from case to case. This phenomenon will be named "the lexical polysemy". It includes the notorious effects of homonymy, shading, polysemy, etc.

These two phenomena are to be considered in the following sections.

13.3 The grammatical space untopologizability

By way of illustration let us consider the feature "case" of Russian nouns (there are six cases: nominative, genitive, dative, accusative, instrumental, prepositional). It is hardly possible to give a sensible answer to the questions: "What cases are close to each other?", "How can they be arranged?", etc. For instance, is the instrumental case closer to the genitive case than the prepositional one? We must mention some publications on the numerical scales for verbal constructions: the so called linguistic variables based on the fuzzy set theory and the pseudo-physical, in particular, spatial logics ([20, 21]). However, all these papers deal with language objects expressing measurable physical (geometrical, biological, etc.) quantities such as distance ("rather far"), size ("he is tall"), age, weight, etc. Generally, the problem of scaling a linguistic category can not be solved and even formulated. This fact remains true in both conventional and orientated linguistics as well as in any other type of linguistics.

Now we see the untopologizability preventing Postulate P13.1 from being used effectively. Thus the implicit likeness of linguistic objects and their features can not be established. Any progress in this direction stops at some very general and obvious facts. For instance, it was discovered that verbs and their derivatives were members of t_k subtexts (the reaction algorithm name) rather frequently (but not always).

Probably every utility of those facts was explored in works like [12, 8]. In these investigations the computer understanding means assembling the name of an action and the names of its actants. The potential roles of the actants are distributed to form the so called "action-actant ensemble" ("conceptual dependence" in [8], "deep case" in [12]).

From our standpoint, this generally useful scheme has an inherited flaw caused by the lexical polysemy. We are going to consider this phenomenon in the next section.

13.4 The lexical polysemy

As the grammatical space untopologizability has its roots in the very nature of grammatical features, it dominates both conventional and orientated linguistics. By contrast, the lexical polysemy is an interpretive category, and different kinds of linguistics surmount this polysemy in different ways. Therefore we shall consider this phenomenon for conventional and orientated linguistics separately.

Let us take the conventional case. The polysemy shows up as soon as the above mentioned ensembles are constructed. In fact, one can not provide an action with any certain list of participants and their roles. For instance, the action "to lead" changes its list in accordance with the situation considered:

- "he led a child by ..." (the possible arguments: "by what", "when", etc.)
- "the path led to ..." (the arguments "by what" and "when" make way for "through what", for example)
- "he led her to do ..." (another list)
- "he led a quiet life" (still another list)
- "he led hearts" (...) and so on.

One should not think the polysemy to be peculiar to the action names (verbs). It is also natural for other lexical objects, for instance, the names of actants. Suffice it to remember the wide set of meanings that such common words as "table" and "chair" can be used in.

Once aimed at the entire language, conventional linguistics cannot overcome the lexical polysemy. But it is this polysemy that causes this non-uniqueness investigated in Chapters 7–9, where the sense non-uniqueness was proved to be insurmountable within the framework of conventional linguistics.

Now let us consider the case of orientated linguistics. In Section 13.1 it was demonstrated that the orientated understanding problem was correct, because it could be reduced to the pattern recognition problem. It means that the lexical polysemy does not prevent a text from being interpreted uniquely. Let us work out why it is possible in orientated linguistics.

Certainly, this advantage is due to the concept of OD–NPD. For instance, the above examples with the verb "to lead" belong to different NPD's. Within these NPD's the actant lists are fixed and any argument has the only meaning. Expanding this observation to the general case we can introduce the term "uniexpressive NPD". More exactly, an NPD is called *uniexpressive* (UNPD) if any lexical object has a single meaning in the dictionaries of this NPD.

Experience suggests that any FPD can be decomposed into UNPD's. Furthermore, a word possessing several meanings can hint that the given NPD consists of smaller self-contained NPD's and the further decomposition can simplify the filters and recognizers. For instance, in our analyzing one of the NPD's in the OD–FPD "oil-products transportation", the Russian word "данные" (*dannyje*) was discovered to have two meanings: "data" and "given". This fact broke the NPD into 2 UNPD's. The first UNPD covered the transportations themselves and the second UNPD dealt with information on those transportations.

The UNPD concept is also supported by the language genesis. From primitive texts of the thing—action level ("TA-level" which means physical actions with things) NL progressed to the modern intellectual use with metaphoric situations prevailing over TA-situations (see Section 9.2). In the course of its evolution NL avoided new words and attributed new meanings to existing words, making the UNPD concept responsible for the selection of the necessary meaning. For instance, the words "to put" and "to carry" are used in this way: "to put a book on a table" and "to put one's money into something", "to carry a load" and "to carry a conclusion". Notice that a person's speech development is similar, from simple TA texts to metaphoric texts [22, page 178].

So, orientated linguistics resolves the lexical polysemy automatically by means of the NPD (UNPD) selection and identification.

Unfortunately, as we have seen, the grammatical space untopologizability is still an obstacle in both conventional and orientated linguistics, thus keeping Postulate P13.1 from being applied effectively. In accordance with Section 13.2, we have to establish likeness explicitly. Of course, the available implication elements (Section 13.3) must be taken into account because they can decrease the volume of the explicit form.

The explicit establishing of likeness is to be considered in the next section.

13.5 The explicit establishing of likeness

Thus, the implicit establishing of likeness is available neither in conventional nor in orientated linguistics. As indicated above, a transition to the explicit establishing is necessary. However, we are going to prove that only orientated linguistics can implement this transition; within the framework of conventional linguistics it is impossible.

One can see right now that it is impossible to establish likeness explicitly for the entire language considered in conventional linguistics. First of all, there are many semantically similar words and word-combinations. Even the very idea of semantic equality (i.e. synonymy) can not be fixed and provided with a non-discrepant definition, though this fact runs counter the scholastic linguistics and the existence of synonymy dictionaries.

We already met this fact when proving Theorem 7.1 (Section 7.2). There the very definition of FPD synonymous sentences included the condition of their inequality in another FPD. For instance, the sentences "He lost his tooth here" and "His tooth was kicked out here" are semantically equal in the street scuffle

FPD. At the same time this relation is broken in the dentist's FPD, where the second sentence does not work at all.

What was said is true not only for sentences but for word-combinations and even words as well. Two words semantically equal in one FPD (NPD) may not be synonymous in another one. The book [8], for instance, proposes the symbol PTRANS to denote all the words like "to go", "to walk", "to tramp", "to stride", "to pace", "to stalk", "to trudge", "to hobble", etc. The author of [8] proclaim them to have the same meaning. But it is clear that these words are related only in the most primitive aspect — the TA-aspect. Other aspects separate their meanings. And it is not evident that these words carry mainly the TA-aspect in every sentence they occur in. What is more, their very existence in the language proves that their subtle aspects are more important than the TA-aspect. Otherwise, the only word "to go" could substitute all of them. This situation is rather typical. The substitution of one word by another modifies the sense provoked by the whole sentence. For instance, if we substitute the words "to produce", "to fabricate", "to make", "to manufacture" by a common code ("to produce", for example), we shall run the risk of misunderstanding. A substitution like this must be supported by a thorough research of how these words are used in their FPD's. If some industrial environment includes an oil-refining plant and a tank-cars manufacturing plant, it is not so easy to understand the sentence "The plant has manufactured ten tank-cars" if "to manufacture" is coded by "to produce". The inverse statement is also true: despite two words do not seem close in their meanings, they can become synonymous in some FPD. For instance, a dictionary of synonyms will never say that "to be" and "to see" are synonyms. However, the texts "Has Johnson been in your surgery today?" and "Has Johnson seen you today?" are semantically equal in the FPD "Seeing a doctor".

Thus, any definition of synonymy is false while it treats this concept as a constant and invariable characteristic of a word pair. It means that the "entire language", as well as conventional linguistics at all, lacks a chance of establishing likeness explicitly.

As for orientated linguistics, the concept of UNPD improves the situation. Any word or word-combination of S_A's filter subdictionaries has a single meaning in any particular UNPD by definition. The inverse statement is false: if a word or word combination t' has some single meaning in a UNPD, there can be found a set $\{t\}'$ of words and word combinations a) occurring in this UNPD b) having the same meaning. This assertion is nothing but the first part of Postulate P7.2 (Section 7.2), extended from whole sentences over their fragments, words and word-combinations.

This assertion suggests two conclusions.

The first conclusion has theoretical significance. It says that the orientated linguistic concept of UNPD allows formulating a non-discrepant definition of synonymy:

Definition 13.1 *The set $\{t\}'$ including words and/or word-combinations of the same meaning in some UNPD is called the set of synonyms of $\forall t' \in \{t\}'$ in this UNPD.*

Therefore the synonymy can be defined only with reference to a particular UNPD.

The second conclusion is practical. It states that the set $\{t\}'$ of any word or word-combination t' taken from S_A's filter subdictionaries is *finite* in any UNPD. This follows from the finiteness of the SST T (Section 10.2). The same concerns the NPD filter subdictionaries with respect to the appropriate FPD.

The finiteness of the set $\{t\}'$ permits the explicit establishing of likeness. Thus, in contrast to conventional linguistics, it turns out to be possible in orientated linguistics. Furthermore, it seems adequate. In fact, in order to interpret a text in some UNPD correctly, a human being must memorize all the words and word-combinations of $t_{(b..)}$, t_k, t_{am}, t_w subtexts together with their meanings in this UNPD.

Practice calls for a reasonable compromise between the above mentioned poor, but economical implicit establishing of likeness/difference and the flawless, but sometimes huge explicit establishing. All the data necessary to produce these two likeness/difference establishing components are obtained during the training. The fundamental grounds of the training are discussed in the following section.

13.6 Training and Postulates P13.2 and P13.3

One of the most fundamental and smart ideas of the pattern recognition theory is that of the training and the training set. As far as we know, the concept of a representative training set, created four decades ago, was the first realization of rather a modern idea of the experts' informal knowledge acquisition.

The significance of a representative training set for the orientated recognizing procedure is extremely impressive. NL is known as a huge informal system. Thus its rules and regularities cannot be expected to form a finite and observable set. That is why even an enormous fund of registered conventional linguistic knowledge leaves a nonzero probability of meeting a text with some new phenomenon for the analyzer to interpret it in the wrong way. But orientated linguistics moves down the tree of OD–FPD–NPD–UNPD domains to obtain an extremely narrow, "zero-dimensional" section through the NL set. It gives hope of obtaining a bounded and observable subset of language rules and regularities inside this "section". It is the training set of texts that exposes this subset. The training set comprises the texts that occurred during the training period, launching an algorithm from some NPD.

The experience indicates that a representative training set is able to expose the mentioned subset of rules and regularities. This observation will be formulated as a postulate which establishes the *completeness* of a sufficiently long training set. Let us consider an infinite sequence Z of tasks. If there appears a problem from the k-th class, the probability of this event is designated as

p_k. Since a K-stationary environment is under discussion, p_k is a nonzero finite number, $\forall k \in \overline{1,K}$. This fact allows us to apply the usual N,ε-formulation of the wellknown property of a stationary discrete random variable.

Namely, let $P_k(N)$ stand for the probability of a task from the k-th class occurring in a sequence of N tasks at least once. Then the postulate can be formulated as follows:

Postulate P13.2 *For any finite (nonzero) numbers $p_1,\ldots,p_k,\ldots,p_K$, natural K and $\varepsilon > 0$ there exists some finite natural N_0 such that*

$$\forall N > N_0 : \quad 1 - P_k(N) \le \varepsilon\,,\ k \in \overline{1,K}\,.$$

The sequence of N tasks ($N > N_0$) forms a complete training set. With a proper N_0, the probability of the set missing a class can be made as small as desired.

In Section 5.2 we mentioned that both strong and weak stationarities could be considered as K-stationarity for the appropriate level of problems. This fact and the finiteness of the SST T make the term "problem" fit the task of scanning an input text for some subtext of it to match a foreknown pattern. Then the k-th class of problems for the considered level implies a complete collection of those texts of the sequence Z (here: all the phrases in succession) where exactly the given subtext can be found. From this it follows that Postulate P13.2 is applicable to the sequence Z treated as a sequence of phrases. And this means here that there always exists a *finite* length of the sequence of phrases such that the sequence includes all possible versions of all necessary subtexts.

It is obvious how to use this effect. The training set being accumulated, its texts are handed to experts. They underline all the wordings of all necessary subtexts, group them into classes and supply the classes with proper subscripts to indicate their roles after the role list Eq. (12.1). The lists of UNPD's, algorithms and arguments are also provided.

Though Postulate P13.2 fixes the finiteness of the training set, it does not expose the length of the set. In practice the experts' intuition is responsible for the training period duration. Their saying "Well, that's it" is the starting point of the second set accumulation. This set is called "testing".

This method is also supported by Postulate P13.3. It expresses a smart and very important idea. Suppose we have a recognizing algorithm with variable parameters modifying its work so that any limited group of the texts from the training set is processed into answers which match those of an expert-"teacher". This can be implemented, for example, by memorizing all the texts and the appropriate answers given by the teacher. Then the essence of Postulate P13.3 is as follows:

Postulate P13.3 *With some natural suppositions about the statistics of problems, the probability of the algorithm making an error at control sets is a* non-increasing *function of the number of texts in the training set.*

From Postulate P13.3 it follows (with the mentioned suppositions) that the algorithm training process *converges* to some error probability, which is minimal for the given algorithm. More detailed and formal information on this issue can be found in [19, 23], for instance. To the best of our knowledge, the literature lacks any exhaustive explanation for the phenomenon stated by Postulate P13.3. We think it derives from the environment stationarity.

The properties of the described training process yield a theoretically errorless solution of the NL understanding problem in a K-stationary environment. As for practice, the error probability can be made as small as desired. This conclusion was supported experimentally by the observed practical reliability of the real orientated system mentioned in Section 12.4.

13.7 Heterogeneous problems of the pattern recognition. Pre-recognition

The pattern recognition problem is rather simple in comparison with incorrect problems, but it does not mean its absolute simplicity. A recognizing procedure grows complicated as the number of classes in the problem runs up. This trouble is generally inherent in the pattern recognition. The existing tools try to overcome this obstacle by means of converting input information into a more adequate form or squeezing the "feature space" or improving the representation of classes in that space.

All those tools were invented and developed for procedures with constant bodies. When applied to different input objects, such procedures change only the values of their arguments. We call them *invariatable* procedures.

Though such an approach is powerful enough to be used in our application, we prefer another method to solve the pattern recognition problem in orientated linguistics. This method exploits the fact that the filter–recognizer system in the right-hand side of Fig. 12.1 is recursive. The method is based on the concept of problem heterogeneity [24] and is allied with the tree-decoding method of the signal reception in a communication channel.

To start up with, let us define the concepts of homogeneous and heterogeneous problems.

Let $\{\Pi\}$ be a bounded set of invariatable procedures that recognize objects t from some set $\{t\}$. Let $\lambda(\Pi, t)$ be a fixed criterion testing the quality of a procedure $\Pi \in \{\Pi\}$ applied to an object t in the given recognition problem. The criterion λ should depend on both reliability and complexity of the procedure Π recognizing the object t.

The procedure is called λ-*adequate* to the object t if the criterion λ choose it as the best one for this t. For instance, when more than one procedure from $\{\Pi\}$ can be applied to the object t and the other conditions (for example, reliability) are equal, the adequate procedure has the minimal complexity.

We shall call a recognition problem *homogeneous* with respect to $\{\Pi\}$ or (with $\{\Pi\}$ fixed) simply homogeneous if there is at least one procedure in $\{\Pi\}$, which is λ-adequate to $\forall t \in \{t\}$.

Otherwise, a recognition problem is called *heterogeneous.*

The first definition can be illustrated by the problem of portrait identification under the condition that all faces are equivalent in terms of presence/absence of hair, moustache, eyeglasses, etc. If this restriction is removed, the problem will become heterogeneous. If one deals with graphemes and machinery drafts and men's faces simultaneously, the problem appears to be heterogeneous too, because these groups of objects have different adequate procedures.

It is evident that the average complexity will be minimized if every input object t is processed by its adequate procedure. It means that first it must be worked out what procedure is adequate to the current input object. Here arises another pattern recognition problem: among the entire set $\{\Pi\}$ one must recognize the subscript of the procedure adequate to the object t.

Thus, a heterogeneous pattern recognition problem solution algorithm has to consist of at least 2 levels: the first recognizes the procedure to be applied to the input object and the second launches this procedure to recognize the object.

The problem being solved at the first level can be named the *pre-recognition problem.* It is evident that this level processes any t in the same way because nothing is known about the object. Consequently, the first level always solves a homogeneous problem. The selected procedure $\Pi \in \{\Pi\}$ is applied to those t, which it is adequate to. Therefore, the second level solves a homogeneous problem too (we call it a final recognition problem). *Thus, a heterogeneous problem can (and must) be decomposed into a sequence of no less than two homogeneous problems.*

The pattern recognition problem connected with the NL text understanding problem in a K-stationary environment is often heterogeneous. If we consider the identification of the proper reacting algorithm subscript k as the final recognition, the identification of $(b..)$ turns out to be a pre-recognition. If the values of the arguments w and am are also necessary for the final recognition to launch the k-th algorithm, the identification of k becomes a pre-recognition for the levels of w and am, because it clarifies the argument lists. In its turn, the level of $(b..)$ may not be the first one because it can be preceded by the FPD level. The latter can follow the level the OD identification.

Just as any tree decoding process, the described procedure needs a very high probability of correct decision at all the levels. At the same time the decision features must be rather simple. Probing into man-to-man NL communication below, we shall see that NL is actually equipped with extremely effective and simple pre-recognition tools.

Now we are finishing our brief discussion of the orientated linguistic philosophy and theory of man-to-computer NL communication. In the next part of the book we shall demonstrate how the basic principles of this linguistics display themselves in man-to-man NL communication.

Part IV

ORIENTATED LINGUISTICS OF MAN-TO-MAN COMMUNICATION

Chapter 14
MAN-TO-MAN COMMUNICATION FROM THE ORIENTATED LINGUISTIC STANDPOINT

14.1 Goals and reactions in the process of man-to-man NL communication

The main feature of the man-to-computer dialogue is that every address to the computer derives from some goal of the speaker and expresses a task for reaching this goal or its part. It was this observation that allowed us to erect orientated linguistics. Thus, the "goal–reaction" couple frames everything in man-to-computer communication .

We already noticed in Sections 8.3 and 10.1 that a study of man-to-man communication could not be described in the "text–sense" paradigm. *Every* text of man-to-man communication implies a real goal too, and the addressee turns out to be either a tool or an object of this goal.

In fact, a human being's sensible actions are goaled. If a person can reach his goal himself, he does it without getting into a speech act. He just fulfills his desire and reaches the goal.

However, sometimes a person (called the author below) needs or wants somebody's help or participation. If he uses an NL text (gesture, miming, signal, etc.) to involve another person, the author's intermediate goal is to make this person carry out the desired action. That is what the author pursues while forming the appropriate NL text.

Not only physical actions are concerned here. The author's goal may be to initiate some mental process in the interlocutor's brain, for example, to put a piece of information into his memory, to make him perform a logical reasoning, etc. The author himself may act as a text addressee, and even this "self-conversation" implies a reasonable goal: to cheer oneself up, to quiet oneself down, etc. What is more, there may be no real addressee at all, or it can be represented by a group of people. This situation is natural for a published text. The author has to refer his text to an imaginary "average" reader. It is natural that the author can fail to reach his goal with some particular reader who differs from the "average" one in his interests, skills, curiosity, etc. The same thing happens to a teacher who speaks in a simple manner for the sake of his average pupils but bores his best ones though he has not pursued this goal.

Thus, a sane man's shaking air by words or marking paper always pursue a goal. This *goal* is a *reaction* of the interlocutor whether he is another person, or the author himself, or a group, or an anonymous reader, etc.

Now we see that both man-to-computer and man-to-man communication use NL in the same way: any NL text conveys a reaction task, but in man-to-man communication this reaction involves informal components as well as formal ones (Section 8.4). With this fact taken into account, we are going to consider orientated linguistics of man-to-man communication.

14.2 Is it profitable to apply orientated linguistics to man-to-man communication?

The man-to-computer NL communication scheme discussed in the preceding chapters was connected with the business dialogue, i.e. with the man and computer's interchanging addresses. Any NL address was considered as rather a short text. Since addresses appeared in texts one by one, the computer was working in the interpreting mode. In its turn, NL behaved very specifically, calling for the new term "address language" to be introduced.

This kind of dialogue seems natural for man-to-man business communication as well. By the way, Chapters 10 and 11 were illustrated with the dialogues of this particular sort (the sketches of "the car service"). The only principal difference between man-to-man and man-to-computer dialogues is that informal components of reactions are impossible to take into account. Therefore, we think it is more interesting to devote our consideration of man-to-man NL communication to "dialogueless" lengthy texts. The interlocutor (reader) is not supposed to react immediately to every sentence or group of sentences of these texts. Of course, this type of texts includes dialogues with addresses looking rather like monologues.

In this part of the book we shall try to expose the utility of orientated linguistics in the processing of lengthy texts of man-to-man communication.

First of all, this utility depends on whether the text processing regards for the above discussed informal reaction components.

In fact, the role and importance of informal components changes substantially when the "address language" makes way to the language of man-to-man lengthy text. Talking to a computer the man can not help being aware of the computer's capacity to get and realize only formal components of reactions. That is why he offers only problems that are solvable with this restriction.

When man-to-man texts remove this restriction, the role of informal components becomes very great, but the computer continues to manipulate with only formal components. Therefore, man-to-man lengthy texts worth studying only if there are any applications of these texts, which require no more than formal components. Luckily, such applications exist and are wellknown. Thus the issue of the lengthy texts computer processing is still on the agenda, and we are going to discuss it.

14.3 K-stationarity in orientated linguistics of lengthy texts

The basic concept of orientated linguistics is the environment K-stationarity. Nothing can prevent from applying this concept to man-to-man lengthy texts. However the concept of K-stationarity must be slightly redefined in this case. Why? The so called reaction component synchronism compels us to do that.

When a dialogue consisted of short addresses, the start and the finish of a reaction to any address were established naturally and even automatically by the following agreement. A party's reaction to the other party's n-th address started after this address and finished before the $(n+1)$-th address. Therefore we could consider the $(2n+1)$-th party alternation act as a signal of the given party's finishing its n-th reaction (Section 7.1). Though different components of the n-th reaction could actually start and finish at different moments of time within the start–finish interval, we might not take this into account in that part of the book. By default we supposed that all reaction components simultaneously started at the moment the reaction started and simultaneously finished at the moment the reaction finished. Then we could speak about reactions with synchronous components.

Just the same, the components of a reaction to a lengthy text can start at different moments for different durations. However, there are no timing tools like a party alternate act. So, here we have to speak about reactions with asynchronous components.

For the value of K to be estimated in the environment of some text, one should count and classify the reader's reactions in the process of his reading the text. So, the case of asynchronous components calls for new agreements on combining components and comparing reactions.

In the current reasoning we are interested only in the qualitative side of the matter. The questions are whether a lengthy text can be characterized by a finite value of K and how to estimate this value. Answering these questions we shall obtain the desired agreements. In so doing we must remember that the designation of a text processing computer system affects the accounted set of formal components: the same text may have different sets of components and different values of K.

The agreement can proceed from the following. A reaction is determined by the subset of components it involves. A change in this set can be considered as a transition to another reaction. Now we suggest a mental experiment.

Let there be a set of all components. Let us divide a lengthy text into N segments for each of them to involve an invariable subset of components taken from the total set. A component is considered as involved if its weight is greater than some threshold. Let us settle that each of these segments causes a single reaction. Two reactions are equivalent (of the same class) if their subsets of involved components are equal or alike (a component may have different weights in these two subsets). The number of obtained classes is taken as K of the given lengthy text. If $N \gg K$ is true, the text will be said to represent a K-stationary environment. The term "environment" is understood as the "environment of reactions to the author's text" (meaning what we described in Section 6.1).

Thus, K-stationarity can be defined for lengthy texts as well. Now a man-to-man lengthy text can be qualitatively estimated in unusual terms of the stationarity degree of the environment of caused reactions.

For instance, a "very long" or even "infinite" text (like a voluminous novel) causes an infinite number of reactions. It is natural to associate this text with a non-stationary environment for the reasons closely similar to those given in Section 8.1. However, rather long but not "infinite" texts are wide-spread in practice. Their environments are characterized by finite, though high values of K. We shall call them "high K environments". Texts and environments of this kind are of particular interest to the study of man-to-man NL communication. Therefore, we shall try to project the basic principles of orientated linguistics onto this kind of texts.

We have seen three practical situations gravitating to the idea of high K environments or even of non-stationary environments. We shall discuss them in the next section.

14.4 Lengthy texts in practical research

The above mentioned practical situations occur in the computer systems called multitopical, goal revealing and automatic translation systems. We are going to consider them one by one since they differ in their reasons for having a high K.

We are starting with the *multitopical* systems because this situation is the clearest one. It results from a natural attempt to develop a topic-independent, universal NL understanding system. As the designers do not possess the FPD concept, they have to construct a procedure to be a priori capable of processing any text, i.e. an universal and standard procedure. We designate this procedure as $\widehat{\Pi}$ with $\lambda(\widehat{\Pi})$ denoting its average complexity. Notice that developing a universal system implies the system's environment non-stationarity.

What actually happens is that the system works in a K-stationary environment (see Section 4.3), though its K can be high. If K is high but finite we can treat a text as a consequence of reactions of K different types (see the previous section). Each type of reaction may be associated with a separate procedure. Let Π_k denote the procedure for the k-th type of reactions, $k \in \overline{1,K}$. Let its average complexity be designated as $\lambda(\Pi_k)$. As it was said in Section 13.7, if we abandon the "universality" of the procedure $\widehat{\Pi}$, it will result in

$$\forall k: \quad \lambda(\Pi_k) \leq \lambda(\widehat{\Pi}) .$$

At the same time here arises the already familiar problem of recognizing the subscript k of the adequate reaction algorithm for each segment of the text. In Section 15.1 we shall discuss how adequate reactions can be used profitably in the multitopical systems in spite of this additional recognition problem.

Let us speak about the *goal revealing* systems now. For definiteness sake we shall consider the systems designed to accumulate information from NL publications and to answer a user's NL query with the necessary piece of this information. These systems usually serve certain object and problem domains. For our experiments we took the domain "Reading automata theory and construction" and used the articles from [25, 26] as data sources.

Let us look through any of these articles. By way of example let it report new theoretical results. It is sure to comprise several parts of different topics often presented as separated sections. The whys and wherefores of the problem come first; the second place is occupied by a review of earlier publications with a piece of information about their drawbacks; next the presentation of the obtained results comes, etc. Each of these parts has its own set of data types, each data type has its own system format with its own algorithm of extracting, forming and fixing data. As for other articles of similar (here: theoretical) stuff, they have practically the same structure. If one collects a lot of corresponding parts (for instance, reviews), it will be clear that the number of their data types and, consequently, the number of their representing algorithms converge to some finite number. It means that the reaction environment is K-stationary. The value of K may be very high in a goal revealing system because of 1) a great number of possible data types within each class of parts, 2) a great number of these classes in each class of articles (theoretical presentations, for example) and 3) a great number of classes of articles within the field of reading automata: theoretical, experimental, bibliographical, historical, algorithmic, etc. Thus, even if a goal revealing system works in narrow object and problem domains, it may have a high K because of a wide range of possible goals with respect to information presented in a text.

To complete the picture we must add that in the considered systems the mode of answering an NL query (this answer may be formatted: Section 6.2) does not differ from the mode of accumulating information in the terms of the problem considered. Both situations expect the desired fragment of the data base to be recognized on the base of the NL text. The only difference is that the first mode uses the recognized fragment to complete it with new information and the second mode uses it to output this fragment partially or entirely. We shall discuss the goal revealing systems more thoroughly in Section 15.2.

At last we are coming to the *automatic translation systems.* The fact of the greatest significance is that this type of systems does not permit any division of the text into segments to classify them in accordance with the reaction they cause, as it was done above for the goal revealing systems.

In fact, the identity of the data types of all the text segments from some subset $Z_k \subset Z$ means only the identity of the business components of the man's complex reactions to those segments; other components may differ. Furthermore, we can not test this algorithmically, because human reactions always contain a huge subset of informal components. Just like fiction, scientific texts subdues this fact, at least in the aspect of associations and emotions like "Oh, I've got it now!", etc. That is why the computer never can determine whether two text segments from Z_k need the same or two different algorithms to provide an adequate reaction to each of them (an adequate translation is meant here), i.e. whether these segments are of the same type. The conclusion is that the environment of automatic translation is non-stationary, i.e. not a simply high but gigantic K (like $K \approx N$) takes place.

This does not concern the human translation. The man's brain is capable of dealing with both formal and informal reaction components. Therefore the man always can determine whether two problems are of the same type. Unlike the computer, the man can classify text segments in accordance with their desired reactions. In Section 15.3 we shall prove that the adequate automatic translation from one national NL to another is unlikely to be performed with the present-day computer architecture conceptions.

Chapter 15
ORIENTATED LINGUISTICS OF HIGH K ENVIRONMENTS

15.1 The multitopical systems and pre-recognition

As discussed above (Section 14.4), a procedure designed especially to react to one type of lengthy text segments is on the average simpler than a universal procedure designed for any type of segments. With small values of K this fact means that the text segment "understanding" should use a special algorithm to recognize the segment types and react to any segment by means of a procedure designed beforehand for this particular type of segments. This is what was done in the case of dialogues.

As mentioned in Section 13.7, a greater number K of classes does not simplify the pattern recognition problem. In particular, it complicates the input data preprocessing and adds dimensions to the decision-making space called the "feature space" in the pattern recognition theory. Therefore, a high K can make the text segment recognition problem tedious enough to nullify the effect of applying a specially designed reacting algorithm to each type of text segments.

Generally, we have got known the way out. The high K situations must be thought of as heterogeneous problems with one or more *pre-recognition* levels. However, the pre-recognition procedure can be enough complex itself. Its utility depends on how frequently it is launched in the course of the text processing. We can not neglect the worst case, when each text segment requires the pre-recognition procedure to be run. Then the utility shows itself in its worst proportions.

Luckily, a thorough investigation of many lengthy natural discourses of various contents (everyday, professional, literary, etc.) enables us to conclude that any discourse, whatever it is devoted to, concerns some narrow problem-object domain at every instant. This domain will be denoted by the familiar abbreviation "NPD" after all the necessary refinements are made. More specifically, any discourse text consists of *relatively long segments*, each of them belonging to an *NPD limited* by some topical and problematic framework. These segments are separated by rather short segments of transitions. The similar phenomena of focus stability and shift are wellknown in conventional linguistics [27].

This observation seems natural. In fact, it is not easy to imagine a multitopical discourse with sentences from different NPD's alternating. The reasons for this organization of texts are also clear. The author of a text, as well as its reader, can "load" and store in his "internal" memory the piece of information connected with a single NPD, including a fragment of the world model and adequate reactions, knowledge, data, associations, emotions, etc. When one has to change information complexes of this type too frequently (sometimes this takes place), the communication becomes difficult because of fatigue and a consequently great number of mistakes.

Since this argument seems evident for fragments of the world model, it must be true for the corresponding fragments of the language set. In fact, a change of the current NPD not only changes a part of the dictionary in use but modifies the meanings, the subcategorization frames, etc. See UNPD's, for instance (Section 13.4). Frequent and hasty modifications and loadings of this language data are as disadvantageous as those of the knowledge about the world.

Inasmuch as the said observation concerns absolutely natural and free-styled NL texts, it reflects an objective property of NL and must be treated as a *phenomenon of Nature.* Orientated linguistics can explain this phenomenon by means of the K-stationarity and NPD conceptions, thus contributing to the research of man-to-man texts.

In this way, the NPD pre-recognition procedure works only at the time of changing the NPD, i.e. rather seldom. We can therefore conclude that the pre-recognition is *efficient* as a tool of processing man-to-man lengthy texts. Now we shall reveal the real mechanisms that perform the NPD pre-recognition.

Our research discovered three of them. The first mechanism is based on the so called "bifunctional" words, the second one exploits special words (word-combinations) termed "NPD alternation indicators", the third one uses dedicated words (word-combinations) referred to as "new NPD pointers". These three mechanisms may be used separately or in combinations. Let us consider them.

15.1.1 The bifunctional words

While discussing the address language we mentioned that some words had two functions. Their basic function was, for example, to name an argument of the reacting algorithm. Besides, they could confirm or object the choice of the reacting algorithm (Section 12.2). This could happen, for instance, when an argument of the given type was peculiar to the given algorithm only. This fact remains true for man-to-man texts, in particular when some relevant words occur exclusively in a certain NPD or a group of NPD's. Thus, these words obtain another function in addition to that of naming a reaction type or an individualizing or working argument: they point to the current NPD. For instance, after a paragraph devoted to sales, a company annual report can contain the phrase "Last year the transportation department overconsumed 100 tons of gasoline ...". The main function of the word "overconsumed" is to make the department employees react properly ("gasoline" is an argument of this reaction). At the same time it has another function, as it signals of a transition from the

NPD of sales into the NPD bundle of transportation. In its turn, the word "gasoline" provides the selection of the specific NPD from the bundle. This is the second function of the word "gasoline", because the first one is to be an individualizing argument of the expected reaction. Note that in the given example the NPD was identified in two stages because the final recognition was preceded by the pre-recognition which determines the NPD bundle.

Studying scientific and technical texts indicates that most bifunctional words are terms (their basic function is to ascribe values to the reaction arguments) or term-like words (for example, "dilution" or "cooling" in chemistry).

The idea of using names of things, phenomena, etc. to characterize the theme of a text resembles the wellknown idea of sentence functional perspective (i.e. exposing the theme and the rheme of a sentence). In terms of this theory, the *theme* of a sentence is what the sentence says about, and the *rheme* is what is said about the theme. What the sentence says about often can be represented by the names of objects. Thus the NPD recognition and pre-recognition features are usually words which also transmit the text actual content, and this is characteristic of the multitopical situation. We shall see below that the goal-revealing systems use pre-recognition features of a different nature.

15.1.2 NPD alternation indicators

Undoubtedly and naturally, the author of a lengthy text wants his interlocutor to catch the moment of NPD alternating immediately. Otherwise, the first part of his text concerning the new NPD can be just missed. Of course, the listener can catch this moment via the speaker's intonation or look or whatever. If the speaker feels that all these are not enough, he precedes the main text of the new NPD by special phrases to warn the listener of the NPD alternation, for instance, "The next topic is ...", "It's time to discuss another point", etc. We call them the NPD alternation indicators. It is not an accident that these phrases are so long: they give time for the listener to clear his memory from the "outfit" of the previous NPD and to prepare it for that of the new one. The NPD alternation indicators are usually followed by "bifunctional" words. It enables the listener to carry out the second part of the pre-recognition problem, i.e. to find the new NPD "outfit" in his "external" memory and to load it into the operational zone. Here we see the two mechanisms combined; we have already noticed this opportunity.

It is important to note that all the three NPD indicating mechanisms (two of them have been described above, the third one is going to be considered) are used unfailingly, though unconsciously. For instance, try to remove the phrase "And now to another point" from the text "She looked at me with love and tenderness. And now to another point. Something is wrong with my car". The result makes an example of "disjointed speech" which is a symptom of one's being mad or drunk. The fact that people unconsciously use NPD alternation indicators (and new NPD pointers, see below) in their speech demonstrates a certain reality of NL and can be regarded as a *phenomenon of Nature*. Our conceptions of K-stationarity and NPD help us to explain this phenomenon, and this is a contribution orientated linguistics makes into studying man-to-man communication texts. We have already encountered the same situation in the first part of this section.

15.1.3 New NPD pointers

These word-combinations differ from the NPD alternation indicators because they simultaneously warn the listener of the NPD alternation and help to recognize or pre-recognize the new NPD: "I've come to talk about the time-table", "I've got a problem with the report", "Let's discuss our financial situation". Practically, the two aforementioned pre-recognizing mechanisms are combined here to form a single phrase.

New NPD pointers are commonly used as headings and titles. This tree-like structure of a multitopical text reflects the author's idea of decomposing the general problem domain of the text into NPD's and enables the reader to see the adequate (in the author's opinion) layout of the NPD pre-recognition and recognition levels.

We would like to underline a specific feature of words like "time-table", "report", "financial" in the above examples. They reflect the contents of their NPD's thus looking like usual keywords. However there is a fine difference between these parts of the NPD pointers and the keywords. The matter is that a keyword is typical of the text and occurs there rather frequently. Contrastingly, words of the discussed sort may be found in the text only once. In fact, they indicate the NPD and make way to more specific words. For instance, the word "report" may not be used in the text any more because the particular items of the report will be discussed.

We have presented the NPD pre-recognition mechanisms of the multitopical systems. Let us consider the goal revealing systems now.

15.2 High K in the goal revealing systems

The goal revealing systems need the multilevel pre-recognition as well. Some of its levels are reserved to clear up the text topics or sections. The designation of these "topic" levels is similar to that of the multitopical systems. Therefore, they can be developed in the same way, and we do not consider them. Here we shall concern ourselves with the rest of the pre-recognition levels called "goal levels".

By way of example let us consider the level that recognizes the types of article fragments. The recognition is especially difficult if all the fragments deal with objects of the same topic. Then the recognizing procedure has to recognize not the objects themselves but what the author wants to say about them, i.e. his *goals*. This procedure should use the fragment rheme not theme. In this way, the rheme of the first sentence of any fragment performs two roles. On the one hand, it carries a piece of data to form the proper reaction. On the other hand, it pre-recognizes the type of the fragment. It means that the first sentence

Table 15.1

Subgoal	Name	Examples
s_3	Recommendation	"For the prototype to be made, it can be necessary to ..."
s_{15}	A method reminder	"An efficient approach to the problem is described in ..."
s_{16}	The beginning of a method description	"The method of statistical analysis by Dr. Johnson is as follows: ..."
s_{21}	A notation	"The displacement is denoted as C_r" "Let M be a maximal number of unengaged prototypes ..." "... where N is the power of the training set ..."
s_{32}	Informing, stating	"This simplifies the problem of constructing a character-reading automaton as a specialized input device"

contains some elements responsible for the pre-recognition of the goal. As there is no saying better, we refer to these elements as *modalities* [28].

The pre-recognizing procedure works as follows. Each sentence is sought for modalities indicating the goal of the sentence (termed "subgoal"), and the combination of subgoals determines the goal of the whole fragment.

The revealed goal shows the desired reaction general orientation. For instance, the author may expect the reader to memorize the bibliography given in the article, or to get the advantages of an approach, or to follow a logic reasoning, or whatever.

Let us consider this pre-recognition mechanism in detail. In Section 14.4 we mentioned that our investigation had been based on the stuff of the articles [25, 26] in the problem domain "Reading automata theory and construction".

The first task of this investigation was to compile a catalogue of subgoals in the given problem domain. The task was carried out in an informal and intuitive way. Namely, two people processed the same stuff independently and reconciled their results to obtain the final catalogue that finally contained $I = 32$ subgoals. Table 15.1 describes some of these subgoals. The record $s(t) = s_i$ means that the sentence t was written to pursue the subgoal s_i. If more texts had been processed, I could have been greater. However, we think that it would be of the same order because the increase of I slowed down even after 3–4 articles (25–30 pages).

The second task was to reveal subtexts responsible for recognizing sub-

Table 15.2

Subgoal	Formula
s_3	$((\gamma_4 \wedge \gamma_5 \wedge \gamma_{17}) \vee (\gamma_4 \wedge \gamma_{16})) \vee (\gamma_4 \wedge ((\gamma_5 \wedge \gamma_{17}) \vee \gamma_{16}))\ldots$
s_{15}	$\gamma_{20} \wedge (\neg\gamma_{14} \wedge \gamma_{19})\ldots$
s_{16}	$\gamma_{20} \wedge \gamma_{14}\ldots$
s_{21}	$(\gamma_6 \wedge \theta) \vee (\gamma_{13} \wedge \theta \wedge (\gamma_8 \vee \gamma_{18})) \vee ((\gamma_7 \vee \gamma_{28}) \wedge \theta \wedge (\gamma_8 \vee \gamma_{18}))\ldots$
s_{32}	none

goals. The investigation proved that any two or more sentences of the same subgoal always included the same words and word-combinations. Unlike NPD indicators, these modal words and word-combinations (simply modalities) usually do not convey any message of topic but indicate the goal orientation. We found out (in the same intuitive way) $U = 29$ of them; the u-th modality is designated as γ_u. Some of them are shown in Table 15.1. For instance, the subgoal s_3 employs the modalities "can" (γ_4), "for ... to ..." (γ_5), "suitable" (γ_{17}), "necessary" (γ_{16}) and some others. The subgoal s_{15} employs "efficient" (γ_{17}), "approach" (γ_{20}), "described" (γ_{19}), etc. The subgoal s_{32} has no stable combination of modalities, it just informs the reader about such-and-such facts. If a sentence does not have the subgoals s_1–s_{31}, it is associated with s_{32}. The record $\gamma_j(t) = \gamma_u$ means that the j-th modality of the sentence t is γ_u.

The more formal is the problem domain business language the stabler are its modality constructions. Among them there are stock phrases such as "Answering your request No. ..." in business documents or "A still further object of the present invention is to provide ..." in patent papers.

The recognition of subgoals by the use of modalities can be implemented as a logical procedure with a system of formal operations. The discussed case demands no more than three operations: AND (Q_1), OR (Q_2) and NOT (Q_3) denoted as $\wedge$, $\vee$ and $\neg$ respectively. In the course of "training", each subgoal s_i gets its own logical formula

$$\gamma_{u1} Q_{b1} \gamma_{u2} Q_{b2} \ldots \gamma_{un} \Rightarrow s_i \,.$$

For instance, the formula $(\gamma_{u1} \vee \gamma_{u2}) \wedge (\neg\gamma_{u3}) \Rightarrow s_i$ can be read out as "If a sentence has the modality γ_{u1} or γ_{u2} and lacks the modality γ_{u3}, then the subgoal of the sentence is s_i".

Usually one can invent several versions of any formula of this kind: different modalities and sentence identity transformations are available. Table 15.2 shows a few examples of subgoal formulas. Versions are given here as disjunctions. The letter θ designates any mathematical symbol or expression; dots mean that other versions are still possible.

Every sentence t is analyzed as follows: we reveal its modalities, composing the expression

$$F(t) = \gamma_1(t) \wedge \gamma_2(t) \wedge \ldots \wedge \gamma_n(t) ,$$

where $\gamma_1(t) = \gamma_{u1}$, etc.; then we compare $F(t)$ with the logical formulas of Table 15.2 by means of some special, though evident, rules; if the comparison is successful, it means that $s(t) = s_i$, $i \in \overline{1,31}$; otherwise, $s(t) = s_{32}$.

Finally, the pre-recognition procedure combines the subgoals to determine the general goal. For the given texts we used the simplest conjunctive formulas

$$s_{i1} \wedge s_{i2} \wedge s_{i3} = \wp_v ,$$

$\wp_v$ is the v-th goal from the list of possible goals. For instance, the goal $\wp_2$ ("a method description") is determined by a sequence of the subgoals s_{16} ("the beginning of a method description"), s_{32} ("informing, stating"), s_{17} ("the end of a method description").

Unfortunately, the small volume of the processed data prevents us from reporting any final results. The above given numbers of $\wp_v$ and s_i are no more than estimates, but we continue researching.

As for applications, the goal revealing systems can be helpful in the automated text reviewing, for instance.

We would like to make a comment on the matter. NL gave up the existence of modalities in the text as soon as the orientated linguistic concept of pre-recognition demanded them. This is another contribution of orientated linguistics to the studying of man-to-man communication. Note that people insert the modalities into their texts unconsciously, and this fact should be treated as a *phenomenon of Nature* too.

Now we are going to discuss the systems for automatic translation from one national language to another.

15.3 Automatic translation systems

In Section 14.4 we found out that the reaction environment connected with the automatic translation problem was non-stationary. Here we shall look at what this fact results in.

Let us remember the statement of this problem in conventional linguistics.

Many of the wellknown automatic translation systems are based on the concept called "Text—Sense—Text model" [11, 29]. Here is the essence of this concept. Every sensible text is associated with some invariant, which is the "text sense" in theory and the "the text semantic representation" (SemRep) in practice. By definition, synonymous texts have the same SemRep, including those in different languages. They build the SemRep of a text in the source language by means of the linguistic analysis, and then form a corresponding text in the target language with the use of synthesizing procedures.

From our standpoint, the text sense as an inseparable part of brain is full of informal components. Thus, we should be very careful and watchful about the above described concept.

Suppose there is a text t. We designate a complete (i.e. man's) reaction to it as $r_h(t)$, considering it as a collection of both formal and informal components (as in Section 7.2). A computer reaction $r_c(t)$ to the same text t can be made up of only formal components from $r_h(t)$. We proceed from the assumption that the author of the text t wants the complete reaction $r_h(t)$ but will be satisfied by some minimal subset $r_{min}(t) \subset r_h(t)$. Thus, a computer reaction satisfies him only if

$$r_c(t) \supseteq r_{min}(t) .$$

The subset $r_{min}(t)$ can be characterized by the following: 1) each text has its own $r_{min}(t)$, 2) only the man is capable of estimating whether the given $r_{min}(t)$ satisfies the author of t, because only the man realizes the contents of $r_h(t)$ and its reducibility.

This is a vicious circle. In fact, we want any NL text to be reacted by the computer not the man. However, for the quality of this reaction to be estimated, we have to show the text to the man. So, what on Earth must we show it to the computer?

Let us consider the automatic translation problem from this point of view. To start with, we must define the notion of adequate translation. Suppose that a text t in one language is translated into another language as t'. The source language native speaker's reaction to t is $r_h(t)$, the target language native speaker's reaction to t' is $r(t')$. Then orientated linguistics suggests the following definition:

Definition 15.1 *The text t' is an adequate translation of t if $r(t')$ is the same as or very close to $r_h(t)$. This is symbolized as*

$$r(t') \cong r_h(t) . \tag{15.1}$$

If the text is translated by the computer, the reaction is $r_c(t)$ (the formal part of $r_h(t)$). Then the target language speaker who forms the text t', can proceed only from the expression

$$r(t') \cong r_c(t)$$

instead of Eq. (15.1). This proves that an adequate computer translation is *impossible* if $r_h(t)$ contains informal components. At the same time, only the man can judge whether any informal components are present in the text or not. Thus, for the computer to produce an adequate translation, the man's participance ("post-editing") is *necessary*.

In this light it seems useless to improve the syntactic and semantic parts of the computer translation systems, which is what practically all the known investigations are aimed at. Quite the reverse. The "smoothness" of these parts can do a lot of harm because it allows a post-editor to relax and distracts his attention. As we have seen, the computer translation systems can be used only as a more or less sophisticated tool to get a draft translation. As for the mentioned smoothness of the ultimate text, it results directly from the post-editor's intellect and competence.

The consideration made in this chapter suggests that orientated linguistics can be helpful in studying man-to-man free communication, despite it is a theory of man-to-computer business dialogues. In the next chapter that winds up this part of the book we shall try orientated linguistics to clarify some problems of man-to-man communication philosophy.

Chapter 16
SOME ISSUES OF MAN-TO-MAN NL COMMUNICATION PHILOSOPHY

16.1 Mastering Language

Conventional linguistics seeks to create a universal method of analyzing NL texts. All possible texts are processed by the same procedure, whatever the goal and the contents of the text. Moreover, such a procedure is supported by universal (for "the entire language") data and knowledge bases. From the pattern recognition standpoint this approach means treating the NL understanding problem as homogeneous. Since conventional linguistics pretends to be a model of the men's language behavior, it thinks of the men's understanding procedure as homogeneous too.

In computer understanding this approach has not yet proved its practical utility and scarcely can do it, as our theory says (Section 9.6). As for men's understanding, this approach seems theoretically imaginable but very ineffective. In fact, it is a deadly sin to neglect useful information, for example, the text fragments intended especially for the pre-recognition.

In contrast to this, orientated linguistics treats the understanding of routine NL texts as a *heterogeneous* problem with the pre-recognition hierarchy. Thus it obtains two principal advantages:

1) the understanding problem is solved in each NPD as a pattern recognition problem, exploiting the brain tools that are far more ancient than speech itself and are widely used by the human brain,

2) data and knowledge of the only current NPD are involved, and their volume look tiny in comparison with that of the universal data and knowledge bases.

It is extremely unlikely that the speech evolution rejected these radical advantages in favour of the homogeneous scheme.

In the light of these facts we are going to review *the language mastering process*, i.e. how the language skills progress from the childish understanding of primitive phrases to the understanding of "the entire language". Many works (for instance [8, 12]) suggest that this process goes from phrases of simple semantics and an unlimited topical range to phrases of complicated semantics and the same unlimited topical range. They follow therefore the philosophy of the problem homogeneity that prevents their models from reaching the deep intelligence. In fact, the reported "understanding" of the mentioned models corresponds to a child's level, and in our opinion it will never be higher despite their authors' hopes. The unlimited width of the simultaneously processed topical range is a fundamental obstacle because there is a natural tradeoff between the depth and the width.

On our grounds we can conclude that there must be another way to the entire language. Namely, it is the "depth instead of width" method. A child learns object domains one by one, starting from the simplest ones such as meals, contacts with the parents, surrounding things, etc. His language expansion looks rather like collecting new object domains. Originally, each object domain is learnt to some necessary depth, but nothing can prevent a person from getting deeper in every NPD: each age and social position imply their own command level. Just the same, different NPD's may be conjoined, generalized and equipped with tree-like structures to support the multilevel pre-recognition.

Of course, nobody can master all existing domains to cover the entire topical range. But shall we? A single person does not and need not understand the entire language, though he may sincerely believe in the reverse. Only the society as a whole has the capacity of understanding the entire language. So, one's limited topical range is not a disadvantage if it is caused by "depth not width" studying language. Quite the reverse. On the one hand, these limits are natural and rightful, they are a tribute for the depth of understanding with one's intellectual resources limited, though huge. On the other hand, they are not dangerous because the environment of one's existence is usually stationary in terms of occupation, everyday life, surrounding people and problems, etc.

We described the process of mastering language from the orientated linguistic standpoint. The next section is devoted to the question of coding of reaction tasks, viewed from the same standpoint.

16.2 The NL coding of reaction tasks

We are interested in this question because we hope that NL tasks are organized parametrically. No wonder: if a set has its objects organized in this way (for instance, a function family), this set is less dimensional and simpler to operate with, the properties of its objects are easier to observe.

Fortunately, orientated linguistics helps to see the parametric organization of NL texts as reaction tasks. Really, any text contains subtexts t_k, t_{am} and t_w to name the reacting algorithm and the values of its arguments. It means that the set R_G of reactions is coded in NL with the use of parameters. In fact, the k-th reacting algorithm "is responsible" for the whole subset $\{r\}_k$ of reactions from R_G, whereas the parameters (argument values) of this algorithm provide a transition from one reaction to another within this subset. In reference to computer understanding we would like to remind that the polytrapezium element of the same function as $\{r\}_k$ used to be designated $\{\alpha^*_{(b..)}\}_k$ in Section 11.3.

The parametric organization of the set R_G can be explained by a great cardinality of this set. When R_G is not so huge the non-parametric organization may turn out to be more efficient, with each reaction having a uniquely named algorithm of its own. Domestic animals' understanding seems to be established like this: a phrase containing a familiar sound is "understood" as the algorithm name and launches the appropriate conditioned reflex. The military drill commands are another example of the non-parametric NL form, though they were originally parametric, for example, "Eyes right", "Eyes left" and "Eyes front": "Eyes" is the algorithm name and "right", "left", "front" are the possible values of the parameter. Now they are probably perceived as the names of self-contained algorithms because a soldier is unlikely to execute immediately the command "Please, eyes, if possible, right". There are some reasons for thinking that a baby behaves similarly at early stages of his speech development.

Another question concerns connected texts, i.e. sequences of logically and topically connected sentences. Following orientated linguistics we proceed from the statement that the understanding of any text, including a connected one, means *reacting to it adequately.* If the author of a text can provide this by means of a single sentence, he manages with this sentence. However, a desired reaction can be compound, requiring a sequence of several steps. If the recipient can not be allowed to perform this sequence himself, the author directs him permanently, forming a sentence or a group of sentences for each step, i.e. a connected text.

In this way, our approach does not discriminate between connected texts and single sentences. In both cases the understanding means "realizing" the expected reaction, i.e. selecting the proper reacting algorithm and evaluating its arguments. Certainly, connected texts raise some additional problems, e.g. the ellipsis, the demonstrative pronouns, etc. However, these questions are secondary and do not obscure the issue. Besides, orientated linguistics has rather efficient tools to handle them: the NPD–UNPD pre-recognition, the elimination of t_{NIL} subtexts and others. We have already seen them working out a case of the ellipsis.

From the said facts it transpires that orientated linguistics treats the understanding of connected texts as the recognition of subtexts determining tasks. This brings us back to the question "Why does the pattern recognition play such a great role in NL communication?". We have already discussed the constructive side of this question in connection with K-stationarity and routine discourse addresses. Here we shall concern its philosophical side.

The pattern recognition problem is often thought "unphysical" and shallow. However, it possesses a great power and some people do not realize that. This power comes from the ideas of the training and of the representative training set. The matter is that a training set is collected not for an entire phenomenon (language, for instance) but for a section of it. As soon as the training set is collected and proclaimed representative, it becomes the only (and finite, unlike the phenomenon itself) object of investigations. Thereafter only problem-relevant regularities of the phenomenon should be exposed and implemented, and it is those regularities that the training is to reflect.

That is why it is so important to clear up whether a problem can be reduced to a pattern recognition problem. Then one can state the problem formally, however informal the basic phenomenon (for instance, NL). This gives an opportunity of investigating only a very limited number of the phenomenon regularities (we can call them "projections" of these regularities onto the training set) instead of the infinite variety of the entire phenomenon regularities. And the pattern recognition "unphysicality" is just a tribute for this remarkable advantage that orientated linguistics rests on.

In the next section we shall prove that some elements of orientated linguistics and its model of activity, as well as of the pattern recognition theory, are useful for discussing the heuristic activity.

16.3 The heuristic thinking and the "break-down" hypothesis

The notions of object and problem domains (Sections 3.4 and 4.2) were introduced too formally, with no comments on their essences and differences.

In this section we shall illustrate these notions and their relations thus making up for our fault. In so doing we shall lift (in this section only) the requirement of the activity being routine, though we have been sticking to this requirement through the whole book. We shall consider the case when a desired reaction does not belong to the set of known reactions. It means that S can neither associate the situation with any familiar class nor use a before-made reacting algorithm: a heuristic act is necessary to create a new algorithm.

The creative process can not be logically investigated in general, but we shall focus on its small part connected with the activity polytrapezium and the OD–FPD (or OD–NPD) relationship.

The above formulated Indirect Action Principle shapes any purposeful action as a polytrapezium, no matter whether the operations of the polytrapezium are made in advance or invented *ad hoc*. It means that any heuristically invented reaction takes the polytrapezium shape. Here arises the following idea. Before S develops an absolutely new polytrapezium, he estimates the possibility of utilizing an existing one. Then S transports a suitable polytrapezium from its OD Σ_M to the OD $\Sigma_{M'}$ where the current heuristic situation occurred.

It brings us back to the pattern recognition problem. The only difference is that the level of situations makes way to some superior metalevel (the level of polytrapezia). The problems are how to select the most suitable polytrapezium among those collected during the subject's life and how to transport it into the OD $\Sigma_{M'}$.

Note that the mentioned metalevel offers the same data as the routine case, nothing else. Namely, it is the current situation description including the information about S's present state (the initial state) and about the desired state (the goal state). Thus, we are speaking about comparing the new situation description with descriptions of old, polytrapezia-equipped situations. The same was observed in the routine case, but here the comparison differs qualitatively.

First, let us consider the formal aspect of this difference. In the case of the routine activity all classes of situations belong to one and the same OD with all operations being performed within the subspace Σ_M of this OD. The heuristic activity involves different subspaces of the embracing space Σ.

As for the substantial side, it shows itself in the use of comparison features working in OD's of different contents and levels.

The notion of problem domains (FPD or NPD) provides a suitable method of establishing likeness.

Here is an example. Suppose that the object domain Σ_M is defined for the objects and specifics of highlands. Any problem domain defines a sort of activity in this OD, i.e. a complex of problems to be solved in the OD environment. As an illustration of such FPD's we refer to the mountain construction works, the mountaineering, mountain excursions, etc. Any FPD can be subdivided into these or those problem subdomains associated with NPD's. One of them can be named "One's actions in dangerous places", for instance, in places of frequent avalanches. Lastly, a reaction in this NPD can consist of several fast and long jumps to leave a dangerous place.

Now imagine an OD $\Sigma_{M'}$ defined for the objects and characteristics of a city street. Certainly, if a highlander S finds himself in a city for the first time in his life, he has to solve problems from the collection (FPD) "One's actions in a city street" in the heuristic way. This FPD never fails to include the NPD "One's actions in dangerous places". By the way, city-dwellers often use these places to cross a street despite the forbidding rules.

Since S does not have any skills of crossing a street and has already seen trams and cars rushing madly, he will probably perform an inadequate action, in a city-dweller's opinion. In fact, it is funny to see a country-looking old lady jumping across a street though there are no transport (i.e. danger) nearby.

Our explanation of this effect rests on the hypothesis that an essential likeness of problem domains from different OD's causes a "short-circuit" distorting the space Σ for a while. As a result, S thinks of the "connected" OD's $\Sigma_{M'}$ and Σ_M as closer to each other than to any other OD. This likeness between OD's displays itself in NL as their names likeness.

This resembles an electric break-down, when a "bridge" appears between normally isolated parts of an electric circuit. If an emergency system works in time, the unit will function properly after the accident. But if the short-circuit lasts for long enough, it is likely to destroy the isolation and the "bridge" will exist forever. Just the same, if one jumps to escape a real emergency, for instance a rushing tram, people will think it natural, but if this "break-down" becomes a habit and one always crosses a street by jumps, it looks like (and conceivably is) schizophrenia.

There are strong grounds for believing that a "break-down" can appear for some other reasons, in particular, due to metaphors. However, any investigation of this field will be too far from the main line of this book. Therefore, in the next section we shall return to other issues of the man-to-man NL communication philosophy.

16.4 Of what the parties to a routine dialogue inform each other

Orientated linguistics says that they let each other know of the following things:

- the selection code t_k of the current reacting algorithm f_k;
- the selection codes t_{am} and t_w of the specific reaction r' from the reaction class $\{r\}_k$;
- the selection code $t_{(b..)}$ of the NPD (sometimes).

We face a paradox when comparing this statement with the common idea of speech as a means to share new information.

Here is this paradox. For the interlocutor to understand a text, the author may use only words and constructions that the interlocutor is familiar with. Otherwise, the codes t_k, t_{am}, t_w and $t_{(b..)}$ will never be recognized. Furthermore, the author may hope only for the reactions the listener knows beforehand, because a routine text usually does not contain a reacting algorithm description (see Section 10.4).

On the one hand, the above conditions are prerequisites for the mutual understanding in a dialogue. On the other hand, they mean that the author can tell the interlocutor nothing new. In fact, the latter knows everything he is told about or can form this with the use of his own language skills and reaction fund. Thus, routine dialogues seem purposeless.

As routine texts are a considerable part of all texts, it is important to resolve this paradox.

We suggest the following solution. Before the interlocutor receives a text, he "does not know" that it is time to activate one of his reactions. The author lets him know that the world has changed and needs this reaction of him. *The author informs the listener of this only thing.*

We would like to notice that this solution corresponds well to Shannon's smart idea he based his definition of "information" on. According to this idea, a recipient *foreknows* all the code words transmitted through his communication channel as well as their a priori probabilities. The information transmission is just a probability redistribution to decrease the entropy. The simplest case is just the recipient's selecting one word among all the foreknown words. Thus, the information transmission means not informing the recipient of anything new but providing sufficient data for him to make this choice.

Another closely connected issue concerns the moment when the interlocutor completes his understanding of a text. Intuition suggests that there are many levels of understanding, and this fact is reported in the literature. For instance, everyone can understand the language of the text "If a is greater than b, c is an integer". It is clear that some object has some property if some other object satisfies a certain condition. Nevertheless, this understanding does not clarify the essence of the theorem, its mathematical message and significance.

Conventional linguistics has no satisfactory definition of "understanding". Therefore, it hardly knows what kind of understanding is expected from a computer system or whether this general understanding is representable as a collection of independent understanding blocks.

Orientated linguistics elucidates the issue. It separates the "language understanding" to be subproblem and considers the "language understanding" completed as soon as the language part of the system extracts the reacting algorithm name and the values of its argument from the NL text. If the main ("business") part of the system has the necessary algorithm, it can execute the expected reaction and complete the "deep" understanding. If it does not, this is the business part's fault, and the language part is not responsible for that.

We are often asked whether our practical orientated linguistic system can respond questions, besides "where", "when", "who", etc.; the question "why", for instance. The answer is evident. If the system's environment changes to raise "why" questions (now it does not), then a new, $(K+1)$-th reacting algorithm will be developed for the business part of the system. As for the language part, the recognition of "why" as an algorithm name does not differ from the recognition of "where", "when" and "who".

Of course, the understanding levels can be differentiated more subtly than the described levels of the "language understanding" and the rest. For example, people differ in their ability of forming complex reactions and in what they think sufficient for an adequate reaction. Let us imagine a person reading a great mathematician's reminiscences, where life episodes are mixed with mathematics. If the reader is not a mathematician himself, his sufficient reaction to the mathematical episodes is to recognize and skip them. Being a mathematician, he pays great attention to these episodes, he thinks that the author included them into the book because they were no less important. Generally, the question of understanding levels is worth a separate discussion. We stop it here because this book is devoted to the "language understanding".

The next section concerns a few language phenomena connected with compound reactions.

16.5 The language use axis and poles

Though in Sections 8.4 and 15.3 we noticed the great role of reaction informal components, we used to pay more attention to formal ones because they were considered as a part of any reaction to any NL text.

In this section we shall turn to NL texts with no formal components at all. By way of example let us refer to poetic works created to produce a pure acoustic effect or to play the music of words with the use of alliteration, assonance, etc. The author of such a poem may be not interested in any semantic interpretation of the words and, as a result, a reader fails to interpret them. For instance, some poems by Cummings fall in this category. All texts of this kind have a feature in common: no one can get or retell their plots. Nevertheless, many experts and amateurs admire and study them. That is why they are an important language phenomenon too.

The preceding observation illustrates that the introduced address language is not the only self-contained language unit. Let us imagine an axis with the language activity of intellectual, pragmatic, "left-hemisphere" thinking on one of its wings and that of the emotional, aesthetic, intuitive, "right-hemisphere" thinking on the other. Then the address language is situated not far from the first wing pole because the computer rejects all informal components and synchronizes formal ones.

As for the second wing, its pole naturally carries the mentioned language of poems. This language can be called "ultrapoetic". The authors' antisemantic extremism provides a filter for all formal components. Other components are asynchronous because unconscious. Thus, in accordance with metaphysics, there are two languages corresponding to two antisymmetric poles of the axis.

Exercising the fantasy, we can imagine the main part of the language situated between these two poles. Closer to the pole of the "address language" there are texts of the so called "business prose" because their business and formal components prevail over emotional and ethic components though do not suppress them. On the wing of the "ultrapoetic language" we see the inverse situation. Here lies the language termed "poetic" in the literary criticism. Texts of this language involve some rational semantic components, but these components are auxiliary because the message is conveyed by informal ones. Thus, our reasoning shows that the word-combination "poetic language" is more than just a metaphor. Namely, it is a mark of informal components dominating.

As for the middle of the axis, the imagination suggests placing there our everyday language: it is fairly businessful, fairly poetic, etc.

We would like to emphasize another point. What the literature (i.e. language) masterpieces are notable for is a wonderful proportion of components in reactions they cause. There are both formal components (for example, a response to detailed situation descriptions) and the power of emotional components. Besides, these works provoke reaction components of the group termed "abstract-eternal". This group includes the feelings of divinity, majesty, goodness, purity, spirituality and other eternal things of the sort: remember works by Dante or Goethe, for instance.

The aforesaid describes the existence and development of language from the standpoint of orientated linguistics. In the next section, which is the last section of this part of the book, we shall try to look at the "non-language" creative activity from the same viewpoint.

16.6 Orientated linguistics and art

If we expand the above presented ideas to all possible NL texts (scientific, everyday, fiction, poetic), we shall catch a glimpse of likeness between literature and other spheres of human creative activity, in particular, painting and music.

Like literature, painting possesses an axis. Its first pole holds pictures by genrists who reproduce the real world just photographically; one can retell the plots of their pictures in every detail. The reproduction accuracy is rather a formal characteristic of a picture; estimating this accuracy makes a good deal of a spectator's reaction. Thus, this pole can be associated with the pole of the address language in the case of NL. The other pole supports the abstract painting. Here it is scarcely possible to retell the plot of a picture or even to say whether the picture has any plot at all. Spectators' reactions contain no semantic components but only emotional ones. It resembles the ultrapoetic language. Other genres and styles of painting lie between these two poles because they are partly rational and partly emotional. As for the masterpieces of painting, they are characterized by an ideal proportion between the rational and emotional reaction components. Like those of literature, they contain a good deal of abstract-eternal components. Mona Liza by Leonardo is a brilliant example.

Similar things, though more veiled, can be noticed in music. On the one hand we have the so called "program" music that induces associations with some scenes and situations of the real life. It imitates everyday sounds and wellknown musical phrases, for example, drill bugle signals or fragments of famous songs (*La Marseillaise* in "1812" overture by Chaikovsky). This kind of music occupies one pole of the axis. On the second hand, there are musical works by dodecafonists who consciously destroy melodic and harmonic (and sometimes rhythmic) structure of music. They appeal to physiological reflexes or to biological rhythms. This music falls onto the other pole. The most of music still lies between the poles, because elements of both natures are involved. The masterpieces ideally combine the two wings and complete them with the abstract-eternal components. The best example is the music by Bach.

Now we are finishing our consideration of the theoretical line "The routine thinking — the action as a result of the thinking — the dialogue as a part of the action — the NL of the dialogue — orientated linguistics as linguistics of this NL — the entire language in the light of orientated linguistics". The next part of the book is devoted to practical implementations of our theory.

Part V

PRACTICAL DEVELOPMENTS IN ORIENTATED LINGUISTICS

Chapter 17
SOME PRACTICAL RECOMMENDATIONS

17.1 Strategy and tactics of collecting a training set

In the preceding parts of the book we discussed the subject's routine activity and, in particular, man-to-computer NL communication in the course of this activity. However, we did not take into account the specific essence and stuff of tasks in a given environment, though it is the accomplishment of those tasks that actually forms the subject's activity. This situation is quite natural because all the aforesaid things present an abstract philosophy, rigorously proved and applicable to environments of any stationarity type (see Part IV).

Of course, the subject himself needs neither orientated nor conventional linguistics to perform his activity. Even if he gets to know anything of them, he will be surprised no less than the character of Molier's comedy, who learns that he has been speaking prose throughout his life.

Quite a different situation takes place when a specialist or a group of specialists (just "developer" for brevity sake) is designing a system for reacting to the subject's NL addresses in the process of his routine activity in a certain object domain. For such work to be carried out, the developer has to realize both object domain and its address language. In this chapter we are going to find out what particular knowledge of this sort is necessary for the orientated linguistic ideas to be put into life. As we shall see, the developer's job becomes much simpler.

If the developer is armed with orientated linguistics, his task includes the following subtasks:

1) accumulating a set of the user's possible NL addresses,

2) clarifying a set of adequate system reactions,

3) mapping the first set onto the second one.

We shall denote these subtasks as ST_1, ST_2 and ST_3 respectively. After the final subtask ST_3 is accomplished, the constructed mapping should be built in the system recognizer, making it react properly. It is evident that the recognition quality will strongly depend on the subtasks ST_1 and ST_2, in particular on whether the mentioned sets are completely determined. However, the set of

NL addresses appears to be of a great cardinality, which prohibits listing its members. As for the second set, in case of K-stationarity the total number of reacting algorithms is substantially smaller than the number of possible NL addresses. (Other cases leave no hope for practical success). Nevertheless, until the developer discovers a bounded set of reacting algorithms, he will deal with a lot of specific reactions and will have no idea of what algorithms actually generate those reactions. This fact follows from a great variability of reaction arguments and their combinations within a reacting algorithm.

Carrying out the subtasks ST_1 and ST_2, the developer should therefore classify only relevant subsets of the appropriate sets, not the whole sets, since they are hardly denumerable. In its turn, this calls for some similarity relations to establish two elements (addresses or reactions) as those of the same class. Orientated linguistic readily proposes such relations. In fact, two reactions are considered similar if they are produced by the same algorithm even with different values of arguments. And two subtexts of the address language are thought of as similar if they launch the same reacting algorithm. Furthermore, two addresses are regarded as completely synonymous if argument values of the algorithm remain the same with both of them.

Thus, here is the first thing we would like to recommend. A training set reflects the served problem domain and the address language in use for the most part implicitly. What the developer must do is to extract useful information in any handy way and to represent it in the explicit form. We suggest accumulating an exhaustive training set of the user's possible addresses to the system in project. Each address should be accompanied by a description of its resulting reactions. This training set is classified in accordance with the mentioned similarity relations. Then the training set should be completed and classified again until it covers all the classes of reactions (i.e. every reacting algorithm has at least one address sample).

A certain technique can be recommended for the first stage of the training set accumulation. It is very helpful if the developer makes himself familiar with the problem domain and the subject's activity beforehand. First of all, he should answer the following questions:

- what problems does this domain generate?
- what objects exist there?
- how many of them?
- what classes or groups do they belong to?
- what is the subject's activity in the domain?
- how does the subject solve his problems?

- what kind of reactions does he need?

- how does he express his necessities in NL? and so on.

Some answers can be found in the literature, protocols or other documentation. Discussions with would-be users are very advisable too. And it is requisite that the developer get a direct access to the user's working place. It will allow him to acquire true information by writing or recording the user's addresses when the user is solving his problems as usual. Here we mean that at this stage the training set of NL texts should be really "natural", not artificially constructed.

Such a recording of the user's addresses should be continued as long as possible. Our experience shows that it is the shortest way to describe the address language: NL addresses are rarely repeated at this stage of the subtask ST_1 solution. Generally speaking, the more is the number of collected NL texts, the less is the probability of a new thing occurring in further work. Unfortunately, a representative training set is usually impossible to accumulate at the user's working place because of time limitations. That is why ST_1 requires another stage.

Thus the first stage is just a passive recording of pronounced or written NL texts. As opposed to this, the second stage of the training set accumulation subtends an active generation of such texts. The basic fact is that the investigated address language is actually a subset of the entire language, and the developer is this language speaker. We advise the developer to write down the collected texts and analyze them word by word, asking himself the following questions:

- can a word be removed from a text without any loss of the sense?

- can a word be substituted by another word?

- is the position of a word fixed?

- are some transformations still possible?

- how can I rephrase a sentence?

Answering these questions, the developer actually does two things. Firstly, he enriches the training set with new examples of NL texts. Secondly, he makes several lists of "basic" objects. Members of such a list can change each other in a fixed text structure. Let us discuss these two things in detail.

When generating new texts the developer should not be misled by his language intuition. Even if he thinks of a new text as synonymous to one of the already collected texts, this new text can actually be beyond the problem domain or involve some everyday lexicon words instead of professional terms, etc. That is why all new text constructions should be verified by an expert of the problem domain.

As for "basic" objects expressed by some words or word-combinations, one should differentiate three situations.

1. A subtext can be changed for another one or just removed from the address without any change in the sense of this address. In such a case it is likely to belong to the class t_{NIL}. The developer can just ignore them when collecting the training set. However, he should keep them in mind because those subtexts may help to recognize the problem domain (i.e. some of them may belong to the class $t_{(b..)}$ rather than t_{NIL}).

2. Changing or removing a subtext change the reacting algorithm. Then the subtext probably belongs to the class t_k. Each algorithm has its own list of synonymous subtexts (we would like to remind that this synonymy is true within an object domain only). The developer should keep completing these lists with new subtexts while he faces any.

3. Changing a subtext for another leads to another reaction though the same algorithm is launched. Then both subtexts are likely to belong to the classes t_{am} or t_w that cover all possible values of the reacting algorithm arguments. In this case it is no use collecting exhaustive lists of objects on the base of the training set only. Much more reliable sources are lists, indices or thesauri of the given object domain or of more general domains. For instance, a reacting algorithm argument can name a company, or a sort of production, or a city, etc. Of course, the developer should start from listing all the served companies, all the produced goods or all the involved cities. Then these lists should be verified by an expert who will append or reject some objects or will add new NL synonyms of the listed objects, using his professional slang.

One way or the other, the developer should accumulate a representative training set of the user's addresses to the projected system. As soon as he sees addresses repeating completely or basically and watches no new examples coming into the training set, it will signify the end of the subtask ST_1. Then it will be high time the developer analyzed the accumulated training set, thus carrying out the other subtasks. We shall discuss them in the following section.

17.2 The training set analysis and the sought-for mapping synthesis

Now the developer should distribute the texts of the accumulated set among the reacting algorithms. He breaks the training set so that each subset corresponds to an algorithm. It can happen that some subsets contain too few texts. This calls for the developer's continuing to collect NL texts for those reacting algorithms until each subset contains a significant number of different addresses. All the above described methods will do. This work being finished, the developer can think the subtask ST_1 to be accomplished.

Now he should switch off for a while the subtexts responsible for the argument value recognition in each subset. Then NL texts of a subset are scanned for subtexts that recognize its reacting algorithm. Here the developer should seek a compromise between two contradictory requirements. On the one hand, such subtexts must consist of as few words as possible. This requirement provides the proper algorithm recognition even if a user skips some optional words of the subtext in his address. On the other hand, the sets of subtexts for different algorithms cannot intersect; otherwise a misrecognition becomes possible. There is a tradeoff between the "missing" and "false alarm" errors, which is typical of pattern recognition problems. Thus the developer should minimize lengths of the subtexts, but make them long enough as to recognize a reacting algorithm correctly.

However, there may appear a situation when an address cannot recognize its algorithm uniquely whatever the accepted address length. It actually means that more than one object domain are involved at a time. As the final choice depends on what particular domain is concerned, the developer should analyze the address context to detect a subtext that indicates the object domain. (NB: Due to this necessity of a complete address context, the developer is recommended to use an audio or video tape recorder in his collecting a training set). Such subtexts form the class $t_{(b..)}$, which eliminates the very problem.

There are some special cases to consider. The first one takes place when the set of reacting algorithms is organized modularly, i.e. a reaction consists of several blocks connected as an algorithmic chain. Then any attempt to regard such a chain as a single reacting algorithm will be inefficient if there are many ways of combining and linking algorithmic modules.

Here we recommend the developer to figure out what modules the system reaction consist of. Analyzing the collected training set can be of much help as well as consulting an expert who knows the reacting component of the system. We advise the developer to reveal the aforementioned subtexts t_k responsible for the selection of each particular module. Special attention should be paid to the relation between the text order of those subtexts and the algorithmic hierarchy of their modules. Besides, it should be taken into account that a user can unconsciously provide his NL address with some subtexts (they belong to t_k class as well) to specify the order or structure of the modules. If this relation and/or these subtexts have been discovered, it is sure to simplify the algorithm assembling out of the fixed modules.

Another special case emerges when there are few or no subtexts of the class t_k. In such a situation the proper reaction choice is mainly determined by the arguments specified in an address. (This case is not forced: a practical example will be given in Chapter 20). As it may seem, the considered system can be thought of as a system with a sole and general reacting algorithm that accepts all discovered argument values. However, the problem should not be treated like this. In fact, the developer has to construct the general algorithm *himself*. Though reasonable for an absolutely new system, this approach looks clumsy if the developer is creating an NL interface for an existing system with ready reacting algorithms. And what is more, it is not easy to find a point where to attach the mentioned algorithm. Therefore, the developer would rather clear up how the set of address arguments relates to the set of reacting algorithms. If such a correspondence is found, it may be embedded into the system recognizer as described in the following chapters.

Let us speak about the subtask ST_3, which is the address-to-algorithm mapping construction. The developer's analyzing the training set of NL addresses and system reactions results in explicit production rules like "If an address contains the subtexts A and B or C, the reaction D is required". A complete set of such rules defines the sought-for mapping, but is very redundant and difficult to use. In Chapters 18 and 19 we shall propose a formalism to represent this mapping implicitly. We shall also prove this formalism, called ATNR, to be extremely suitable to our purposes.

17.3 The result estimation and the additional training stage

The tasks ST_1–ST_3 being carried out, the constructed mapping can be embedded into the NL understanding subsystem. However, the developer should not think his work finished, because another piece of work still lies ahead.

After the system is brought into service, the developer is recommended to set up an automatic recording of users' addresses. Thus obtaining real statistical data, he will be able to estimate the system operation quality. Furthermore, those data can help the developer to discover situations of the system's misunderstanding of addresses. As a rule, there are two main reasons for system errors.

Strange as it may seem, most system errors stem from the developer's faults. In fact, even if the system knows all necessary subtexts, some combinations of them may point to a wrong reaction because the developer did not consider them. That is why in addition to the training set tests we strongly recommend testing the system NL analyzer by as many training set derivatives as possible.

System errors can also be caused by a poor training. The developer should remember that new types of addresses will unfailingly appear in every system reaction class. Therefore he must provide a facile tool to involve new subtexts in the recognition process. (Our idea of such a tool is presented in Chapters 18 and 19). If the system environment is K-stationary, this fact exposes itself as a lower demand for additional training procedures in the course of time. The longer is the period of the developer's monitoring the system and training it up, the less is the wrong reaction probability. At last this probability becomes low enough as for the developer to leave the system alone. For how long? We think forever or at least until the current K-stationary period of the environment evolution gives way to an explosion period, as it was described in Chapter 4.

In this chapter we have sketched the development process. And now we are going to consider it in detail.

Chapter 18
EXPANDING THE ORIENTATED SYSTEM NL REPERTORY

18.1 The readjustment problem

An NL understanding system will not be too efficient if its orientated text analysis algorithm is renewed each time the current NPD is changed for another. In Chapter 13 we saw that with the system's problem domain naturally breaking down into several NPD's (or even UNPD) it was advisable to equip the system with one or more pre-recognizing levels. The less expensive is the pre-recognition with respect to the final recognition selecting the adequate reaction in the NPD, the more productive is the heterogeneous construction scheme. However, a switch to another NPD can demand a complete reloading of the final recognition software thus nullifying the advantages of the pre-recognition.

Furthermore, any designer usually seeks to create his system in such a way as to enhance it in the future. The more sophisticated the system, the more thorough is the development and the stronger is this wish. This well known fact has an obvious explanation. Actually, the designer knows that the system will unfailingly require an improvement as soon as the environment evolves. That is why he puts into his product some ideas to simplify this improvement and in this way to prolong the environment K-stationarity. Besides, he wants the system to meet currently unknown domains.

The structured and object-oriented programmings are traditional tools for this purpose. Of course, one can and should involve them to implement orientated NL text analysis algorithms.

Nevertheless, the implementation stage is preceded by inventing these algorithms, and even at this stage one should provide a standard structure of the algorithms for them to depend on an object domain address language as little as possible.

Algorithm *parameterizing* is a common way of doing so. It means isolating some parameters to make them input data of the algorithm with its main body remaining the same. Then any readjustment is performed by means of modifying or changing these parameters [30].

So, if the suggested approach is followed, the preliminary design should include:

1) selecting a parameter set if it has not been selected before or hardly suits the problem,

2) adjusting this selected set to the NPD of interest.

When necessary (for instance, when new NPD's are attached), the designer returns to item 2) to readjust the system.

We think that this readjustment technique has two aspects. First, the algorithm must always be able to provide an NL address with an adequate reaction on the assumption that the address belongs to the appropriate NPD. This assumption is backed by the second aspect recognizing the current NPD and involving the parameters of only this particular NPD. Thus, to adjust a universal algorithm to some desired NPD means to complete the main pre-recognition algorithm with a new pre-recognition module and to develop a final recognition algorithm, terminating the added branch of the pre-recognition tree.

The readjustment problem was raised to change creating and debugging new programs in both cases for simply forming new parameters, i.e. new input data for programs made in advance.

Evidently, the information stuffs of the parameters qualitatively and quantitatively differ in different NPD's. In its turn, this imposes special requirements on the formalisms describing parameterized systems. These requirements are going to be discussed in the next section.

18.2 Requirements on choice of parameters

Demand D18.1 *Generative power.*

Whether the system serves several NPD's at a time or is just an "empty" commercial software product ready to work in any NPD, a sufficient generative power must be provided for the formalism parametrizing the embodied NL text analysis algorithm. With the algorithm body being constant, the generative power of the parameters determines the algorithm capacity of searching a text for subtexts $t_{(b..)}$, t_k, t_{am}, t_w (see Part III of the book) complex enough to pre-recognize the proper NPD and to react there correctly. Of course, it is impossible to test the algorithm for all texts of an NPD, and one has to do it for the training and examination sets only. Thus, various implementations of the algorithm may be qualitatively compared by testing their parameterization generative power. This characteristic actually relates the quality of the recognizing algorithm to its recognition domain adjustability.

The following degenerate example illustrates the said. Suppose that our algorithm starts with copying the received text to the Turing machine tape with the final situations of the machine mapped one-to-one onto the set of the system reactions. Let us use the description of this Turing machine (in any common form) as a parameter. If the orientated text analysis problem has a solution in some given NPD, there exists a Turing machine that solves it; the description of this machine gives us the desired parameterization. This parameter system has an extreme generative power to the detriment of the other requirements as we shall see below.

Demand D18.2 *Parameterization adequacy.*

This is essential to what degree the parameter system fits the very problem of a purposeful search for an object in an NL text, i.e. the recognition problem. In particular, a text analysis procedure may be sequential as a grammar parser, running through a text from the beginning to the end and collecting all necessary data on the text structure. As opposed to this, it may be constructed to extract only currently urgent information requested by the general plan of the main heterogeneous recognizer. The second scheme appears to be more beneficial and we shall consider a parameterization to be more adequate if it leads to a procedure of this kind. Another aspect of the adequacy is that the more adequate the parametrization, the less expensive is the parametric organization in comparison with redeveloping the algorithm for every new NPD.

It is rather possible to estimate the parametrization adequacy at early stages of the algorithm development. If the parameters explicitly reflect the characteristic features of the looked-for subtexts or directly include the decision rules, the parametrization is expected to be adequate. Then one can readjust the algorithm, extracting the mentioned features from a training set and constructing appropriate decision rules. Thus he does not need to touch the very body of the algorithm.

Demand D18.3 *Parametrization efficiency.*

We think that the algorithm parametrization efficiency is more than the experimental work comfort or the parameter system simplicity and clearness. Compactness and visibility must be taken into consideration too. These characteristics come as a result of a modular structure that enables a designer to combine identical or similar pieces of the description (perhaps, in the recursive form).

However, one should remember that constructing the parameter system as a combination of typical fragments slows down the algorithm (a similar effect is observed when a computer program is organized as a collection of subroutines). Such a tradeoff between memory and performance is usual for computer practice and means that one should avoid an excessive modularity of the parameter system structure. The same reason often keeps programmers from using recursive parametrization.

Generally, this criterion is rather subjective, though sometimes it helps to compare parameter systems. Another important question is whether a formalism is familiar and tested.

Demand D18.4 *Nondeterministic description support.*

As mentioned above, a properly selected NPD guarantees a unique final reaction. Nevertheless, it does not exclude nondeterministic situations at the intermediate stages of processing, though different ways may give the same result, i.e. the same reaction. For such situations to be described and processed effectively (in terms of the previous demand), the formalism must admit some elements of nondeterminism. This demand also helps to evade misunderstanding when a user changes the NPD but the system does not catch this. In such a case the system either offers all suitable reactions for the user to select the proper one or makes the choice itself, for instance, proceeding from probabilities of the reactions in question.

We have shown the main requirements imposed on a parametrized algorithm performing the orientated NL text analysis. In the ensuing sections of this chapter we shall construct a parametrization method complying with Demands D18.1–D18.4. Then we shall demonstrate a parameter system used in actual practice. The important but secondary question of algorithm body construction will be postponed till Chapter 20.

18.3 Hyperdictionary as an explicit parametrizing component

It is apparent that a change of the NPD modifies the lexicon in use (the training set never fails to reflect this fact). Therefore, an NL text analysis dictionary is usually considered as a possible component of the parameter system. Any attempt of not isolating the dictionary (for instance [30], where each wordform is a terminal formal grammar symbol) is sure to result in unfounded duplications because many NPD's share words, for example, prepositions. The more frequent this situation, the more efficient is a stand-alone dictionary in terms of Demand D18.3.

The dictionary is a functionally delineated component of any system, fairly separated from other parameters. Therefore, its formal description scheme is practically independent of the formalisms used for the rest of the parameters. This reason keeps us from implementing the attractively looking idea of the same formalism for all the parameters, as it was suggested in the ATNL language [31, 32]. Nevertheless, this approach remains good for experimental systems where it completely displays all its advantages such as the universality and the uniform structural organization.

There are various types of computer dictionary structure. To a certain degree the preference depends upon the served NPD and the used language. An investigation reveals two tendencies in constructing a dictionary record: they are respectively allied with declarative and procedural nature of the lexical analyzer. We shall briefly characterize these two approaches referred to as morpheme-based dictionary (MBD) and word-based dictionary (WBD).

In practice, an MBD usually consists of several files representing morphemes of the same kind (stems, prefixes, inflexions, etc.) and an additional file of combination rules that define how separate parts can be combined to form a whole word. MBD reduces the volume of the dictionary but complicates the analyzer and decreases the word recognition performance. This method is widely used for Russian and some other highly inflexional languages.

A WBD is just a storage of all possible wordforms to be recognized. This method trivializes the lexical stage of analysis and accelerates it considerably but consumes a lot of memory. WBD is normally applied for less inflexional languages, English, for example.

Conventional linguistics usually seeks for an MBD–WBD combination to find the best memory/performance compromise. In orientated linguistics WBD is preferred because of Demand D18.2. In fact, why morphology attracts conventional linguistics is its utility for describing and explaining the rules of word-changing and word-building in the "entire language". But we are discussing practical systems for the address language that exists and functions in the course of a subject's routine activity in a K-stationary environment. As we know, the address language considerably differs from "the entire language". Thus, orientated systems may not support any morphological analysis. Actually, the orientated NL text analysis looks for subtexts of some known types and each of those subtexts consists of no less than one word.

As for the dictionary occupied memory, the orientated approach suggests some natural methods to reduce the volume of the dictionary. These methods are based not on any general language knowledge but on the training set. We shall discuss them later. Now we would like to notice that the dictionary organization choice depends also on whether the system is equipped with any facility to suppress users' misspellings, which is a prerequisite for the NL understanding system reliability. This issue is discussed in Part VI of this book and we shall see that the WBD organization is preferable as well.

Now we are going to describe a dictionary populating strategy. Let us first introduce some notation. Let $V = \{V_i\}$ be a finite set of all wordforms with the operation of concatenation (symbolized by $\|$) defined there. The transitive closure of V with respect to this operation is V^*. The set V^* comprises chains of any length produced by a multiple concatenation of elements of V. Unlike V, the set V^* is infinite (though denumerable). In particular, it includes any set of NL texts. Let us denote the length of a chain $\omega \in V^*$ (i.e. the number of its words) as $|\omega|$ with duplicated words considered to be different. Furthermore, for the sake of the symbolic notation simplicity we introduce a multivalent mapping $L : V^* \mapsto V$. When applied to a chain $\omega = V_{i_1} \| V_{i_2} \| \ldots$, it produces the set of words used in the chain: $V_\omega = \{V_{i_1}, V_{i_2}, \ldots\}$. The cardinality of this set is $|V_\omega| \leq |\omega|$ because the chain can include the same word twice or more (the operator L looks like an inverse concatenation disregarding the order). Let T^* signify a representative training set of texts from an NPD or a group of NPD's where the system is to work.

In accordance with the orientated NL text analysis principle a dictionary will comprise only wordforms necessary for the subtext recognition. Therefore, the maximal contents of a WBD is determined by the set

$$\widehat{V} = \left(\bigcup_{t \in T^*} L(t_{(b..)})\right) \bigcup \left(\bigcup_{t \in T^*} L(t_k)\right) \bigcup \left(\bigcup_{t \in T^*} L(t_{am})\right) \bigcup \left(\bigcup_{t \in T^*} L(t_w)\right), \quad (18.1)$$

where $t_{(b..)}$, t_k, t_{am}, t_w are the subtexts to be recognized in each text t of the training set T^*. We emphasize that no word, except those included in Eq. (18.1), has to be recognized during the orientated analysis. All other words will be just ignored while the dictionary is being collected.

Comparing the cardinalities of the sets $\widehat{V}$ and V one can conclude $|\widehat{V}| \ll |V|$ because the dictionary lacks words of t_{NIL} subtexts and words from outside the given NPD. Thus the transition to the subset Eq. (18.1) considerably reduces the WBD volume. Using $\widehat{V}$ as a base we shall construct a special *hyperdictionary* H_V comprising word-combinations as well as words, i.e. elements of V^*, not V.

The formal hyperdictionary populating algorithm is made up of three steps:

Step 1. $H_V = \widehat{V}$. At first the hyperdictionary comprises all the words from Eq. (18.1). These chains have the length of 1 by definition.

Step 2. For an ordered pair $\varphi, \psi \in H_V$ and for all the texts $t \in T^*$ the following conditions are tested. If for $\forall t \in T^*$ either

$$\begin{cases} L(\varphi) \cap L(t) = \emptyset \\ L(\psi) \cap L(t) = \emptyset \end{cases} \quad (18.2)$$

or

$$t = \lambda_1 \|\varphi\|\psi\| \lambda_2 \quad (\lambda_1, \lambda_2 \in V^*) \quad (18.3)$$

is true then the conversion is made:

$$H_V \to (H_V \cup \{\varphi\|\psi\}) \setminus \{\varphi, \psi\}\,.$$

It means that two hyperdictionary records corresponding to the chains φ and ψ are replaced by a record of their concatenation. If both conditions Eqs. (18.2) and (18.3) are false, another pair of chains is taken and so on.

Step 3. If there is no pair satisfying either Eq. (18.2) or Eq. (18.3) for all the texts from T^*, this is the end of the procedure, otherwise it goes to step 2.

It is apparent that $|H_V| \leq |\widehat{V}|$ because every success at the second step decreases the number of hyperdictionary records by 1. In practice, the more of stable word-combinations are used in the given NPD to form mentioned subtexts, the greater is the hyperdictionary reduction. Judging by our practical systems, the volume of hyperdictionaries is rather acceptable even for such an inflexional language as Russian.

Nevertheless, that is not the limit: a further compression of the hyperdictionary is still possible and seems to be beneficial in some NPD's, though currently we do not need it. Evidently, WBD multiply duplicates information as word-changing affects only a small part of a word (what MBD eliminates is this redundancy). If a hyperdictionary contains a considerable number of similar entries despite the described filtration, it is advisable to apply any encoding procedure to compress the information. For instance, the well known method is to substitute a frequently used letter combination for a single code letter. As a result we shall have the hyperdictionary represented in the code alphabet. The dictionary retrieval algorithm is also evident: it must previously encode a received text with the use of the same alphabet.

Now let us discuss a hyperdictionary typical record. Besides a word or a word-combination itself, it is equipped with *lexical* and *role* features. Let us begin from the former ones. Their nature bears an essential impress of orientated linguistics: on the one hand, the set of features differs from that used in conventional linguistics; on the other hand, it is dominated by the pattern recognition ideas. Thus, the common morphological features (for instance, case and number) that sometimes can be helpful for a purposeful search, there can arise some new features derived from the analysis of the given NPD lexicon. They may be unusable in another NPD and such a situation is typical for the pattern recognition. Those features are neither universal nor generally linguistic, and each NPD may have a feature set of its own. At the same time, some features important for conventional linguistics (like gender or animacy) can be neglected in some NPD's as they do not affect the reaction choice. (The same is true for uninformative features in the generic pattern recognition problem).

As for role features, their set and representation strongly depend upon a specific NPD. For example, in the case of a NL driven DBMS they may include the database name, the active domain, the search keys and so on. Here we are not discussing this type of features in detail, but in Chapter 20 we shall describe the hyperdictionary role features used in one of our practical systems.

The above described hyperdictionary as an algorithm parameter, has a certain peculiarity. The matter is that its information is represented for the most part in the explicit form. The main source of this explicitness is a training set. Just as in the generic pattern recognition problem, the training set also contains a lot of information, which can be represented more efficiently (in terms of Demand D18.3) in the implicit form. The next section is devoted to implicit components of the parameter system.

18.4 Possibilities for implicit parametrization

The hyperdictionary stores information explicitly and represents it so as to optimize the memory/performance relation. Thus its representation method has only a weak dependence of any particular NPD. Contrastingly, the implicit form of data representation requires a formal approach; otherwise one has to investigate each NPD *ad hoc* and no parametrization will be obtained at all. There are some formalisms invented and tested in conventional linguistics but still adaptable to our purposes. The best known of them are formal grammars, semantic networks and augmented transition networks. We are going to compare them in terms of Demands D18.1–D18.4.

Formal grammars transform a text analysis algorithm into a grammar parser clarifying whether a text could be generated by the given grammar and decomposing the text into the nonterminal alphabet symbols. The formal grammar theory is well elaborated and widely used but this formalism complies with only a part of our requirements.

In fact, the generative power (Demand D18.1) of such a parametrization system can be as high as desired, if the appropriate formal grammar belongs to the class of grammars with non-restricted rewrite rules. Demand D18.4 is fulfilled as well because formal grammars can be built isomorphic to nondeterministic automata (finit-state, push-down, linear-bounded or even Turing machine in dependence of Chomsky class of grammars). At the same time, formal grammars do not meet Demand D18.2 because they express subtext characteristics indirectly (the process of generating a subtext usually employs many rewrite rules). The non-redundancy of formal grammars would provide rather a high efficiency (Demand D18.3) if it were not for the necessity of a *complete* text decomposition. This would demand all wordforms of t_{NIL} subtexts to be included in the terminal alphabet (or an isolated dictionary) in addition to words of $t_{(b..)}$, t_k, t_{am}, t_w. It is clear that processing those words would be just a waste of time and memory, decreasing the parametrization efficiency.

Semantic networks appear as another popular description formalism. Researchers tried semantic networks of frames, of conceptual dependencies, etc. They proved that this form of the NPD linguistic and pragmatic knowledge representation mainly answered the purpose. Nevertheless, the original designation of semantic networks mismatches the very nature of the orientated analyzer and this fact prevents them from being sufficiently effective.

Actually, a semantic network is considered to be a means to visualize a general set of conjectured "text senses". According to the model, each text corresponds to a subgraph of the network. Even if we neglect the evident infeasibility of encoding an adequate text sense to something different from the text itself (see Part II of this book for more information), we will have to construct a parametrizing semantic network not out of nodes and edges mapped one-to-one onto the sought lexical objects, but out of subgraphs corresponding directly to the system reactions. The only way to assemble those subgraphs into a whole network is to glue their nodes of the same name with all the existing edges preserved, what is not acceptable either because of a low efficiency.

The same problems will arise if one attempts to equip a semantic network with nondeterministic elements. Nothing can be made about this, except for involving all alternative subgraphs however small differences between them.

Now we are coming down to the third formalism, **Augmented Transition Networks** [33]. Its basic concept is a transition graph that is a description of the decision making sequence in terms of states ascribed to the graph nodes. The graph edges are associated with conditions; therefore, a transition along an edge symbolizes that all the edge-associated conditions are considered to be true. This analysis strategy resembles the recognition strategy which fact makes us suspect the ATN formalism to fit the subtext recognition problem. Thus, Demand D18.2 may be thought of as satisfied.

The same concerns Demand D18.4 because a node can emit several edges with simultaneously true conditions, thus allowing nondeterministic situations. What is more, an ATN description can be easily equipped with various rules of processing nondeterministic situations for a dialogue to control the nondeterministic situation processing strategy just in operation with no modification of the program.

The ATN generative power is extremely high because this formalism is proved to be equal to a Turing machine (remember the example illustrating Demand D18.1 in Section 18.2). At the same time, edges of POP and PUSH types make it possible to combine similar parts of a description into fragments looking like recursive subroutines. The literature suggests a lot of other points in favour of the ATN model, for instance, its clearness, experimental work easiness, readjustment simplicity, etc.

We can not help saying that the classical ATN model needs elaborating for our purposes. In fact, this model is developed to scan a text from its very beginning and to reach the end if and only if all the elements of the text have initiated a successful transition along some edge of the network. This structure evidently contradicts to the very idea of the purposeful search and, in this way, to the essence of the orientated text analysis. Furthermore, this model requires the network to cover the set of all possible NL constructions as in the case of formal grammars. This means, in particular, that edge conditions will use words from t_{NIL} subtexts, which is unnecessary and unprofitable.

To overcome this obstacle we propose a modified version of the classical ATN model. It is called the *Augmented Transition Network with Returns* (ATNR). Not contradicting to the basic merits of the classical model, it fits the recognition-based analysis algorithm to much a greater extent and this fact was practically proved (Chapter 20).

18.5 The ATNR formalism and how to use it

The discussion begins with an informal description of the ATNR. Like the classical ATN, this transition network is organized as a collection of directed multigraphs with their nodes marked by names of decision making process states and their edges indicating possible transitions. An edge connects two states termed original and resulting ones and is directed from the former to the latter. Each ATNR edge is associated with some conditions (may be identically true). If these conditions are actually true, the appropriate transition is considered to be permitted. Besides, an edge may have some actions attributed to it; they are commands to be executed when going along the edge if it is permitted.

We shall distinguish edges of TST, PUSH and POP types. Transition along a TST-edge is permitted if all the associated conditions are true. CAT-edges of the classical ATN model can be treated as just a special case of TST-type edges because the latter can convey the desired lexical category of the current word as a condition imposed on the lexical features taken from the hyperdictionary entry of the word.

A transition along a PUSH-edge demands one more special condition to be fulfilled. This condition is that the edge is marked by the name of a state named "submerge". The condition is tested by a transition to the submerge state with the resulting state name stored in a special stack (that is a LIFO-queue). Then the decision making process runs as usual until a POP-edge transition is permitted. Edges of this type have a dummy resulting state whereas a genuine resulting state name is popped from the mentioned stack before the process goes along the POP-edge. If the process returns to the resulting state of the PUSH-edge responsible for the submerging, the special condition is said to be true. The side effect shows itself in executing all the actions attributed to the edges of the subgraph the process submerged to. Thus, the special condition of a PUSH-edge is checked by a recursive call of the subgraph marking the edge.

As for conditions not related to submerging, their arguments may be lexical and role features of the current word, this word itself, constants and literals, system registers (logic, character or numeric variables) or list-like structures made up of them. We dedicate the register named WORD to store the hyperdictionary record of the current word and to become empty when the end of text is reached (this event puts the true value in the "End-Of-Text" register named EOT). The admissible condition set may involve algebraic and set-theoretic operations and relations as well as parentheses and logic operators AND, OR, NOT to form compound conditions.

We have already mentioned that an ATNR edge may have some attributed actions to be executed during a transition along the edge. As a rule, those actions are intended for modifying the system registers on the current or adjacent recursion levels. New values of the registers are calculated from the above described arguments by usual arithmetic, logic and character (string concatenation and splitting) operations.

In addition to this, the ATNR is equipped with some special actions:

NEXT - to put the next non-deleted word in the register WORD (go to the next word);

EXCL - to delete the current word from the text;

BACK - to go back to the beginning of the text remainder and to put its first word in the register WORD.

Certainly, there may be auxiliary special actions for the message interchange with a user, communication logging, etc. As they are secondary, we shall skip them here.

Making an ATNR description, one should point to the initial state S that the process starts from. When a text t comes, its first word is put in the register WORD. An ATNR parametrized algorithm tests conditions on the edges originated from S and accomplishes one of the permitted transitions, executing all the attributed actions. In a new state the process does the same and so on.

If a POP-edge transition is permitted and the state name stack is empty, the algorithm terminates its work with the text t. The ATNR should be developed so as for the appropriate system registers to store the goal reaction name and its working arguments values at this moment.

If no transition is permitted in a state, the built-in backtracking mechanism is activated to return back to the nearest state with non-tried edges. There another option is selected and the process goes ahead. If the backtracking comes back to S and there are no alternative ways, it means that the system lacks an adequate reaction to the text.

EXCL and BACK actions make the main difference between the classic ATN model and the ATNR formalism. Firstly, they provide a direct (non-recursive) unordered text analysis by means of scanning it more than once. Secondly, these actions make it possible to eliminate text elements irrelevant to the reaction choice. An EXCL action reduces the text before a reiteration so that already recognized subtexts are skipped. Thus, the ATNR formalism looks more adequate to the orientated text analysis strategy based on the purposeful search; we are going to illustrate this by examples below.

Here is another observation. The later works [34, 35] completed the classical ATN model with the network cascaded connection: a special action (TRANSMIT) furnished an intercascade transmission of analysis results. Formally, the ATNR may be considered as a cascaded ATN (CATN) with TRANSMIT concerning a partially reduced text but not the deep information extracted from the text by the previous cascade as it was in Woods' model. In the general case, the ATNR can be represented as a CATN non-uniquely because such a representation strongly depends on the input text in both number of cascades and

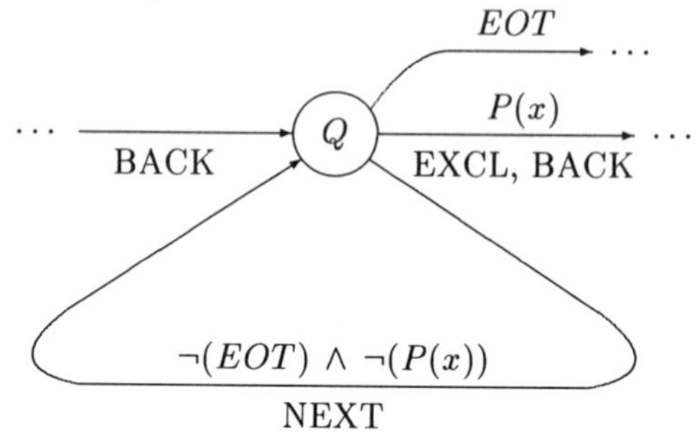

Figure 18.1

their sequence. The work [34] proposed the CATN cascades to be morphologic, syntactic, semantic and discourse analyzers. This proves that the CATN remains an exhaustive text analysis tool, whereas the ATNR exploits the cascade-like organization as a mean of purposeful search for the desired reaction. This observation explains why the ATNR should be treated rather as a self-dependent model.

Figure 18.1 depicts a typical fragment of the ATNR, namely, the purposeful search for a word with its lexical features combination x making predicate $P(x)$ true. When on graphical display, conditions (if any) are written above the edges, and attribute actions stand below them. One can see the ATNR implementing a single search operation in the loop form. As there are no a priori information about the sought word location in the text, this is an exhaustive search loop.

When developing and discussing network fragments, an ATNR graphic view is very illustrative and convenient but these advantages are sure to evaporate with whole networks, huge and multidimensional. It forces us to accept another formal language. Being written in this language, the ATNR can be used as the second parameter of an orientated algorithm. However, this language will be essentially affected by the computer architecture and the parameter processing strategy, as we shall see below. Therefore, it may be either insufficiently illustrative for the development with no computer or rather ineffective for the implementation on a given computer. That is why we do not propose any universal formal language, though in Chapter 20 we shall say a few words about the ATNR representation languages used in our practical systems.

This chapter answers a question of great importance to everyone who deals with the computer NL interface problem. This question is how a system NL repertory can be expanded to extend the object world of the system. The answer is:

> A computer system object world expansion does not contradict to the routine activity conditions. However, the present NPD bounds moving apart is not a proper method of such an expansion. Instead, more NPD's must be collected and provided with an adequate NPD pre-recognition mechanism. This process becomes easier if the orientated NL text analysis algorithm is designed readjustable, for instance, with the use the above described parametrization system including a hyperdictionary and ATNR.

Nevertheless, it is no use readjusting a system to a new NPD if the system does not support goal reactions of this NPD yet (that is a usual situation). So, new reaction algorithms must be developed when the system is expanded. It often leads to a complete change of the reaction subsystem and this is another important problem. This problem would not be of our concern at all, if it were not for one reason. Our NL communication system is made up of two self-contained components: the NL subsystem responsible for the orientated NL text analysis and the "business" subsystem that performs reactions. Both components are of substantial complexity and either of them needs to be improved or even substituted independently in a case of expansion. Therefore, it makes sense to clear up whether these subsystems can be connected lest an improvement of one of them affect the other. This will be done in the following chapter.

Chapter 19
ASSIMILATION OF ORIENTATED NL SYSTEMS

19.1 The NL interface assimilation problem

Let us look at man-to-computer NL communication at another angle. In the preceding parts of this book we presented orientated linguistics that provides a reliable theoretical base for man-to-computer NL communication within a pre-chosen object domain. Some other results, collected in the final part of the book, make the computer understanding almost independent of input errors. This facility is very important for the keyboard input and absolutely needful for the speech (acoustic) input because pronunciation is usually more flexible than orthography. Thus, we have a good theory that stood a practical scrutiny. Nevertheless, the recent years have shown that NL driven systems remain exotic in actual practice.

What is the matter? We know that the urgency of the problem goes up not down every day. New computer generations are attracting more and more users whose activities are farther and farther from computer science. However, a really free NL interaction with PC is still difficult to find in the market. For instance, in 1987 there were presented no more than 10 NL-equipped packages among thousands of software products [16]. The passed seven years have not improved this ratio.

Undoubtedly, the first reason for this deadlock is the absolute prevalence of the keyboard input, whereas the NL communication can be really free only with a continuous speech input. This field has its own bottle-necks and the problem of errors is not the lowest of them. (Some keys to this problem will be discussed in Part VI of the book).

Neither the mentioned reason nor hardware limitations (like equipment shortage or high prices) complete the list of troubles inhibiting the popularization of NL systems. This chapter covers a trouble never specially discussed before. That is the *assimilation* of NL driven systems by the present-day hardware and software. (Do not be misled by the word "assimilation". We are going to consider no more than the technical aspects of the NL technology penetration into the computer world, leaving the psychology and the organization of this process outside the discussion). Now about what the problem is and where it comes from.

The computer NL interface is not the end in itself, it is just a facility that helps a user to simplify and improve his running a system of some practical designation. Such a system always has a formal operating means because it is just a collection of hardware and software. So, if a system serves some problem domain and is operated by means of a formal language ("menu", for example), we call it *a business* system. A variety of business systems for various applications have been designed since the beginning of the computer era; nowadays the software market is full of them. Database management systems (DBMS's) make a typical example. Business systems dominate over other software products because these systems serve the user's needs, accomplish his tasks thus pursuing the original purpose of computerization.

What place does the NL interface occupy with respect to business systems? We think there are two basic lines. The first line tries to break through the problem of translation from a professional NL into the business system formal language, for instance, into the SQL language supported by many relational DBMS's. A query processing is said to be completed when the translated task, being input in the usual way (via the keyboard, for example), produces an adequate system reaction. This line proposes no practical methods of linking up the NL interface and the business subsystem (except for rather rare cases of a business system allowing an external program to pre-process input addresses). Projects of this line do prove that the computer NL communication is possible, but they are no more than experimental models. This sin is typical of conventional linguistic works. These text analysis systems are so huge that even very powerful business systems look insignificant in comparison with them. It is doubtful whether this line will help NL to become as customary as menus.

The second line covers all existing practical projects (among them our systems described in Chapter 20). Within this line a system includes its business subsystem as an integral part created *ad hoc*. Thus, the business subsystem usually can not function separately; sometimes its formal interface is the designer's secret. Therefore, this line suggests nothing but waiting for new good business systems to equip them with NL facilities. A good business system is very difficult and expensive to create, whereas the present-day market offers a lot of business systems that users have got accustomed to. It is clear that this line is not a way of accelerating the NL interface assimilation process either.

On these grounds they conclude in [36] that formal language controlled applications do not need any NL interface at all. We think this is just a delusion. Suffice it to remember that staff rotations in any object domain result in newcomers' studying the formal language of the business system in use. It is more logical to improve the interface instead of training users to a bad one. Of course, such an improvement must maintain the old business system functions and result display.

Thus, the fastest way for computer business systems to assimilate NL is an improvement of the existing systems. So, the problem is to equip a functioning business system with an NL interface (i.e. *to embed* the latter into the former). This problem is going to be discussed.

19.2 The embedment problem

Let us consider a business system working in an interactive mode as a "black box" that receives formal addresses and reacts to them adequately. There are many ways to communicate with such a system. If there is any input formal language, a user may address the system explicitly, via the keyboard. Otherwise, the system is operated by means of function keys, touch-sensitive screen or a mouse-like manipulator. For the sake of definiteness we shall discuss the case of the keyboard. A reaction shows itself as launching an appropriate system algorithm: calculations, result display, printing, etc.

The *embedment problem* is raised to provide NL communication facilities for existing business systems not equipped with such facilities originally; in so doing no internal modifications of the business systems are permitted. Though the essence of the problem is clear, our experience shows that people who meet the problem for the first time usually fall in one of two opposite opinions.

The first one is: "What is the problem here? Since a formal interface is available, the NL text analysis must translate a text into the formal language of this interface. That is it". The question of how the translation results are transferred to the business system is usually answered that the developer of the business system could have provided an interface for an NL understanding program. And if the developer is far away or hates to review the already forgotten product, the only way out is to call a hacker...

No comments. A standpoint like this fits the first method among the two considered in the preceding section and has nothing to do with orientated linguistics.

The second opinion is: "Since the business system lacks any address preprocessing means, it is impossible to put in an NL interface with no modifications". We think it is too pessimistic to agree with. Certainly, we are far from saying that any software product, on any computer, can be successfully equipped with an NL interface, however it is quite possible in many cases, as we shall see below and as practice proved.

Let us consider different ways of handling the problem. We discriminate between two techniques: "hard-embedment" based on special hardware and "soft-embedment" using only software tools. We shall discuss both techniques in the following sections, paying special attention to those implemented in actual practice.

19.3 Hard-embedment and speech input devices

The very idea of hard-embedment looks rather natural. Actually, why cannot we design a dedicated processor (may be even on-chip) and charge it with processing an input task (written or oral), ignoring errors, translating the task into the necessary formal language and transferring the formalized task to the main processor that controls the business system?

If the embedment problem seems forced, these doubts will evaporate as soon as a large-scale production of continuous speech perception devices is concerned. Nowadays such devices stand apart from the available software; they are designed emphatically universal. Therefore, all speech input equipped business systems have to be developed anew. It is difficult to reconcile with an oral speech interface rejecting all existing software. We think that this fact, as well as rather low characteristics of continuous speech recognizers, is a serious obstacle to assimilating NL as a tool for man-to-computer communication. That is why the hard-embedment is also a way of integrating speech input devices into existing business systems.

From the main processor's standpoint, the dedicated NL processor must completely *simulate the keyboard.* Such an implementation solves the embedment problem because the business system cannot distinguish the dedicated processor's formal language output from the usual keyboard signals. However, a mass production of such chips is just a dream because it actually has to be a complete computer of high performance and with its own external memory, perhaps.

Another implementation method suggests constructing a complex of two universal computers. The first one services the business system as usual and the second one takes care of the NL subsystem. In this case one should develop only an interfacing circuit for the second computer to simulate the keyboard of the first one and to provide their handshaking. If the business system is designed to operate in a local domain network with free commutation and redirection of transactions in addition to file sharing, no extra hardware is necessary at all.

However, the keyboard simulation approach has a strong disadvantage. The keyboard is a read-only device; its input channels, if any, service only technical needs such as informing the keyboard about a successfully read character, etc. Thus an NL text analyzer based on an independent processor lacks a feedback channel and the whole tandem looks clumsy. The feedback runs through a user, though sometimes the business computer reporting on the current situation in the business system (working, waiting or failure) severely affects the orientated text analysis procedure.

The hard-embedment runs into special difficulties connected with an inevitable adjustment of the text analysis equipment to the object domain of interest. Actually, expenses on the development and production of a special on-chip processor for some particular NPD will hardly be justified. Generally speaking, such an adjustment can be made by overwriting the system ROM, but even a hyperdictionary can take a ROM space of megabytes: too expensive, isn't it? Furthermore, if the dedicated processor is expected to work in several NPD's with their pre-recognition and switching, it must be equipped with its own external memory that requires a power supply, etc. As before, we have got a complete computer instead of a chip desired. In addition to the said, whatever hard-embedding technique is used, the hardware readjustment to a user's NPD becomes a manufacturer's problem. That will not do.

Though both hard-embedment techniques (based on a chip and on an additional computer) are rather attractive, they demand significant investments. Therefore, they can be used when a new hardware is developed for some other reasons. Hence we do not reject the hard-embedment but think of it as a long way in the future.

It is more interesting to embed the NL interface into a business system based on the same processor with no hardware modifications. In fact, it will allow the NL interface assimilation right now. Of course, in this case we can discuss only written NL texts coming from the keyboard.

Let us look at the embedment problem solutions based on software tools only.

19.4 Soft-embedment: question of power

Soft-embedment techniques treat the NL interface as a self-contained software subsystem for processing users' addresses. The key question is here the question of power, i.e. which of the two subsystems is the *master* in the control hierarchy: whether the NL subsystem or the business system or both. Let us consider these options one by one.

A. Let the NL interface be the master. When "understanding" an address it recognizes the appropriate reacting algorithm and works out its working arguments. The only way to transfer this information to the business system (which is to execute the recognized algorithm) is to call it at its entry point and slide down the tree of options until the necessary algorithm is reached. This solution is inefficient for business systems with powerful menus because this sliding takes a considerable amount of time. Another reason is that a properly designed menu system is organized so that a user works in a small vicinity of a point in the tree and changes branches rather rarely. Thus, multiply sliding to the work point from the very root is unnecessary. The consideration scheme fits only menuless business systems such as those controlled through the entry point (very exotic case) or organized as a library of stand-alone modules for standard algorithms ("toolboxes"). Certainly, we skip the question of modifying any existing software packages (for instance, hooking intermediate entry points), because it is unprofitable and often impossible, not to mention copyright violations.

B. Now let us suppose an implementation with the business system as the master. Then the business system works as usual but contains an NL module to be called when a user is wanting to communicate with the system. This module receives an NL address and converts it into a formal language query or into a menu option. The advantage is that the translation results are given on the proper level of the business system, increasing the total efficiency. However, most software products are put up for sale as executable modules not allowing any address pre-processing, which fact inhibits a implementation like this.

C. Two masters can be implemented only in a multitasking environment, where both subsystems are actually subordinates of the operating system task scheduler that calls them in accordance with their priorities and input/output events. If the operating system allows reassigning input/output devices (including the keyboard) to a temporary file, it suggests rather a simple embedment based on information interchange through a disk file. There are grounds to think it will work with OS/370, UNIX, OS/2 operating systems but experiments lie ahead. Yet, it is a wellknown fact that a program execution in a multitasking environment is slower than that in a single-program environment because of the housekeeping overhead. Thus, this approach suits only business products designed for multitasking operating systems.

When comparing the above options, one can see that option B is preferred in a single-program environment (we explored this case as the most wide-spread). We think that all the mentioned implementation problems can be overcome by means of operating system facilities, because in contrast to typical business systems, any operating system is designed multipurpose and includes powerful instruments for its adjustment, modification and improvement. The designers conceal some of those instruments, but the rest are available for system programmers who can create their own modules to extend the initial capabilities of the operating system. Of course, no comprehensive instructions can be given nor all the present-day operating systems can be observed. Therefore, we are going to describe a soft-embedment technique for IBM PC compatible computers controlled by the MS DOS operating system version 3.0 and above.

19.5 An embedment system for PC

The MS DOS operating system by Microsoft Corporation is one of the most popular operating environments for IBM-compatible PC's. Its Technical Reference suggests only one way to extend the original capabilities of the operating system. Namely, it is to develop new installable input/output device drivers (see Chapter 2 of [37]). This facility was designed to support nonstandard input/output devices, but one can use it to drive the standard devices in unusual modes. The keyboard is one of these devices, of course.

At first we tried this soft-embedment technique, i.e. we treated the NL processor as a possible keyboard driver. There were no problems with interfacing the business subsystem, but we ran across other difficulties, discussed below.

1. A device driver must be an executable module of the certain structure, including the specific header. This structure is difficult to construct by means of only high level programming languages, C language among them.

2. In addition to the main function of address translating from NL into the formal language, a device driver must execute the virtual device control functions such as initializing, testing status, opening/closing the device, etc. Otherwise, the driver will not run properly. These important things have nothing to do with our purpose, but take a lot of human efforts and computer resources.

3. A driver program, the stack and data segments included, cannot exceed 64 Kbytes. This restriction forbids using a time-to-memory exchange to accelerate the program even if the business subsystem leaves a lot of free memory space.

4. A driver cannot be quickly added to or removed from the current configuration of the operating system. While passive, it still occupies a certain amount of RAM. Removing it means editing the configuration file and reloading the operating system, which is not very convenient.

Taking into account all these disadvantages we rejected the driver-based embedment technique. Another possibility, though it is poorly documented, considers the NL processor as a "Terminate-and-Stay-Resident" (TSR) program activated by a hardware or software interrupt. This method helps to overcome the above listed difficulties. In particular, with this technique the soft-embedment was implemented for MS DOS, using C language† and just a bit of Assembler language (a few instructions). Before discussing this technique, let us consider the existing interrupt mechanism of the PC keyboard interface control (Fig. 19.1). Each pressing or releasing a key causes the hardware interrupt numbered 09. The control is given to the interrupt handling routine (denoted as INT09) with its start address stored in the fixed place of the so-called interrupt vector table. Interrupt 09 is normally handled by a special piece of Basis Input/Output System (BIOS) located in the computer ROM. This program reads the key number from the prescribed input/output port and converts it into an extended ASCII code in accordance with the BIOS table and special keys pressed. Before the return, the program saves the obtained code in the circular buffer located at the fixed RAM address. The buffer is reserved to contain as many as 16 characters and if it gets overflowed, you hear a beep.

Whatever language the business system is written in, when its input module needs a character from the console it invokes the interrupt with hexadecimal number 16H (directly or via the MS DOS standard functions). Three invocation modes are possible:

†We used Turbo C compiler version 2.0 by Borland International

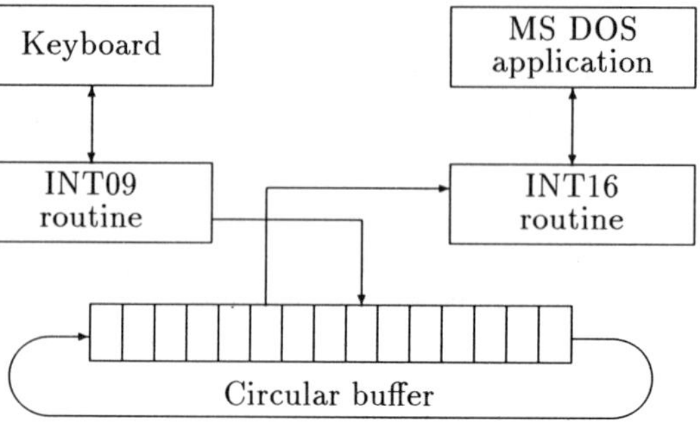

Figure 19.1

(0) reading (and erasing) the next character from the buffer if there is any; otherwise waiting for a character;

(1) testing whether the buffer holds a character and reading it if success (without erasing);

(2) testing the control keys pressed.

It is mode (0) that transfers the next character to an application program. The standard handling routine is also incorporated into BIOS (in Fig. 19.1 it is denoted as INT16).

In other words, the character input consists of two asynchronous phases. On the one hand, the application program reads a character from the buffer or waits for it if the buffer is empty. On the other hand, a key press/release makes BIOS interrupt all running programs and place the corresponding character into the buffer. And a natural-to-formal language translation program may work between these phases. The MS DOS standard control sequence can be changed by modifying the interrupt vector table so that it points to new INT09 and INT16 interrupt handlers. This is a common trick in this operating system.

However, the above described technique is not very easy to implement because of other 09 or 16H interrupt handlers installed. Among them there may be national alphabet or alternative keyboard layout drivers, "hot key" pop-up programs and so on. Furthermore, some other interrupts may occur (timers, self-test circuits, local area network adapters, etc.). Therefore, one who modifies the operating system must be considerably experienced in system programming and operating system conventions (even those not documented completely). And now we are going to present our soft-embedment technique.

The main problem is to minimize the interference with the MS DOS routines and the business system components. There are two aspects:

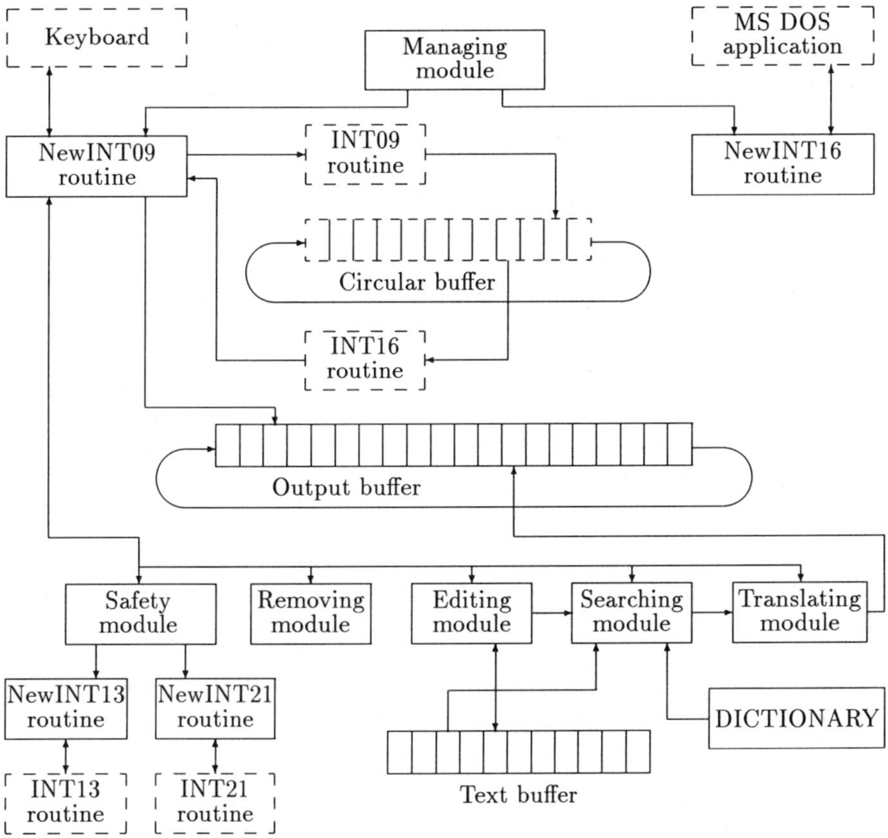

Figure 19.2

1. One should preserve the old calling chain; all the previously used programs must work in the usual order, though the NL processor modules can run in breaks between them.

2. One should not violate the current time relationship between the processing stages. In particular, it means that there are must be no delay for the existing high-performance modules such as character echoing. Otherwise, a keyboard buffer overflow can occur.

With these things taken into account, we implemented the embedment configuration shown in Fig. 19.2, where new blocks are drawn in solid lines and old ones in dashed. The embedment system starts with the managing module initializing the NL subsystem: allocating memory, opening necessary files, modifying the interrupt vector table, etc. The module terminates its work, leaving the other modules resident. Those modules are not active yet and let through all keyboard characters without any processing (the "transparent" mode). Then the business system is launched as usual.

With the transparent mode on, the business system works as follows. A key press/release initiate interrupt 09. The new INT09 handler (NewINT09) supports the usual input processing scheme by calling the old interrupt handler (INT09). As a result, the extended character code falls into the circular buffer as before. Next, NewInt09 module calls the old INT16 handler to get the character from the buffer. This technique is consistent with other resident programs catching keyboard interrupts, in particular, with national keyboard support programs.

While the embedding system is not active, any character is tested for its being a control signal. There are two control signals: the activation/deactivation signal and the removal signal, both ascribed to some "hot keys". If the control signals have not occurred yet, the character is copied into the output buffer. This buffer looks like the system circular buffer, but is of a greater size in order to hold NL text translation results longer than 16 characters.

When the business system needs a character, it invokes interrupt 16H handled by the embedment system NewInt16 module. If the system is not active yet, this module works as the INT16H standard handler, but instead of the standard circular buffer it uses the mentioned output buffer. Thus, the embedment system transparent mode does not affect the business system keyboard interface. The emergency case exception is the business system directly interacting with the keyboard.

If the removal signal hot key combination is pressed, the NewInt09 module runs the removing module that is a resident part of the embedment system too. This block rebuilds the old interrupt table and removes the embedment system from the memory. Then the computer is ready for new applications.

If the activation signal comes, the embedment system becomes active. This activation must not interfere with other running programs, including the operating system routines. Let us discuss this condition in detail. Since MS DOS was designed as a single-program environment, most of its functions are not reentrant. Therefore, one should avoid a situation when an operating system routine is interrupted by a program calling an operating system routine, because MS DOS routines often call each other. So, a prerequisite for a safe activation is that all MS DOS functions must be terminated by the activation moment, except for the keyboard input and display output routines (it is this exception that enables the print spooling and disk operations while the command line editing). Besides, all disk operations must be finished; otherwise, a data loss is possible. Sometimes this condition does not follow from the first one because they may directly use interrupts to access disks. There are a few more conditions, but we skip them as their corresponding situations occur rather rarely.

The embedment system safety module is responsible for checking these conditions. This module includes handling programs for interrupts 13H (low level disk activities) and 21H (MS DOS function call). Though this method is not very easy to implement in a high level programming language, it seems more reliable than using the undocumented operating system facilities such as function 34H or interrupt 28H ("idle").

If the system is safely activated, on the screen there appears a special window to type an NL text (another version has its NL input window in the formal input screen area). From this point on the business system communicates with the keyboard in the following way.

Everything is the same until NewInt09 module checks the character returned by the old INT16 handler. If the character is the deactivation signal, the embedment system switches to the transparent mode and the text input window disappears. Otherwise, the character falls to the special text buffer displayed in the screen window. The window reflects all changes while a user is entering an NL text, which is supported by the editing module. This module has two peculiarities. Firstly, it cannot call any operating system functions to display the window text; it has to do with direct BIOS calls. Borland C compiler offers the console input/output library (*conio.h*) for this purpose. Secondly, the processing rate must be maximized to preclude a keyboard input delay. Therefore, the window re-displays only altered characters.

As words are entered, they go to the searching module that looks them up in the dictionary. This module ignores misprints using methods described in Part VI of this book. Due to the text buffer, the retrieval process does not impede the user's typing. Thus, the input and the recognition are combined asynchronously.

After the address is entered and its words are identified as well as possible, the translating module takes control. This module performs the orientated analysis, recognizes the adequate reaction and forms the formal language query as if it were a sequence of pressed keys. This sequence is placed into the output buffer and the mentioned NewInt16 module returns the control to the business system. The latter gets the formal address from the output buffer through NewINT16 handler and performs an appropriate reaction.

Additionally, the embedment system has a mode of entering a sequence of formal addresses. If this mode is on, the output buffer is refilled with another address after the previous one is processed. The mode is useful in situations of a sought-for reaction demanding no less than a few formal tasks.

We have presented the embedment system for the MS DOS operating system environment. The resident part of our system did not exceed 64 Kbytes. We tested it on IBM PC/AT with the wellknown DBMS dBASE III PLUS by Ashton-Tate as a business system. During the experiment we did not observe any impact of the embedment system upon the database operations.

Thus, we have considered the NL interface assimilation problem and the embedment as one of its possible solutions. In the next chapter we shall describe practical systems for the orientated NL text analysis.

Chapter 20
PRACTICAL IMPLEMENTATIONS

20.1 The problem domain description

The ideas of orientated linguistics were implemented in the field of management where a computer data base was run by inexperienced users (office employees, top-ranking officials, etc.). This class of problem domains usually implies non-verbal reactions (tables and diagrams) and rather short queries (one–two sentences or even a few words) in the NL version known from Chapter 6 as the address language. This sort of NL communication takes place in many fields: industrial management, business, information service, scientific research, etc. In fact, practically all DBMS's support the interrogation service.

More specifically, we explored the problem domain that covered a part of the data base owned by the Russian State Committee for Oil-Products Supply. We call this problem domain "Oil-products transportations" and designate it and its appropriate object domain by Ω (for convenience sake we use a notation not connected with the rest of the book). The schematic structure of the managed field is as follows.

In the problem domain Ω there is a set of suppliers $A = \{a_i\colon\ i \in \overline{1,m}\}$, a set of consumers $B = \{b_j:\ j \in \overline{1,n}\}$ and a set of oil-products $C = \{c_k:\ k \in \overline{1,k}\}$. Those sets are naturally bounded ($m = 327$, $n = 2309$, $l = 786$). An elementary managerial action ("delivery") in the problem domain Ω is described as a vector function $G = G(a_i, b_j, c_k, \nu)$, where ν is a moment (or a sequence of moments) of discrete time.

The vector G components represent the delivery characteristics (the kind of transport, the measurement unit, the amount, etc.) and the data type (planned, actual, total, etc.). Experience suggests that a single value of the function G usually gives a user too little information; he or she can invent an effective managing action on looking through sufficiently considerable time period information given as a single list. Furthermore, such a list must include information of various data types for the user to compare it. Thus, the data base represents an object as a vector-function independent of time (at least explicitly). Its vector includes uniform data for all the time moments and all the mentioned data types (in other words, uniform data for different time moments are stored in different data base fields, not in different records). This block function will be written as

$$g_{ijk} = g(a_i, b_j, c_k),\ a_i \in A,\ b_j \in B,\ c_k \in C\ .$$

The investigated data base fragment is denoted as $D_\Omega = \bigcup_{i,j,k} g_{ijk}$.

Proceeding from the ten year experience of operating the considered data base, we examined the goals that users pursued in their routine activity within the problem domain Ω. The examination proved that practically all these goals could be reached by means of 14 algorithms listed in Table 20.1. Each row of this table defines a subset of one-type reactions produced by a certain algorithm with several arguments (from 1 to 3). Each argument may be presented in any of three possible forms:

1) a value,

2) a list of values,

3) a generalizing flag to denote a request for either a list of all possible data or a sum of those data.

Table 20.1 represents possible values of arguments in the following notation:

$a = \{a_{i_1}, \ldots, a_{i_r}\} \subseteq A$ — a list of suppliers ($1 \le r \le m$);

$b = \{b_{j_1}, \ldots, b_{j_s}\} \subseteq B$ — a list of consumers ($1 \le s \le n$);

$c = \{c_{k_1}, \ldots, c_{k_q}\} \subseteq C$ — a list of oil-products ($1 \le q \le l$);

Σ_A — a sum for all suppliers;

Σ_B — a sum for all consumers;

* (asterisk) — a generalizing flag.

The column "Reaction essence" shows the data subset making a reaction to a certain subset of input NL texts. Some examples, taken from the training set T_Ω of texts, are given in the last column (word-for-word Russian-to-English translations).

Of course, numeric data is accompanied by additional information (names of objects and oil-products, etc.). For simplicity sake we consider this information to be a part of the vector-function g_{ijk}. Using the common data base nomenclature we can conclude that each of the listed reacting algorithms defines a *report* to be produced by the DBMS interrogation service. Thus, the problem domain Ω needs only 14 types of reports; this number has not been changed for more than 15 years. At the same time, these algorithms can produce more than 400 000 reports, to say nothing about arguments as lists of a few values. Such a ratio proves that the described environment is K-stationary and Ω is an NPD of

Table 20.1

#	Arguments			Reaction essence	NL text examples
1	a	b	c	$\{g_{ijk} : a_i \in a,\ b_j \in b,\ c_k \in c\}$	What amount of A-76 was delivered from Ufa to Altai and Irkutsk?
2	a	b	$*$	$\{g_{ijk} : a_i \in a,\ b_j \in b,\ c_k \in C\}$	What did Khabarovsk dispatch to Primorje?
3	a	$*$	c	$\{g_{ijk} : a_i \in a,\ b_j \in B,\ c_k \in c\}$	Where did summer diesel fuel go from Belorussia?
4	a	Σ_B	c	$\{\sum_{b_j \in B} g_{ijk} : a_i \in a,\ c_k \in c\}$	What total amount of mazut did Samara factory give?
5	$*$	b	c	$\{g_{ijk} : a_i \in A,\ b_j \in b,\ c_k \in c\}$	From where did Krasnoyarsk region get aviation petrol?
6	Σ_A	b	c	$\{\sum_{a_i \in A} g_{ijk} : b_j \in b,\ c_k \in c\}$	Give me total figures of the road bitumen supply to Perm'.
7	a	$*$	$*$	$\{g_{ijk} : a_i \in a,\ b_j \in B,\ c_k \in C\}$	Delivery from Ukraine.
8	a	Σ_B	$*$	$\{\sum_{b_j \in B} g_{ijk} : a_i \in a,\ c_k \in C\}$	I need a summarized oil-products shipment from Peterburg.
9	$*$	b	$*$	$\{g_{ijk} : a_i \in A,\ b_j \in b,\ c_k \in C\}$	What and whence did the Briansk region department get?
10	Σ_A	b	$*$	$\{\sum_{a_i \in A} g_{ijk} : b_j \in b,\ c_k \in C\}$	How much various products did they totally give to Armenia?
11	$*$	$*$	c	$\{g_{ijk} : a_i \in A,\ b_j \in B,\ c_k \in c\}$	What is the situation with heating fuel?
12	Σ_A	$*$	c	$\{\sum_{a_i \in A} g_{ijk} : b_j \in B,\ c_k \in c\}$	Wanted summarized information on A-92 gasoline consumption.
13	$*$	Σ_B	c	$\{\sum_{b_j \in B} g_{ijk} : a_i \in A,\ c_k \in c\}$	Give a report: total dispatch of TG-22 by all consumers.
14	Σ_A	Σ_B	c	$\{\sum_{a_i \in A} \sum_{b_j \in B} g_{ijk} : c_k \in c\}$	Well, sum up the arctic diesel fuel they sent.

K=14. Notice that this description fits a lot of similar problem domains situated in the fields of supply, scheduling, trade, etc.; they are also K-stationary for the most part.

Now we are going to present the parameter system of the algorithm performing the orientated NL text analysis. We shall use the parametrizing technique discussed in Chapter 18.

20.2 The parameter system description

For the sake of clearness, we shall start from the simplest parametrization to continue with a more sophisticated one (they respectively have nonintersecting and intersecting sets of suppliers and consumers).

Variant 1: $A \cap B = \emptyset$

This case is rather simple because the hyperdictionary naturally falls into independent lexical categories:

(a) geographical denominations or colloquial names of suppliers ("supplier's name");

(b) the same for consumers ("consumer's name");

(c) official (full and brief) and colloquial names of oil-products ("oil-product name");

(d) the training set T_Ω words and word-combinations indicating a summarized information query, for instance, "totally", "in whole", "overall", "sum" ("total data indicator");

(e) words and word-combinations to point to suppliers in general; for example, "supplier", "dispatcher", "from where", "whence" ("generic supplier indicator");

(f) the same for consumers ("generic consumer indicator").

Since these sets of words do not intersect, for the adequate reaction to be recognized an NL text must be searched for words and word-combinations of the listed lexical categories. This variant does not call for any traditional linguistic features and the hyperdictionary may indicate only a category letter ("A", "B",..., "F" in accordance with the above given order). Just as it was supposed in Chapter 18, the role information is represented in the hyperdictionary as D_Ω data base keys of the appropriate objects. The hyperdictionary holds truncated words thus reducing the number of records. In fact, each record corresponds to a word-changing bundle because all words of such a bundle have the same feature.

Besides, this design makes the analyzer more tolerant to errors because cutoff word parts are ignored independently of errors in them.

The orientated algorithm parametrization ATNR is shown in Fig. 20.1. This transition network is 1-connected and involves 3 states and 23 edges. Let us consider the algorithm. When a text comes, the network leaves the state S for the state $Q1$ and initializes the ATNR registers. The designation of those registers will be clear from the further discussion.

The register $WORD$ holds the current word of the text. This word is analyzed in accordance with the order of the edges emitted by the state $Q1$. If it is a supplier's, a consumer's or an oil-product name, the appropriate D_Ω data base key is picked up from the corresponding hyperdictionary record and appended to A, B, C registers respectively. The symbols $cat(WORD)$ and $key(WORD)$ are used in Fig. 20.1 to denote the current word lexical and role features stored in the hyperdictionary record of the word (it is agreed that unknown words are responded by a dummy record). If the current word is either a generic supplier indicator or a generic consumer indicator or a total data indicator, the flag registers $A1$, $B1$ or Q are respectively set to 1. If the word does not belong to any lexical category of the hyperdictionary, the analyzer skips it.

The end of the text being reached, the process leaves $Q1$ for $Q2$ along the first edge. There it refers to Table 20.1 to calculate the reacting algorithm number from the register values. That is it.

The result is that the register N holds the algorithm number and the registers A, B and C store lists of the data base keys corresponding to the values of the algorithm arguments. The DBMS gets this information to produce the desired reaction.

A transition from a state P' to a state P'' along the l-th edge will be written as $P'(l) \longrightarrow P''$. Above the arrow there will be the word caused the transition (if any). The example below illustrates analyzing the text: "Please, inform me whether Tula got any solvent and whence".

$$S(1) \longrightarrow Q1(8) \xrightarrow{\text{Please}} Q1(8) \xrightarrow{,} Q1(8) \xrightarrow{\text{inform}} Q1(8) \xrightarrow{\text{me}} Q1(8) \xrightarrow{\text{whether}}$$

$$\rightarrow Q1(3) \xrightarrow{\text{Tula}} Q1(8) \xrightarrow{\text{got}} Q1(8) \xrightarrow{\text{any}} Q1(4) \xrightarrow{\text{solvent}} Q1(8) \xrightarrow{\text{and}} Q1(6) \longrightarrow$$

$$\xrightarrow{\text{whence}} Q1(1) \longrightarrow Q2(5) \longrightarrow \text{POP}$$

The resulting contents of the ATNR registers are as follows: $N = 5$, A=" "(an empty list), B="051002" (the key of the Tula region in D_Ω data base), C="013007" (the key of the solvent).

It is evident that if the set of suppliers and the set of consumers do not intersect, the described algorithm has a recognizing power sufficient to react correctly to any text from the NPD Ω (the hyperdictionary must be sufficiently exhaustive). Now let us consider the variant of the sets intersecting.

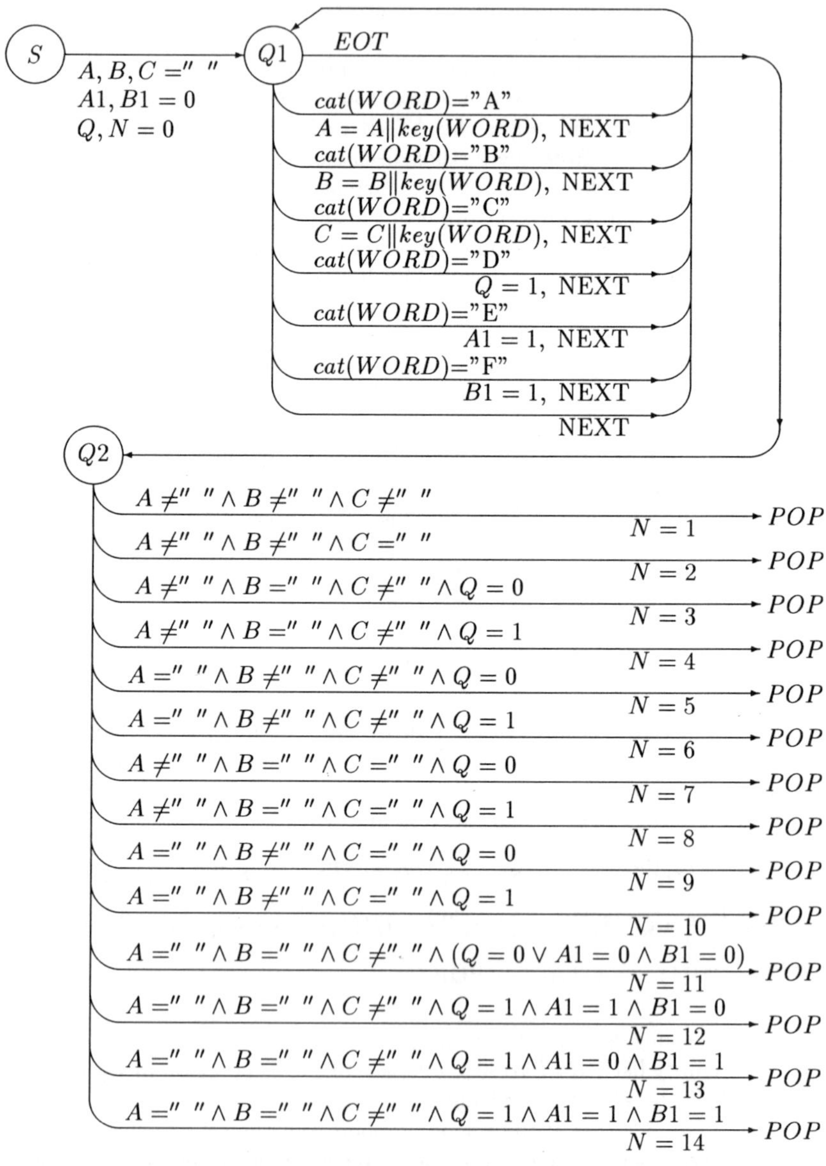
S
Q1
Q2
EOT
A, B, C =" "
A1, B1 = 0
Q, N = 0
cat(WORD)="A"
A = A||key(WORD), NEXT
cat(WORD)="B"
B = B||key(WORD), NEXT
cat(WORD)="C"
C = C||key(WORD), NEXT
cat(WORD)="D"
Q = 1, NEXT
cat(WORD)="E"
A1 = 1, NEXT
cat(WORD)="F"
B1 = 1, NEXT
NEXT
A ≠" " ∧ B ≠" " ∧ C ≠" "
N = 1
POP
A ≠" " ∧ B ≠" " ∧ C =" "
N = 2
POP
A ≠" " ∧ B =" " ∧ C ≠" " ∧ Q = 0
N = 3
POP
A ≠" " ∧ B =" " ∧ C ≠" " ∧ Q = 1
N = 4
POP
A =" " ∧ B ≠" " ∧ C ≠" " ∧ Q = 0
N = 5
POP
A =" " ∧ B ≠" " ∧ C ≠" " ∧ Q = 1
N = 6
POP
A ≠" " ∧ B =" " ∧ C =" " ∧ Q = 0
N = 7
POP
A ≠" " ∧ B =" " ∧ C =" " ∧ Q = 1
N = 8
POP
A =" " ∧ B ≠" " ∧ C =" " ∧ Q = 0
N = 9
POP
A =" " ∧ B ≠" " ∧ C =" " ∧ Q = 1
N = 10
POP
A =" " ∧ B =" " ∧ C ≠" " ∧ (Q = 0 ∨ A1 = 0 ∧ B1 = 0)
N = 11
POP
A =" " ∧ B =" " ∧ C ≠" " ∧ Q = 1 ∧ A1 = 1 ∧ B1 = 0
N = 12
POP
A =" " ∧ B =" " ∧ C ≠" " ∧ Q = 1 ∧ A1 = 0 ∧ B1 = 1
N = 13
POP
A =" " ∧ B =" " ∧ C ≠" " ∧ Q = 1 ∧ A1 = 1 ∧ B1 = 1
N = 14
POP

Figure 20.1

Variant 2: $A \cap B \neq \emptyset$

The first variant looks very simple, though its "understanding" is errorless. The reason is evident: any word has a unique role thus removing the role recognition problem. However, in actual practice such a case is very difficult to meet. For instance, the discussed NPD Ω has the set intersection cardinality of no less than 40% of the union cardinality. That is why we must raise the question of the NL text understanding algorithm parametrization in this situation.

This more complicated problem needs more features to recognize an object as a supplier or as a consumer. With Russian language we may use case endings, prepositions and other parts of speech indicating an oil-product transportation direction (TO the object or FROM it). Necessary information is added to the hyperdictionary. There new lexical categories appear, called a "dispatch-TO indicator" and a "dispatch-FROM indicator" respectively. Besides, wordforms allowed to have two roles are involved in the new lexical category "supplier/consumer's name". For this category the hyperdictionary supports the conventional linguistic feature "case".

Furthermore, the training set contains some examples with the object role determined by the word order ("the route Khabarovsk — Moscow"). All words that can help to identify such constructions in a text form a specific lexical category. Auxiliary words used in the object role recognition are represented by the usual categories "prepositions", "conjunctions" and "punctuation marks" (a complete list of lexical categories is given in Appendix). The hyperdictionary comprises a total of 1800 records corresponding to more than 12 000 words.

The ATNR of the algorithm aimed primarily at identifying an object as a supplier or a consumer. As soon as this problem is solved, we obtain the above considered first variant.

Analyzing the training set T_Ω we revealed certain situations that can be used as object role identification features. Let us denote an NL text as $t \in T_\Omega$ and its objects (i.e. subtexts) as $t_1, t_2, \ldots, t_u$. Then these features are represented by the following predicates:

$U_m(t)$ is true if the text t contains a word order indicator determining the roles of all the objects;

$U_c(t_s)$ is true if an object t_s role (i.e. where the oil-product moves with respect to this object) is uniquely shown by the case of the subtext t_s or by a combination of its case and a preposition;

$U_d(t_s)$ is true if the text contains a dispatch direction indicator corresponding to the subtext t_s;

$U_h(t_s)$ is true if the text contains another object t'_s of some known role and t_s and t'_s are uniform parts of the sentence.

First, the algorithm evaluates predicates $U_c(t_s)$, $U_d(t_s)$ and $U_h(t_s)$ for all recognized subtexts t_s of the text t. Then it calculates the number $\eta(t_s)$ of true predicates for each of them. Here the following options are possible:

(a) $\eta(t_s) = 0$. The subtext t_s role can not be determined yet. This question can be solved later, for example, when the algorithm finds a subtext t'_s with $U_h(t'_s) =$ **true** and with t_s and t'_s as uniform parts of the sentence.

(b) $\eta(t_s) = 1$. The object role is apparent and corresponds to the true predicate semantics (for instance, if $U_d(t_s) =$ **true** and there is a "dispatch-FROM indicator" in the text then t_s describes a supplier).

(c) $\eta(t_s) > 1$. If all the true predicates indicate the same role of t_s, the situation does not differ from option (b). But if they contradict to each other, it means that the text concerns more than one object. Now the problem is to refer these objects to the appropriate indicators. Let us consider this problem in detail.

Just as the usual problem of choosing an adequate reaction, the problem of determining the subtext role can be treated as a heterogeneous pattern recognition problem. Its complexity depends on the number of ambiguously roled objects in the text and on the set of their features given as the mentioned predicates. Namely, the recognition algorithm calculates the number of suppliers (NS), of consumers (NC), of two-role objects (NSC), of dispatch-FROM indicators (NDF), and of dispatch-TO indicators (NDT). Then it solves a recognition problem, one of P1–P4 described below.

(P1) $NSC = 0$. The problem is reduced to Variant 1 because there are no objects of unknown role.

(P2) $NSC > 1 \wedge U_m(t) =$ **true**. Here the problem is reduced to Variant 1 too, because there is an order indicator determining roles of *all* the objects in the text t.

(P3) $NDF = 0 \vee NDT = 0$, i.e. all dispatch direction indicators show the same direction. Then $U_c(t_s)$ is tested for all t_s with two possible roles (a supplier or a consumer): there are NSC of them in the text. If $U_c(t_s) =$ **true**, the role of t_s is clear. Otherwise, $U_d(t_s)$ predicate is tested. If $U_d(t_s) =$ **true**, the role of t_s is determined (see case (b) above), else the next object with unknown role is processed and so forth, returning to skipped objects after the whole list is exhausted.

(P4) $NDF > 0 \wedge NDT > 0$. Usually it is not very difficult to clarify how dispatch direction indicators and objects are correlated; few constructions allow such a "mixing up" and they are rather exotic. Nevertheless, there are no grounds to neglect phrases like "How many railroad tanks of gasoline was dispatched by Omsk and Kurgan received?" (a word-for-word translation from Russian). In Russian original version "Omsk" and "Kurgan" look like uniform parts of the sentence; either of opposite direction indicators ("dispatched" and "received") can be related to both objects by mistake.

Therefore, the ATNR makes a preliminary text segmentation for each segment to cover dispatch direction indicators of the same direction and their relevant objects. In the given example there are two segments: "dispatched by Omsk" and "Kurgan received". This segmentation is always possible because of a phenomenon observed in the training set T_Ω. The matter is that any two of such segments either do not intersect at all or one of them covers the other. A partial intersection never occurs. Within a segment we should solve problem (P3). The only peculiarity of the covering case is that the analysis must start from the deepest segment; processed segments must be excluded from the text by means of EXCL operations on the appropriate network edges.

The ATNR of Variant 2 is 3-connected and consists of 45 states and 162 edges. A full description of the network is given in the Appendix; the notation of the following section is used. The first connected component (starting from the state $POST$) embraces constructions that determine suppliers. The second one (starting at $POTR$) deals with consumers. The main component, including the initial state S, calls these two components more than once (they are essentially its subroutines) and controls the orientated text analysis procedure.

The outlined hyperdictionary and transition network provide the parametrization basis for a practical readjustable system requesting the D_Ω data base in natural language (Russian). The system was implemented in two versions differing in their hardware and in their parametrized description processing techniques. Implementation peculiarities are discussed in the next section.

20.3 The implementation technology description

The first of our developments for the NPD Ω was designed to work on a mainframe computer communicating with remote terminals under the control of OS/360 MVT operating system. As the computer had a sufficient performance but rather obsolete system software, we developed the algorithm to be an *interpreter*. It also helped us to accelerate the development.

Specifically speaking, the hyperdictionary of this version was built as an indexed sequential data set (we used BISAM access method) with a high level index stored in memory to increase the dictionary retrieval speed. As for the ATNR, no attempts were made to convert its description into an executable code; instead, the properly encoded description was processed by a special interpreting program. And it was this program that carried out the orientated text analysis.

For this purpose we developed a collection of Assembler language macro instructions that could independently describe the following things:

- an ATNR register,
- an ATNR state (i.e. a network node),
- an edge linking two states,
- an elementary condition to permit a transition,
- an elementary action to be performed during a transition along an edge.

Macros of two latter types can be repeatedly combined to form complex conditions and actions. In addition to this, there are macro instructions breaking an ATNR description into segments that overlay each other in operation. When the system is being adjusted, each (maybe only one) ATNR segment is specified as a usual assembly control section. Then it is processed by the OS/360 Assembler and Linkage Editor programs. The resulting module is not an executable code but just a control data table. The ATNR-interpreting program uses this table to perform transitions along network edges. In so doing it tests the associated conditions, carries out the attributed actions and changes the overlays if needed.

The interpreting program was written in the PL/1 language for the OS/360 optimizing compiler. It consisted of about 850 operators and had a static volume of less than 70 Kbytes. The transition network (considered in the preceding section — Variant 2) was a control table of about 30 Kbytes. We tested the algorithm for both training and examining sets and did not reveal any misinterpretation of NL addresses. The analysis used to take 0.75–35 seconds per text; about half of that time was taken by the dictionary retrieval. It should be noticed that such a low performance did not look excessive against the slow data base interrogation and report generation (sometimes those operations took more than a minute). What is more, the channels in use did not support more than 1200 baud of communication rate. As a result, sometimes the whole system seemed irritatingly slow but not because of the NL analyzer.

The described version of the algorithm was installed in the Russian State Committee for Oil-products Supply and worked there for a year. Its operational characteristics were qualitatively the same as those shown in our preliminary tests; users gave it high praise though they did not like its slow operating.

Within that period we made a successful attempt to readjust our orientated system; it was done in the context of a Soviet-Czechoslovakian agreement. For this purpose our Czechoslovakian colleagues (we were just consulting experts) collected two training sets: for Czech and Slovak languages. These sets were searched for recognition subtexts and necessary lexical and role features. They also compiled hyperdictionaries for both languages and constructed the appropriate ATNR descriptions. This work took them 1.5 man-month per language. Thus the practice confirmed the possibility of switching the system between national languages as well as between object domains.

As far as we know, such a possibility was demonstrated for the first time. Within the framework of conventional linguistics a change of language is followed by a complete reconstruction of all analyzing levels which is equal to developing the whole system anew.

The experience of the analyzer readjustment into different languages was naturally continued by creating a multi-lingual NL system [38]. Its operating principle is the same as in the case of serving several object domains at a time. We developed a pre-recognition module to provide a fast and reliable identification of an input text language (among four supported languages: Russian, Ukrainian, Czech and Slovak). After the language is recognized, the appropriate hyperdictionary and ATNR are loaded in the memory, and the interpreting program runs as usual. Furthermore, each algorithm has the argument "language" that makes the system react in the language of the query.

In the meantime the serviced object domain was re-equipped with a more sophisticated computers. In the process of decentralizing the managerial structure the local area networks and multi-terminal super-minicomputers became available instead of remote terminals connected with a host computer via communication channels. All these improvements allowed essentially quickening the data base retrieval and the information transmission. So, the problem of accelerating the orientated NL text analysis was brought to the fore.

This problem called for the second version of the orientated algorithm to be designed as a *compiler*. The main efforts were aimed at automating the development of an orientated analyzer program (i.e. of an executable code) by pre-processing a parameter system arranged as an ATNR. Then a ready program could be transferred to all workstations operating the data base independently. This method would speed up the understanding of every input address and remove the interpreting program, saving time and memory.

The practicability of such a construction rests on the following simple grounds. Indeed, when the ATNR interpreter is going along a network edge, it performs certain operators to test the conditions associated with the edge and to execute the actions attributed to the edge. However, in addition to this necessary job it must execute a great number of instructions to set operands of these conditions and actions, to determine the next state, to locate the current position in the control table, etc.

These operations are just a lumber for the ATNR itself. Hence the evident idea arises: to separate essential instructions of each edge and to organize them as a single program in accordance with the network structure. This processing of every edge description into an equivalent sequence of essential operations makes a compilation of the transition network. The compilation process is performed beforehand with the use of a special compiling program or even manually.

The only necessary addition to the compilation result is a module handling explicit components of the parameter system. In our consideration these components are represented by a hyperdictionary; therefore, we shall speak about a dictionary retrieval module. (We believe that in many cases explicit information cannot be effectively converted into an equivalent algorithm).

The compiler was designed to run on the WANG-2200-MVP minicomputer characterized by an extremely small memory available to each terminal (no more than 64 Kbytes). The low-level programming technique is not available on this computer either: a software designer sees any process on any terminal as a hardware interpretation of a BASIC program launched on this terminal. Therefore, the ATNR compiler should produce a BASIC program of a size not exceeding 64 Kbytes (on this computer it is about 5–6 thousand BASIC operators).

This shortage of computer resources prevented the projected compiler from being implemented on WANG-2200 itself. The necessary BASIC program was built by a stand-alone compiler written for the mainframe in the PL/1 language. In order for the compiler to be simpler, the transition network description was endowed with more structurality than the above described assembly macro instructions. Specifically, the ATNR language syntax was defined by the following rules given in the expanded Backus-Naur form:

```
<ATNR>      ::= <bundle> {<bundle>}
<bundle>    ::= FROM <state> <edge> {<edge>}
<edge>      ::= [IF <condition>] [DO <action> {,<action>} <branch>]
<condition>::= <relation> | (<condition>) | ¬ <condition> |
                <condition> ∧ <condition> | <condition> ∨ <condition>
<relation>  ::= <expression> <symbol> <expression> | EOT
<symbol>    ::= < | ≤ | > | ≥ | = | ≠ | ∈ | ∉
<action>    ::= <operand> = <expression> | EXCL | NEXT | BACK |
                UP <register> | DOWN <register>
<branch>    ::= [PUSH <state>] TO <state>   | POP
<operand>   ::= <register>   | PRE <register>   | SUC <register>
```

Let us also agree that:

(a) ATNR states and registers may have names of any length;

(b) expressions are written as it is prescribed by the PL/1 programming language; the operation precedence is also preserved;

(c) operation order changing parentheses may be used with unlimited nesting;

(d) comments are bounded by the character pairs `/*` and `*/`.

Let us consider in brief the semantics of the listed rules. An ATNR description is a collection of as many bundles as needed. Each bundle corresponds to a single network state with all edges originating from it. The very first bundle in the description refers to the initial state S. The edges are tested for being permitted in accordance with their order in a bundle. The logical operations AND, OR, NOT (denoted as $\wedge, \vee, \neg$ respectively) can be used to form a complex condition out of the primitives. An edge description consists of three parts: a condition (optional), a list of actions (optional) and the transition itself. The latter component is referred to as "branch" in the syntactic scheme above and determines the edge type, for instance:

`PUSH Q1 TO Q2` (a PUSH-type edge: a submergence to the state $Q1$, a transition to the state $Q2$);

`TO Q3` (a TST-type edge: a transition to the state $Q3$);

`POP` (a POP-type edge: back from a submergence).

Expressions used in conditions and actions may involve the construction "operand" that specifies a pointed register value at either the current or the preceding (`PRE`) or the succeeding (`SUC`) recursion level. This register must be a list. Additional actions move the current position pointer in such a list-like register from the beginning (`UP`) or in the opposite direction (`DOWN`).

As we have already mentioned, the second considered ATNR variant is completely described in the Appendix. That text was processed by the stand-alone compiler that generated a BASIC program to be run on any workstation.

The compiler works in rather a simple manner. At first each ATNR register is represented as a BASIC variable of the appropriate type. Then each edge description is converted into a single conditional statement:

$$m \text{ IF} < \text{I-condition} > \text{ THEN}\, m+1 \text{ ELSE } < \text{action} >: \ldots : \text{GOTO}\, n$$

Here m is the current line number of the program; <I-condition> means an inverted condition assigned to the given edge; <action>: ... is a sequence of BASIC statements implementing the list of actions attributed to the edge (repeated and special actions exploit the GOSUB statement); n is a program line number corresponding to the first edge of the resulting state.

If a condition or an action list exceed the BASIC limitations, the line is split into two or more lines and the line numbers are properly modified.

As a result, we obtained a BASIC program of 3163 statements (698 lines). It was supplemented by a dictionary retrieval subroutine of 192 statements (78 lines). The whole program occupied 56 Kbytes, which fortunately met the memory per terminal limitation. Otherwise, the network would be segmented and equipped with an overlay structure (as it was done with the interpreter above).

The compiling version of the orientated algorithm was introduced into service to help non-programming users. Among them there is the Minister, his deputies, heads of departments and other top managers. Some examples and results of the system functioning will be discussed in the next section.

20.4 Examples and results of service

The work of the orientated algorithm will be demonstrated by the examples from Table 20.1. We shall consider those addresses one by one as we did in Section 20.2. Since the transition network was designed for Russian and does not work with correct English equivalents, we preserve the initial appearance of the queries but translate their words below. For the clearness sake we underline all words and word-combinations stored in the hyperdictionary in their full or reduced form.

1. Много ли А-76 отправлено из Уфы на Алтай и в Иркутск ?
   (What amount of A-76 was delivered from Ufa to Altai and Irkutsk?)

Here "Много ли" means "What amount", "А-76" is a sort of gasoline, "отправлено" equals "was delivered", "из" corresponds to "from", "в"="to", "и"="and", "на"="to". "Уфы", "Иркутск", "Алтай" are the geographical names of cities and regions.

The transition trace in this case is as follows (here and in the subsequent examples we exclude deadlock branches that launched the backtracking mechanism):

$$S(1) \longrightarrow Q1(10) \xrightarrow{\text{А-76}} Q1(8) \xrightarrow{\text{отправлено}} Q1(10) \xrightarrow{\text{из}} Q1(7) \xrightarrow{\text{Уфы}}$$

$$Q1(10) \xrightarrow{\text{в}} Q1(7) \xrightarrow{\text{Иркутск}} Q1(10) \xrightarrow{\text{и}} Q1(10) \xrightarrow{\text{на}} Q1(7) \xrightarrow{\text{Алтай}} Q1(1) \longrightarrow$$

$$Q2(4) \longrightarrow Q5(2) \xrightarrow{\text{А-76}} Q5(3) \xrightarrow{\text{отправлено}} Q5(3) \xrightarrow{\text{из}} Q5(3) \xrightarrow{\text{Уфы}}$$

$$Q5(3) \xrightarrow{\text{в}} Q5(3) \xrightarrow{\text{Иркутск}} Q5(3) \xrightarrow{\text{и}} Q5(3) \xrightarrow{\text{на}} Q5(3) \xrightarrow{\text{Алтай}} Q5(1) \longrightarrow$$

$$Q6(5) \xrightarrow{\text{отправлено}} Q6(2) \longrightarrow POST(4) \xrightarrow{\text{из}} PS2(1) \xrightarrow{\text{Уфы}} Q7(6) \longrightarrow$$

$$Q6(3) \longrightarrow POTR(7) \xrightarrow{\text{в}} PT4(1) \xrightarrow{\text{Иркутск}} Q12(3) \xrightarrow{\text{и}} POTR(7) \xrightarrow{\text{на}}$$

$$PT4(1) \xrightarrow{\text{Алтай}} Q14(1) \longrightarrow Q12(1) \longrightarrow Q25(1) \longrightarrow Q4(1) \longrightarrow POP.$$

The ATNR output registers get the following values:

N=1 (the 1st reacting algorithm),
A="007009" (the key of "Уфы" in D_Ω data base),
B="063000018001" (the catenated keys of "Иркутск" and "Алтай"),
P="012070" (the key of "А-76" gasoline in D_Ω).

2. Что Хабаровск отгрузил в Приморье ?
   (What did Khabarovsk dispatch to Primorje?)

Word equivalents:

Что	What
Хабаровск	Khabarovck (a city)
отгрузил	did ... dispatch
в	to
Приморье	Primorje (a region)

The transition trace:

$$S(1) \longrightarrow Q1(7) \xrightarrow{\text{Хабаровск}} Q1(8) \xrightarrow{\text{отгрузил}} Q1(10) \xrightarrow{\text{в}} Q1(7) \xrightarrow{\text{Приморье}}$$
$$Q1(1) \longrightarrow Q2(4) \longrightarrow Q5(3) \xrightarrow{\text{Хабаровск}} Q5(3) \xrightarrow{\text{отгрузил}} Q5(3) \xrightarrow{\text{в}}$$
$$Q5(3) \xrightarrow{\text{Приморье}} Q5(1) \longrightarrow Q6(2) \longrightarrow POST(3) \xrightarrow{\text{Хабаровск}} Q7(6) \longrightarrow$$
$$Q6(5) \xrightarrow{\text{отгрузил}} Q6(4) \longrightarrow Q17(3) \xrightarrow{\text{в}} Q17(2) \xrightarrow{\text{Приморье}} Q18(1) \longrightarrow$$
$$Q25(3) \longrightarrow Q4(2) \longrightarrow POP.$$

The output registers contents:

N=2 (the 2nd reacting algorithm)
A="023001" (the key of Khabarovsk)
B="024007" (the key of the Primorje region)
P=" " (empty)

3. Куда пошло дизтопливо летнее из Белоруссии ?
(Where did summer diesel fuel go from Belorussia?)

Word equivalents:

Куда	Where
пошло	did ... go
дизтопливо летнее	summer diesel fuel
из	from
Белоруссии	Belorussia

The transition trace:

$$S(1) \longrightarrow Q1(4) \xrightarrow{\text{Куда}} Q1(8) \xrightarrow{\text{пошло}} Q1(10) \xrightarrow{\text{дизтопливо летнее}}$$
$$Q1(10) \xrightarrow{\text{из}} Q1(7) \xrightarrow{\text{Белоруссии}} Q1(1) \longrightarrow Q2(4) \longrightarrow Q5(3) \xrightarrow{\text{пошло}}$$
$$Q5(2) \xrightarrow{\text{дизтопливо летнее}} Q5(3) \xrightarrow{\text{из}} Q5(3) \xrightarrow{\text{Белоруссии}} Q5(1) \longrightarrow$$
$$Q6(5) \xrightarrow{\text{пошло}} Q6(2) \longrightarrow POST(4) \xrightarrow{\text{из}} PS2(1) \xrightarrow{\text{Белоруссии}} Q7(1) \longrightarrow$$
$$Q25(1) \longrightarrow Q4(3) \longrightarrow POP.$$

The output registers contents:

N=3 (the 3rd reacting algorithm)
A="068008" (the key of Belorussia)
B=" " (empty)
P="031005" (the key of summer diesel fuel)

4. Сколько всего мазута поставили Самарские заводы ?
(What total amount of mazut did Samara factory give?)

Word equivalents:

Сколько	What ... amount
всего	total
мазута	of mazut
поставили	did ... give
Самарские	Samara (a city)
заводы	factory

The transition trace:

$$S(1) \longrightarrow Q1(2) \xrightarrow{\text{всего}} Q1(10) \xrightarrow{\text{мазута}} Q1(8) \xrightarrow{\text{поставили}} Q1(7) \longrightarrow \xrightarrow{\text{Самарские}} Q1(1) \longrightarrow Q2(4) \longrightarrow Q5(2) \xrightarrow{\text{мазута}} Q5(3) \xrightarrow{\text{поставили}} Q5(3) \xrightarrow{\text{Самарские}} Q5(1) \longrightarrow Q6(5) \xrightarrow{\text{поставили}} Q6(2) \longrightarrow POST(3) \longrightarrow \xrightarrow{\text{Самарские}} Q7(1) \longrightarrow Q25(1) \longrightarrow Q4(4) \longrightarrow POP.$$

The output registers contents:

N=4 (the 4th reacting algorithm)
A="039001" (the key of Samara)
B=" " (empty)
P="041006" (the key of mazut).

5. Откуда Красноярский край получил авиабензин ?
(From where did Krasnoyarsk region get aviation petrol?)

Word equivalents:

Откуда	From where
Красноярский	Krasnoyarsk
край	region
получил	did ... get
авиабензин	aviation petrol

The transition trace:

$$S(1) \longrightarrow Q1(3) \xrightarrow{\text{Откуда}} Q1(7) \xrightarrow{\text{Красноярский}} Q1(9) \xrightarrow{\text{получил}} Q1(10) \longrightarrow \xrightarrow{\text{авиабензин}} Q1(1) \longrightarrow Q2(3) \longrightarrow Q5(3) \xrightarrow{\text{Красноярский}} Q5(3) \xrightarrow{\text{получил}} Q5(2) \xrightarrow{\text{авиабензин}} Q5(1) \longrightarrow Q6(3) \longrightarrow POTR(3) \xrightarrow{\text{Красноярский}} Q12(6) \longrightarrow Q6(5) \xrightarrow{\text{получил}} Q6(1) \longrightarrow Q25(1) \longrightarrow Q4(5) \longrightarrow POP.$$

The output registers contents:

N=5 (the 5th reacting algorithm)
A=" " (empty)
B="019007" (the key of the Krasnoyarsk region)
P="011003" (the key of aviation petrol).

6. Дайте суммарные цифры отгрузки дорожного битума в Пермь .
(Give me the total figures of the road bitumen supply to Perm').

Word equivalents:

Дайте	Give (me)
суммарные	total
цифры	figures
отгрузки	of ... supply
дорожного битума	road bitumen
в	to
Пермь	Perm' (a city)

The transition trace:

$$S(1) \longrightarrow Q1(8) \xrightarrow{\text{Дайте}} Q1(2) \xrightarrow{\text{суммарные}} Q1(10) \xrightarrow{\text{цифры}} Q1(8) \longrightarrow \xrightarrow{\text{отгрузки}} Q1(10) \xrightarrow{\text{дорожного битума}} Q1(10) \xrightarrow{\text{в}} Q1(7) \xrightarrow{\text{Пермь}} Q1(1) \longrightarrow Q2(4) \longrightarrow Q5(3) \xrightarrow{\text{Дайте}} Q5(3) \xrightarrow{\text{цифры}} Q5(3) \xrightarrow{\text{отгрузки}} Q5(2) \longrightarrow \xrightarrow{\text{дорожного битума}} Q5(3) \xrightarrow{\text{в}} Q5(3) \xrightarrow{\text{Пермь}} Q5(1) \longrightarrow Q6(5) \xrightarrow{\text{Дайте}} Q6(5) \xrightarrow{\text{цифры}} Q6(5) \xrightarrow{\text{отгрузки}} Q6(3) \longrightarrow POTR(7) \xrightarrow{\text{в}} PT4(1) \xrightarrow{\text{Пермь}} Q12(1) \longrightarrow Q25(1) \longrightarrow Q4(6) \longrightarrow POP.$$

The output registers contents:

N=6 (the 6th reacting algorithm)
A=" " (empty)
B="008004" (the key of the Perm' region)
P="071009" (the key of road bitumen).

7. Поставки с Украины .
   (Delivery from Ukraine).

Word equivalents:

Поставки	Delivery
с	from
Украины	Ukraine

The transition trace:

$$S(1) \longrightarrow Q1(8) \xrightarrow{\text{Поставки}} Q1(10) \xrightarrow{\text{с}} Q1(7) \xrightarrow{\text{Украины}} Q1(1) \longrightarrow Q2(4) \longrightarrow$$
$$Q5(3) \xrightarrow{\text{Поставки}} Q5(3) \xrightarrow{\text{с}} Q5(3) \xrightarrow{\text{Украины}} Q5(1) \longrightarrow Q6(5) \xrightarrow{\text{Поставки}}$$
$$Q6(2) \longrightarrow POST(4) \xrightarrow{\text{с}} PS2(1) \xrightarrow{\text{Украины}} Q7(1) \longrightarrow Q25(1) \longrightarrow$$
$$Q4(7) \longrightarrow POP.$$

The output registers contents:

N=7 (the 7th reacting algorithm)
A="058000" (the key of Ukraine)
B=" ", P=" " (both empty)

8. Мне нужны итоговые отгрузки продуктов из Петербурга .
   (I need a summarized oil-products shipment from Peterburg).

Word equivalents:

Мне нужны	I need
итоговые	summarized
отгрузки	shipment
продуктов	(oil-)products
из	from
Петербурга	Peterburg (a city)

The transition trace:

$$S(1) \longrightarrow Q1(2) \xrightarrow{\text{итоговые}} Q1(8) \xrightarrow{\text{отгрузки}} Q1(10) \xrightarrow{\text{продуктов}} Q1(10) \longrightarrow$$
$$\xrightarrow{\text{из}} Q1(7) \xrightarrow{\text{Петербурга}} Q1(1) \longrightarrow Q2(4) \longrightarrow Q5(3) \xrightarrow{\text{отгрузки}} Q5(3) \longrightarrow$$
$$\xrightarrow{\text{продуктов}} Q5(3) \xrightarrow{\text{из}} Q5(3) \xrightarrow{\text{Петербурга}} Q5(1) \longrightarrow Q6(5) \xrightarrow{\text{отгрузки}}$$
$$Q6(5) \xrightarrow{\text{продуктов}} Q6(2) \longrightarrow POST(4) \xrightarrow{\text{из}} PS2(1) \xrightarrow{\text{Петербурга}} Q7(1) \longrightarrow$$
$$Q25(1) \longrightarrow Q4(8) \longrightarrow POP.$$

The output registers contents:

N=8 (the 8th reacting algorithm)
A="044001" (the key of Peterburg)
B=" ", P=" " (both empty)

9. Что и откуда получало Брянское управление ?
(What and whence did the Briansk region department get?)

Word equivalents:

Что	What
и	and
откуда	whence
получало	did ... get
Брянское	Briansk (region)
управление	department

The transition trace:

$$S(1) \longrightarrow Q1(10) \xrightarrow{\text{и}} Q1(3) \xrightarrow{\text{откуда}} Q1(9) \xrightarrow{\text{получало}} Q1(7) \xrightarrow{\text{Брянское}} Q1(10) \xrightarrow{\text{управление}} Q1(1) \longrightarrow Q2(3) \longrightarrow Q5(3) \xrightarrow{\text{и}} Q5(3) \xrightarrow{\text{получало}} Q5(3) \xrightarrow{\text{Брянское}} Q5(3) \xrightarrow{\text{управление}} Q5(1) \longrightarrow Q6(5) \xrightarrow{\text{и}} Q6(5) \xrightarrow{\text{получало}} Q6(3) \longrightarrow POTR(3) \xrightarrow{\text{Брянское}} Q12(6) \longrightarrow Q6(5) \xrightarrow{\text{управление}} Q6(1) \longrightarrow Q25(1) \longrightarrow Q4(9) \longrightarrow POP.$$

The output registers contents:

N=9 (the 9th reacting algorithm)
A=" " (empty)
B="030002" (the key of Briansk region)
P=" " (empty).

10. Сколько в целом дали Армении различных продуктов ?
(How much various products did they totally give to Armenia?)

Word equivalents:

Сколько	How much
в целом	totally
дали	did (they) ... give
Армении	to Armenia
различных	various
продуктов	(oil-)products

The transition trace:

$$S(1) \longrightarrow Q1(2) \xrightarrow{\text{в целом}} Q1(8) \xrightarrow{\text{дали}} Q1(7) \xrightarrow{\text{Армении}} Q1(10) \longrightarrow$$
$$\xrightarrow{\text{продуктов}} Q1(1) \longrightarrow Q2(4) \longrightarrow Q5(3) \xrightarrow{\text{дали}} Q5(3) \xrightarrow{\text{Армении}} Q5(3) \longrightarrow$$
$$\xrightarrow{\text{продуктов}} Q5(1) \longrightarrow Q6(5) \xrightarrow{\text{дали}} Q6(4) \longrightarrow Q17(2) \xrightarrow{\text{Армении}}$$
$$Q18(8) \longrightarrow Q6(5) \xrightarrow{\text{продуктов}} Q6(1) \longrightarrow Q25(6) \longrightarrow Q4(10) \longrightarrow POP.$$

The output registers contents:

N=10 (the 10th reacting algorithm)
A=" " (empty)
B="061000" (the key of Armenia)
P=" " (empty).

11. Какая у нас картина с печным топливом ?
(What is the situation with heating fuel?)

Word equivalents:

Какая	What
у нас	is
картина	situation
с	with
печным топливом	heating fuel

The transition trace:

$$S(1) \longrightarrow Q1(10) \xrightarrow{\text{у}} Q1(10) \xrightarrow{\text{с}} Q1(10) \xrightarrow{\text{печным топливом}} Q1(1) \longrightarrow$$
$$Q2(1) \longrightarrow Q3(5) \xrightarrow{\text{у}} Q3(5) \xrightarrow{\text{с}} Q3(2) \xrightarrow{\text{печным топливом}} Q3(1) \longrightarrow$$
$$Q4(11) \longrightarrow POP.$$

The output registers contents:

N=11 (the 11th reacting algorithm)
A=" ", B=" " (both empty)
P="036004" (the key of heating fuel).

12. Требуются суммарные сведения о получении А-92 потребителями .
(Wanted summarized information on A-92 gasoline consumption).

Word equivalents:

Требуются	Wanted
суммарные	summarized
сведения	information
о	on
получении ... потребителями	consumption
А-92	(a sort of gasoline)

The transition trace:

$$S(1) \longrightarrow Q1(2) \xrightarrow{\text{суммарные}} Q1(10) \xrightarrow{\text{сведения}} Q1(10) \xrightarrow{\text{о}} Q1(8) \xrightarrow{\text{получении}} Q1(10) \xrightarrow{\text{А-92}} Q1(4) \xrightarrow{\text{потребителями}} Q1(1) \longrightarrow Q2(1) \longrightarrow Q3(5) \xrightarrow{\text{сведения}} Q3(5) \xrightarrow{\text{о}} Q3(5) \xrightarrow{\text{получении}} Q3(2) \xrightarrow{\text{А-92}} Q3(1) \longrightarrow Q4(12) \longrightarrow POP.$$

The output registers contents:

N=12 (the 12th reacting algorithm)
A=" ", B=" " (both empty)
P="012042" (the key of A-92 gasoline).

13. Выдайте справку : итоговая отгрузка ТГ-22 поставщиками .
(Give a report: total dispatch of TG-22 by all suppliers).

Word equivalents:

Выдайте	Give
справку	report
итоговая	total ... all
отгрузка	dispatch
ТГ-22	(a sort of gas-turbine fuel)
поставщиками	by ... suppliers

The transition trace:

$$S(1) \longrightarrow Q1(8) \xrightarrow{\text{Выдайте}} Q1(10) \xrightarrow{\text{справку}} Q1(10) \xrightarrow{:} Q1(2) \xrightarrow{\text{итоговая}} Q1(8) \xrightarrow{\text{отгрузка}} Q1(10) \xrightarrow{\text{ТГ-22}} Q1(3) \xrightarrow{\text{поставщиками}} Q1(1) \longrightarrow Q2(1) \longrightarrow Q3(5) \xrightarrow{\text{Выдайте}} Q3(5) \xrightarrow{\text{справку}} Q3(5) \xrightarrow{:} Q3(5) \xrightarrow{\text{отгрузка}} Q3(2) \xrightarrow{\text{ТГ-22}} Q3(1) \longrightarrow Q4(13) \longrightarrow POP.$$

The output registers contents:

N=13 (the 13th reacting algorithm)
A=" ", B=" " (both empty)
P="044001" (the key of gas-turbine fuel)

14. A сколько всего отправили дизтоплива арктического ?
(Well, sum up the arctic diesel fuel they sent?)

Word equivalents:

А	Well,
сколько	(none)
всего	sum up
отправили	(they) sent
дизтоплива арктического	arctic diesel fuel

The transition trace:

$S(1) \longrightarrow Q1(10) \xrightarrow{\text{А}} Q1(2) \xrightarrow{\text{всего}} Q1(8) \xrightarrow{\text{отправили}} Q1(10) \longrightarrow$
$\xrightarrow{\text{дизтоплива арктического}} Q1(1) \longrightarrow Q2(1) \longrightarrow Q3(5) \xrightarrow{\text{А}} Q3(5) \longrightarrow$
$\xrightarrow{\text{отправили}} Q3(2) \xrightarrow{\text{дизтоплива арктического}} Q3(1) \longrightarrow Q4(14) \longrightarrow POP.$

The output registers contents:

N=14 (the 14th reacting algorithm)
A=" ", B=" " (both empty)
P="034000" (the key of arctic diesel fuel)

The interpretation results are evidently correct. It is notable that the system could understand defected and ambiguous NL addresses as well as grammatically accurate ones. If the NPD Ω pragmatics were not essentially accounted, this effect would never be possible. A facility like this can not exist in conventional linguistic systems: if their parsing process fails, they come to a halt.

The orientated analysis is absolutely independent of users' professional slang or colloquial expressions or text reductions "for short". In Chapter 12 we gave several examples of this sort, taken from the actual practice. Though these addresses are very free, they remain absolutely clear for an expert in the NPD Ω. And the system correctly understands all these examples too.

As for the algorithm performance, the compiler considerably accelerated the analysis in comparison with the interpreter, just as it had been expected. It becomes especially evident if we take into account that WANG-2200-MVP computer is 3–4 times slower than the mainframe of the first version. The average text analysis time decreased to 3–5 seconds and 70% of this time was taken by the dictionary retrieval.

The above presented information brings out clearly that the designed algorithm reacts to absolutely free NL address quickly and correctly. Since the very installation the system has not made a mistake. People use the system every day and enjoy it. The only disadvantage is the keyboard input, because the system lacks any speech input facility. As yet it lacks.

Part VI

ORIENTATED THINKING AND ERRORS

Chapter 21
ORIENTATED LINGUISTICS AND THE ERROR-IGNORE CONCEPTION

21.1 "To err is human"

Having developed or developing a software product the designers are naturally hopeful of its popularity among users. Computer NL understanding systems, which are aimed at non-experts, should have caused this effect. So, what is the problem here?

Partially, it can be put on the above mentioned drawbacks peculiar to all conventional linguistic systems. However, there is another, even more important reason. This reason makes us doubt that orientated linguistics will have more success, though it is formulated theoretically, tested experimentally and implemented in a few cheap and facile systems.

This reason is the evident incongruity between the system capability of free NL understanding and the unnatural communication via the keyboard. In fact, the only actually natural way to input NL addresses is acoustic speech used in man-to-man communication.

As we have already pointed out in Introduction, one can see three rather independent stages in a consideration of the way from the keyboard to the acoustic speech input:

1. Understanding, i.e. a correct interpretation of an input text.
2. Overcoming deviations from the language standards: in written speech there may be misspellings and misprints; oral speech implies personal or regional pronunciation peculiarities.
3. Recognizing acoustic speech, i.e. a translation of a sound sequence to some character string and a fragmentation of continuous speech into words.

As we have mentioned, the gap can not be crossed in three jumps. That is why we can not expect a user to be captured by man-to-computer NL communication facilities until all the three mentioned stages are completely developed and assembled into a single unit.

Of course, it has not gone unnoticed that the already described part of orientated linguistics concerned only the 1st stage. And now it is high time we reported on some new clues that orientated linguistics has for 2nd and 3rd stages, thus opening the way to a complete solution of the NL man-to-computer communication problem.

The problem of errors (2nd stage) can be considered here in every detail because this problem concerns only symbolic chains as before.

As opposed to this, the acoustic speech recognition (the 3rd stage) implies dealing with physical objects. This fact needs a great variety of questions to be discussed, but this book is not infinite. Therefore, in Chapter 28 we shall outline only the foundations of our approach to this problem.

As for this part of the book, we devote it to the problem of errors.

21.2 Human perception of texts with errors. The current situation in the errors problem

Why should we write accurately? In other words, why is there a number of grammar rules, strict and rigid? The common answer is: "These rules enable us to understand what was written by other people", but it is hardly satisfactory.

Firstly, the language is redundant; secondly, a letter is naturally and instinctively changed for an acoustically similar letter (for example, "blend" — "bland"); thirdly, people use acoustically suitable rather than correct letters (for instance, "fone" instead of "phone"). All these facts help a human being to understand the message of a text in spite of errors in this text. What is more, most people (except for announcers, teachers and like them) do not keep to any strict pronunciation rules and it does not prevent them from understanding each other.

The question will be answered more perfectly if we take into account the historical background of the grammar rules. The matter is that written language was designed for long distance communications, whereas oral speech used to exist within rather small communities. And the mission of grammar rules was to provide information interchange between those communities, because their dialects considerably differed (for example, in China). Nowadays these rules have the same value but their function has shifted. The grammar rules form an axis, and all texts float around it because of errors. If it were not for this axis, typical errors would distort the patterns and even recently written texts would be more difficult to read than the 16th century literature.

Grammar skills are not inborn, they indicate one's education and social background. That is why they are of great social and ethical value.

Thus, we care so much for errors not only because they can damage "business" components of the desired reaction but also because of aesthetical and ethical reaction components (AE-components). Here is an example. When applying for an intellectual job, people always try to write and speak correctly. Why? Of course, the "business" message of the application remains clear even if there is a mistake, but the AE-aspect is very much important: if you make mistakes in your documents, you are not a proper candidate for the post. Likely, when writing a letter to foreign colleagues, we check it thoroughly though we understand that they will not judge our professional skills and knowledge from the grammar accuracy of the text. Nevertheless, their reaction AE-components will differ from the desired and it is so important to us that we spend a lot of time and efforts to perfect the letter.

At the same time, if a situation does not impose strong requirements on AE-components, even literate people do not care about mistakes (if this does not damage the message). For instance, one does not waste his time to place commas in notes he leaves to his household.

So, people usually pay much attention to AE-components. That is why almost all PC text editors involve spelling checkers and spelling correctors. But the potentialities of such systems are closely restricted and it is quite clear why.

The designers of correcting systems who rely upon conventional linguistics usually stay on the orthography level. No wonder, trying to climb even the syntax level they run across insuperable obstacles. Syntactical rules are much more complicated because they depend on the deep and surface semantics, i.e. on the text message. Moreover, these rules demand a good intuition rather than good memory. Therefore, it is very difficult (if possible at all) to make a computer correct mistakes on high language levels, especially in difficult situations when mistakes are likely to occur. Nevertheless, if one is determined to provide a complete correction with AE-requirements switched on, he has to dive into all niceties of syntax, semantics, pragmatics and other delights of conventional linguistics.

Fortunately, we are discussing computer, not human understanding and we can admit orientated linguistics instead of conventional linguistics. What is the use of this change? The next section will show.

21.3 Radical and aesthetic errors and the error-ignore conception

Once admitted, orientated linguistics dramatically alters the situation. In fact, orientated linguistics does not discriminate between orthographical, morphological, syntactical and other mistakes. Instead, it classifies them in accordance with how they affect the system *reaction* to a text.

Looking at this aspect of the problem we can see the following. First of all, computers do not care about ethics and aesthetics at all. They can not produce appropriate reaction components, lifting AE-requirements. Consequently, the orientated approach that uses only computer-available reaction components, does not need all errors to be detected and corrected. Only errors damaging the mentioned components should be taken into account. Speaking about a reaction correctness we shall proceed not from any absolute truth but from the business part of a man's reaction to the same text. Therefore, even if a computer reaction is wrong in some absolute sense but matches the man's reaction, *it will not be considered erroneous*: in the NL understanding field there is no use expecting a computer to do better than a human being. Errors affecting the reaction (with the said reserve) will be termed *radical*. Other errors are called *aesthetical*, as they affect AE-components only.

If one substitutes the letters "ff" for the letter "n" in the phrase "If the temperature increases, switch off unit A", it will be a radical error. At the same time, writing "tamperature" instead of "temperature" is an aesthetical error. Intuition suggests that aesthetical errors occur more often than radical.

Using the introduced terms, we can formulate a preliminary opinion on the difference between men's and computers' attitudes to text errors. Human understanding requires *all errors*, both radical and aesthetical, to be corrected. As for computer understanding, aesthetical errors should be just *ignored* and radical errors should be detected. In fact, there is no one who needs them corrected, no one aesthetically sensitive or interested in such a correction.

The qualitative effect of ignoring and sometimes detecting errors instead of correcting them is evident. The quantitative value of the effect depends on the actual proportion between radical and aesthetical errors. In particular, the part of radical errors can be so small that should be neglected too.

We made an experiment to estimate what part of all possible errors in natural texts was taken by radical errors. We explored a considerable variety of NL texts (lecture synopses) handwritten by three people. Our exploration detected no radical errors at all. On the average, there were 2.63 orthographical errors per page, 3.05 morphological errors per page (case incongruities for the most part), 7.81 syntax and punctuation errors per page and 11 semantic errors (i.e. situations when a sentence could not be understood without its context) per text(!). Of course, these data reflect personal features of the authors and depend on what the experts regarded as a radical error, but the final result, i.e. the absence of radical errors, seems impressive. It allows us to admit that a radical error (and a consequent wrong reaction) is negligibly rare and we can do nothing even to detect it. Instead, such an occurrence can be included in an inevitable system failure percentage which is just a characteristic of any system.

The distribution of errors in the mentioned texts can explain this interesting fact, i.e. why there are no radical but a lot of aesthetical errors. While forming a subtext to indicate a reaction, people unconsciously follow morphological rules more strictly and prefer simpler and more reliable (robust) syntactic patterns so that ambiguous situations are quite exotic ("He looked at the man standing on the porch" vs. "He looked at the man, standing on the porch").

The above observations entitle us to assert the following. The conception of error detection and correction is peculiar to human understanding. With computer understanding, it can be changed for the conception of *ignoring errors* (the error-ignore conception).

We should have said "must be" instead of "can be", because the easiest way to solve a problem is to throw it away. This is what the error-ignore conception says. Thus, a man-to-computer dialogue resembles two illiterate men corresponding each other. One of them makes errors and the other does not care, because he does not know that these are errors.

The importance of this result is difficult to overestimate. In particular, it implies that computer understanding does without solving the extremely difficult problem of syntax and semantics computer correction.

21.4 Special features of orthographical errors

In this way, an orientated linguistic NL understanding computer system may ignore all errors. Only one exclusion has to be done: orthographical errors should be detected.

Let us explain this. The reason seems to be rather technological than fundamental. The matter is that the man and the computer perceive the reality in different ways. The man's way is rather qualitative and fuzzy (after Zadeh, [20]), whereas the computer originally identifies an object by its matching a pattern.

Computer-experienced people do know that even a slight error (a missed comma, for example) is enough to cause a system failure, no matter how many commas or whatever are missed, one or two or more. At the same time, such an error is hardly to confuse a human being. The same difference between men and computers is observed in interpreting text words. An occasional misprint or error does not prevent a human being from understanding a text. At the same time, such an error will mislead the computer even if it is equipped with the best possible NL understanding algorithm: a garbled word will be just rejected.

It is this difference that makes us consider the orthographical error detection.

There are only two ways out. The first one suggests developing a new computer generation based on fuzzy logics. Those computers would ignore misspellings like a human being, reacting to an amorphous proximity of an input word to a dictionary pattern. Then the very problem would be eliminated. However, things stand so that the present computer science is aimed at pure calculating problems. It offers digital, "exactly thinking" computers that do not fit such an informal object as NL.

The other way out is that the fuzzy thinking capability can be emulated on a common computer. It means that there must be special software for the computer to interpret an accurately written word and a garbled version of this version in the same way. Of course, errors should not be too severe; otherwise, the word would look rather like another word. At any rate, we find ourselves in the field of the *pattern recognition* again. From here on, we shall discuss the error detection in terms of this branch.

Generally speaking, we could take advantage of the aforementioned spelling checkers if they were sufficiently good. However, they are not flawless, especially when used for our purposes (we shall discuss their drawbacks below). That is why we shall put forward a new approach to the error detection problem in the further consideration. The novelty of this approach is that texts are analyzed to expose the expected reaction components. That is what is said in orientated linguistics.

As usual, this consideration will be preceded by a review of the existing methods.

Chapter 22
CURRENT APPROACHES TO OVERCOMING MISSPELLINGS

22.1 Specific features of the pattern recognition problem in the discussed case

The spelling correction demonstrates some specific features when it is treated as a pattern recognition problem. We are going to discuss these peculiarities together with the current solutions of the problem.

In conventional linguistic systems those peculiarities are determined by a great number of classes resulted from the use of huge dictionaries (thousands and dozens of thousands words). Orientated linguistics says (see Section 13.7) that such problems should be regarded as heterogeneous. Then the final recognition is preceded by a preliminary selection (pre-recognition) letting through few most suitable words ("candidates"). Remember that the purpose of this structure is to speed up the process. In fact, the final recognition usually exploits sophisticated and computer-expensive procedures; pre-recognition procedures take advantage of rather simple features, turning out extremely rapid.

If we look at the available word recognition systems, we shall see them implementing only the pre-recognition with a user responsible for the final recognition. The matter is that those systems are designed as a part of PC text editors to correct texts for men's reading.

There are two types of spelling correctors [41]. The first one, called proofreading, searches a text for misspellings (usually they are just misprints). As a rule, systems of this type (for example, the UNIX operating system built-in corrector) do not propose any correction guesses; a user should correct mistakes by the usual editing means.

The second type is known as the dictionary lookup. Those systems automatically mark words mismatching all the dictionary patterns and proposes several alike words to be selected by a user. A selected word substitutes the wrong word at the current position or all over the text. For example, the Microsoft Word editor's built-in spelling corrector functions like this.

Thus we see both types solving the pre-recognition problem only. The next section is devoted to the ideas that the available misspelling detection and correction are based on.

22.2 Misspelling detection and correction methods

For the most part these methods follow the traditional approach to the pattern recognition, seeking certain characteristics of recognized objects. Such characteristics should be tolerant (ideally, *invariant*) to object changes (here: word changes caused by errors).

The pattern recognition imposes another, somewhat *contrary* requirement on those characteristics. Being invariant to variations of one word, they should have considerably different values for other words of the dictionary (together with their variations) and for meaningless words not involved in the dictionary (the so called "don't know" class). For instance, the property of being made out of letters is invariant for all words and fits to tell words from numbers. However, it is of no use in distinguishing words. So, the main difficulty is to satisfy both requirements at a time. Nobody seems to have worked out this trouble by the present moment, if its general aspect is meant. We shall illustrate this by discussing two most popular lines in the problem of overcoming errors ([41]–[46]).

The first line comes from the computer heuristics concerning the quick memory search problem. A word is characterized there by letter chains of lengths dependent of the dictionary volume. If the dictionary comprises less than 50 words, a simple alphabetical makeup may be used; the probability of a word pair with the same, though differently ordered, letters is too little. If the dictionary is more comprehensive, the order of letters in a word is taken into account. It may be represented as digrams (letter pairs) with dictionaries under 10 000 words and as trigrams with dictionaries under 100 000 words. Normally, those combinations keep the order they have in a word [41]. For example, the full feature list of the word "pencil" is as follows: "□pe", "pen", "enc", "nci", "cil", "il□" ("□" denotes the space character, preceding and following any word).

Certainly, these features are redundant because they are closely correlated. In fact, the question of a letter being a part of the word is answered by three features at a time; the order of two letters can be clarified by two features. As a result, if "n" is substituted for "k", three features will be damaged. Therefore, though these features properly and uniquely identify a correct word, they will fail to do it with a garbled word, as the corresponding groups of features are damaged. They use the so called "rubber" trigrams to make the features invariant to such changes. "Rubber" trigrams are allowed to get extra characters. For instance, the initial trigram "enc" is accompanied by "e∗nc", "en∗c", "e∗n∗c", with "∗" denoting any character. These letter-combinations will be changed back for "enc", and this is the invariance as they see it.

Unfortunately, it mars the feature capability of distinguishing different words. For example, the feature "enc", of "pencil, encounter", etc. will correspond to "enact" as well. Actually, "enact" and "pencil" do not look alike, and this contradiction between men's and computer's perceptions illustrates the main drawback of this line. In practice [41], "southeast" written as "southtost"

(2 mistakes) was recognized as "southernmost". "Sipping" written as "sipning" (1 mistake) was interpreted as "spinning". Even "barret" (no mistake) gave way to "barrette", because the latter had been responded by more features than the former.

In order to lessen such effects, they often weaken the invariance by reducing the allowed word changeability. There are two ways. Firstly, the dictionary may include a word together with its typical erroneous versions. Secondly, the letter order of a word may be regarded more rigidly: they restrict a trigram shift to 2 positions [42]. The spaces of the first and the last trigrams pursue the same goal. Nevertheless, the nature of errors and their corrections remains "unhuman". Moreover, the man's interpretation can hardly be imagined to be based on trigrams and digrams. That is why we can not admit this approach to be adequate to the problem though it offers quick and efficient algorithms [41, 42].

The second line in the problem of overcoming errors leans upon the noise-immune coding theory. We shall discuss it in the next section.

22.3 Overcoming errors by means of the noise-immune coding

The noise-immune coding theory became interesting to our consideration as soon as it started to deal with insertions and deletions in addition to substitutions it had dealt before. The same types of errors are inherent in NL texts. The mentioned theory puts forward certain tools, in particular the sequential decoding to overcome such errors. For instance, [44] proposes to recalculate the known probabilities of character-to-character transitions (the characters represent acoustic segments) into the probabilities of chain-to-chain transitions, which chains are made up of those characters and may be of different length. A word is characterized by its segments, phonemes for instance. This approach disregards the coordination of character transitions, though it is very important (we shall see this below). The order of characters is considered to be the only important thing.

Other works study deletions and insertions in situations even less connected with our problem. Some works investigate the case of uniform codes, i.e. code words of the same length (for example, see [45], page 39). In this case, insertions and deletions are easily detected and corrected by a special coding procedures with certain combinations of informative and test characters as features. Nevertheless, this approach does not work with NL, where word length varies considerably.

As for nonuniform codes, the communication theory does not even raise the question of correcting deletions and insertions [46]. It tries only to synchronize the code reception after such errors.

Completing the review, we have to highlight one fundamental fact. Both pattern recognition theory and noise-immune coding are sure to improve their methods. But as we want to estimate their applicability to the problem of NL word correction, we can not help making the following observation. Any of such methods will work only if recognition objects have sufficient differences. In this way, in the pattern recognition theory those objects should have different feature vectors and in the theory of noise-immune coding there should be a nonzero code distance between them.

Following conventional linguistics, one has to say that the current NL situation is disastrous in this aspect. At the same time, orientated linguistics provides some means of making objects differ. We shall touch this point in the next section.

22.4 Word differences in conventional and orientated linguistics

In Section 21.3 we considered the experimental results and drew the conclusion that any error could be ignored because of an extremely small probability of its being radical. However, it is theoretically important to understand the nature of errors. Here we are going to remind how errors become radical and to show that the NPD concept practically eliminates such errors.

Let us consider (at first, outside the NPD concept) the reasons for radical text errors coming from misspellings.

Evidently, errors come from small differences between words. In NL there are many similar words with one letter differing ("take — lake") as well as a lot of identical words differing in their meanings only (the homonymy and polysemy): "band" — a group of people, "band" — a tape. While the computer dictionary contains more than one entry per such a word, there is a risk of selecting a wrong entry. In its turn, this will result in a semantic error even with no misspellings. The same result will be obtained with "meaningful" misspellings like "take — lake — fake — make — sake — ...".

Designers of linguistic systems use huge and clumsy constructions to avoid such confusions. All of them appeal to the context and, finally, to the pragmatics and a world model [7]. We already discussed the extreme complexity and variety of language regularities on these levels.

Things do not stand better in the noise-immune coding theory which relies on a nonzero code distance. Let us consider this in detail.

The information transmission theory and the coding theory deal with code words which commonly are sequences of ones and zeros. A noise can inverse some of them during a transmission. If such inversions do not result in mixing up two words, they can be named aesthetical errors in our terms. The cybernetic nature of both transmitter and receiver demands nothing more than ignoring them.

Otherwise, when too many characters are inverted and a transmitted word looks more like another code word, the error can be named radical.

The coding theory possesses a powerful tool to prevent radical errors. It is a *freedom of constructing* code words to encode transmitted messages. First of all, one may make code words as long as desired by writing additional ones and zeros. If those additional characters are written in accordance with the theory, they will "strengthen" basic characters so that an error will be detected or even corrected. In fact, writing additional characters, one increases the total number of possible code words many times over as compared with the number of words to be encoded, i.e. any word can be encoded by many code words. A transmission uses only code words with no less than some fixed number of differing positions. This number is called a code distance. If a noise inverses less than half the code distance positions, the resulting error will not be radical.

Unfortunately, this powerful tool does not work with NL words. Firstly, the set of NL words can not be reconstructed with account for "the code distance". Secondly, no one can make a person write (or say) any additional characters. Consequently, we can speak about neither a great nor even a nonzero code distance between NL words and this regrettable fact was illustrated above by the homonymy and polysemy.

How then does NL overcome radical errors, if it is just a mess from the standpoint of the noise-immune coding theory? Any answer appealing to a context or to a word model makes little sense as these terms can not be defined more constructively than the terms "sense" or "understanding".

Orientated linguistics proposes a more substantial answer: any NPD and any orientated analysis level run their own subdictionary which actually concerns a UNPD (see Chapter 12 and Fig. 12.1). Unlike the "context" or the "word model", UNPD is a formal and visible object. In the current discussion it is represented by a *bounded* dictionary and we know where this boundedness comes from. We also know that such a dictionary can include only one meaning of a polysemantic word. Thus, the UNPD conception eliminates the polysemy and the homonymy. A UNPD dictionary lacks *zero code distances* whereas the "entire language" is full of them.

Elaborating this idea, we naturally anticipate that a UNPD dictionary has a much lower percentage of easily mixable words, i.e. words with only one character differing. To test this hypothesis, we carried out an experiment for two English dictionaries. The first one was a comprehensive dictionary of more than 20 000 words and the second one integrated the UNPD subdictionaries of the NPD "Information on the Russian and American inhabited spacecraft", comprising about 2000 words (word-combinations) in total. These subdictionaries were populated on the base of the training set of texts from this NPD. (Today they are used in one of our orientated computer understanding systems with an absolutely free NL communication subsystem). Thus, those subdictionaries contain only words from t_k, t_{am} and t_w subtexts and are complete within this NPD.

Table 22.1 demonstrates the results of the experiment. Both figures in the column "0" were obtained manually. We scanned the texts of the UNPD training set to find words of the same spelling but different meanings. As the table shows, we anticipatedly failed. The figure for the comprehensive dictionary results from

Table 22.1

Number of differing positions		0	1	2
Word pairs percentage	Comprehensive dictionary	32.00	21.51	40.31
	NPD dictionary	0	3.66	26.09

the following. We selected by chance 30 pages of the dictionary† and for each of them calculated:

(a) the sum of essentially different meanings of the words that had more than one meaning,

(b) the total number of meanings of the words on the page.

The ratio between (a) and (b) multiplied by 100 and averaged by all the selected pages is placed in Table 22.1 as the percentage of words having the same spelling but different meanings.

The figures in the columns "1" and "2" were calculated on a computer. Since the experiment was just an estimate, we were taking into account only one type of word differences: different characters at the same position. Though those data are preliminary and estimative, the qualitative effect in clear: the NPD naturally involves only considerably different words. In fact, there are no words of the same spelling but different meanings. With a single letter mismatch admitted, there are approximately 5.88 times fewer word pair in the UNPD dictionary than in the comprehensive one. Certainly, the effect goes down with two positions regarded.

Thus, the UNPD concept proposed by orientated linguistics provides a nonzero and even considerable "code distance" between words, which makes it possible to cope with the problem of misspellings. In the next chapter we shall discuss a practical approach to the problem.

† *English-Russian Dictionary*, ed. O. S. Akhmanova and E. A. M. Wilson (Russkiy yazik, Moscow, 1985)

Chapter 23
DIGITAL EMULATION OF THE ERROR-IGNORE CONCEPT: SETTING THE PROBLEM

23.1 The changeability representation dualism

An orientated linguistic consideration of misspellings should be started with the following remark. A good deal of misspellings are ignored by the very nature of this kind of linguistics. First of all, an orientated system disregards all words irrelevant for the reaction identification. Such words are not included in UNPD dictionaries; consequently, it does not matter at all how they are spelled. Furthermore, if changeable word parts (like endings in Russian) do not determine the reaction, they are ignored together with possible errors.

This specific feature provides orientated NL understanding systems with the so called passive means of ignoring errors, which work before any special procedure runs to recognize a word from its erroneous spelling. Those special procedures make active ignoring means; they will be the focus of our discussion in this and the following chapters.

To start with, let us consider two forms of representing an object changeability and, in particular a word changeability.

In any pattern recognition problem it is very difficult to discover good recognition features. This phenomenon is rather typical than exotic and we shall make an attempt to reveal its nature. In so doing we shall handle objects of the spelling correction problem in terms of the pattern recognition theory.

Let there be a dictionary comprising explicitly all wordforms involved. Any wordform together with catenated spaces (the starting space at the beginning and the finishing space at the end) will be named a *dictionary word.* A set of correctly written words, used in some UNPD, will be called the *UNPD dictionary* and denoted as X_p. If an understanding system has a built-in pre-recognition subsystem (a spelling checker), the term "UNPD dictionary" and notation X_p are associated with the set of words, selected by this subsystem. The k-th word of X_p, made up of R_k letters is

$$x_k \equiv (a_0^{(k)}, a_1^{(k)}, \dots, a_r^{(k)}, \dots, a_{R_k}^{(k)}, a_{R_k+1}^{(k)}) ,$$

with $a_0^{(k)}$ and $a_{R_k+1}^{(k)}$ representing the spaces. It can be called a *pattern word* or simply *pattern* (this is where the subscript p in X_p comes from). A possibly garbled *input word* of length S, which is to be recognized, will be denoted as x:

$$x \equiv (a_0, a_1, \ldots, a_s, \ldots, a_S, a_{S+1}),$$

with a_0 and a_{S+1} as spaces. The set of all input words, occurring in the texts of the given SA, is designated by X. Evidently, $X_p \subset X$.

Since errors can occur, the dictionary word x_k corresponds to words from X which differ from x_k in some certain way (besides the exactly matching input word x). The subset of words corresponded by x_k, in a user's opinion, will be designated X_k and named the k-th class. In order to understand in what way the words of X_k can differ from the pattern, we must establish a comparison method. Let us justify two words by the left margin. Thus, a_0 and $a_0^{(k)}$ are beneath each other and provide the starting point for counting character positions of a word. We ought to remind that a_0 and $a_0^{(k)}$ are always equal because both of them are spaces.

Now we can proceed to the question of features. It is not easy to find good recognition features and this fact has a clear explanation. Some variations of a word x_k leave x within its class X_k, but other variations push it out from this class. However, all of those variations have *the same qualitative nature*: insertions, deletions, substitutions or transpositions. Thus, it can be even impossible to find a few features displaying simultaneously an invariance inside X_k and a considerable difference between x's outside X_k and x's inside it. In theory, it should be put down on the fact [47] that the more complicated an object changeability, the fewer invariant features. Thus, a wide range of errors makes such features difficult to construct.

An approach to this problem was proposed in pattern recognition [47]. It is based on the idea of *two* possible changeability representations. Firstly, a changeability can be exhaustively described in terms of invariant features. This form implies that the number of such features decreases as the changeability gets more complicated (the invariant description *degeneration*), in particular, as it has more degrees of freedom. The remaining features still give an exhaustive description of the changeability but allow alien object to get into a class.

There is *another* changeability *representation form.* It is defined in terms of *transformations*, i.e. of the changeability itself. A description given in this form anticipatedly spreads out as the changeability gets more complicated. The qualitative aspect of those transformations is conveyed by the appearance of their formal expressions (equations); the quantitative aspect comes through the values of their parameters. Both aspects are useful for discriminating between permitted and forbidden changes. An example of the former is any variation of x within X_k. The latter is any variation which pushes x out of X_k.

Representing changeability as transformations helps to overcome the contradiction between the requirements of feature invariance and feature recognizing ability. In the next section we shall represent the word changeability in terms of transformations and consider those transformations in detail.

23.2 Word changeability types and Postulate P23.1

We are going to start with the misspelling statistics. Some authors think it useful to distinguish keyboard errors (misprints) and illiteracy errors [41]. They speculate that the latter are of special nature, more complicated than the former [48], which fact can help to use "rubber" trigrams and digrams more naturally. But the latest statistics do not prove this, at least in Russian. Most errors observed in [45] belong to *the same four classes* as keyboard errors: substitutions, transpositions, insertions, deletions. Nothing formally indicates whether an error (for instance, a substitution of the r-th character in a word) comes from a misprint or from a user's idea of what that character must be. In figures, 86% of errors (according to [45]) are single substitutions, 8%—adjacent letter transpositions, and 4.5%—single insertions and deletions. Other errors occur quite rarely, for example the probability of a double substitution is $\approx$72 times smaller than that of a single one, a nonadjacent transposition is $\approx$20 times rarer than adjacent, etc. Taking into account a low a priori probability of an error itself, we can expect problematic situations to be not very irritating. Thus, the above four classes of errors are enough to develop NL word recognizing systems, at least until the actual practice demands a wider range of errors to be taken into account.

Coming down to a study of the word changeability, we introduce the following notation. A single substitution of a character in a word is denoted as SE(1); single deletions and insertions are designated LSE(1) and RSE(1) as they cause a part of a word to *shift* left and right respectively; at last, a single transposition of adjacent characters is symbolized TE(1).

We can summarize the mentioned misspelling statistics as the following

Postulate P23.1 *A word can contain no more than one error at positions from 1 to R_S; this error can belong to the following types: SE(1), LSE(1), RSE(1), TE(1).*

This means that the probabilities of all other possible errors are declared to be negligibly small. The special note about the range of possible positions highlights that the starting and finishing positions (0 and $S+1$) are occupied by spaces.

The statistics reflected in Postulate P23.1, i.e. a huge gap between probabilities of the involved and other errors, has a good explanation in the nature of a UNPD dictionary. As we remember, an artificial word constructing in the noise-immune coding theory limits the similarity between involved words to half a code distance (measured in mismatching bits). The maximum number of errors in a word that can be admitted is equal to the nearest integer less than half the code distance.

In this light we see most words (about 96%) of the UNPD dictionary (Table 22.1) differing in two or more characters. As for few (3.66%) words differing in only one character, we should take into account that acoustic speech is much older than written one: the UNPD dictionary populating principle is sure to be based on acoustic differences rather than on spelling. Therefore, talking about a similarity of two words we should keep in mind not only the number of differing positions but the acoustic difference between sounds at these positions as well. When studying the mentioned 3.66% of words from the UNPD dictionary, one is likely to note that their mismatching positions, though there is only one pair of them, are occupied by very different sounds. For instance, if we consider the words "mite" and "kite" differing in only one position, the real acoustic difference between "m" and "k" will never let you confuse them. At any rate, this difference sounds no smaller than that between "blame" and "blain", though they differ in two positions.

Now it can be concluded that an analogue of the code distance in UNPD dictionaries must be equal to 2. The actual practice also shows that radical errors occur rarely, meaning that a word usually contains no more than a single error. This is what Postulate P23.1 asserts.

23.3 Representation of errors by transformations

The types of errors being settled, we are starting to construct a model of the changeability caused by errors. In Section 23.1 we said that it would be done in terms of transformations. Let us begin with shift errors. It is evident that errors of this type destroy a word more dramatically than other errors because they change many positions at once. But these changes are coordinated and can be regarded as one complex error. The idea of coordinatedness will be formulated below as a postulate. As for a formal interpretation of LSE/RSE's, it should be taken into account that a character string is naturally associated with a *discrete* one-dimensional space. However, the regularity of a character string shift reminds of *continuous* axis transformations. In fact, if an RSE(1) occurs at the beginning of a word, the whole word will be shifted to the right. It looks like a parallel translation with the translation parameter of 1. When in the middle of a word, an LSE(1) and an RSE(1) respectively shorten or lengthen the word. Then only a part of the word moves, i.e. we are talking about *piecewise linear transformations.*

LSE/RSE's make topological transformations, which preserve the relation "a character a_s is on the left hand of a character a_{s+l}" ($l > 0$). This circumstance allows us to apply the continuous group theory [49], developed earlier for other objects of topological nature (pictures and acoustic sounds).

We now turn to transposition errors (TE's). A transposition breaks up the axis topology. Errors of this type easily occur when keys are pressed in a wrong order, like in the word "aglorithm". They also appear, though more rarely, in acoustic speech ("sytsem" instead of "system"). We have already noticed that only adjacent character transposition should be taken into account, because a far transposition ("argolithm", for instance) has rather a negligible probability.

The changeability connected with shift errors and TE's is *regular*, meaning that resulting changes are correlated. The continuous group theory considers *occasional* changes as well, treating them as a result of some noise. Substitution errors (SE's) are likely to be discussed in this manner. It is this random noise model that is applied to this type of errors in the coding-decoding theory (with no deletions and insertions) that deals with both single and batch substitution errors. In accordance with Postulate P23.1 we admit only single errors and no more than one in a word. Trying to maintain the terms and notation we shall say word changes caused by SE's to be transformations too.

A transformation t, when it converts a pattern word x_k into a word x, will be written as $x = tx_k$. If the transformation t complies with Postulate P23.1, the word x will be said to be a *natural derivative* from x_k. Then the class X_k appears as a set of all natural derivatives from x_k. The set of all transformations converting x_k into its natural derivatives will be named the k-th *admissible transformation class* and denoted as T_k. If x contains no errors, i.e. $x = x_k$, then t_{0k} in $x = t_{0k}x_k$ is an identical transformation and, of course, $t_{0k} \in T_k$. The sets T_k and X_k are mapped onto each other in the one-to-one manner.

The class X_k is a subset of another set that is also associated with the pattern x_k. It is a set of all words that can be compared with x_k during the dictionary retrieval. We shall call this set the k-th pattern *working area* and denote it as $\{x\}^{(k)}$. If we had a simple retrieval procedure comparing its input word with each word of the dictionary, $\{x\}^{(k)}$ would be just the set of all words possible in the given OD and would not need the superscript k in its designation. But in practice merely a part of all the words should be compared with the pattern x_k. For instance, if an input word x is made up of 15 characters and x_k comprises only 5 characters, x is unlikely to be an effect of errors occurred in the pattern word x_k. Of course, in addition to the word length some other simple features can be used to eliminate knowingly wrong words. It has been already noticed that this elimination is a result of the pre-recognition. Below we shall see some other effects of the pre-recognition concept.

The set of words from the k-th pattern working area, which do not belong to the class X_k, will be denoted as $X_{\neg k}$:

$$X_{\neg k} = \{x\}^{(k)} \setminus X_k \ .$$

Formally speaking, each element of $X_{\neg k}$ can be associated with some transformation of the pattern x_k. The set of these transformations will be designated as $T_{\neg k}$.

Thus we have come to the "transformational" formulation of the problem. It is evidently adequate, because the problem wants a formal method to get clear what characters of x and x_k should be compared, and transformations give such a method. Furthermore, the continuous group approach seems to be organic to this problem.

Within the context of this approach the problem solution is organized with two basic stages:

1. A comparison of x with the current x_k indicates the transformation t that relates them.

2. The relation $t \in T_k$ is verified. If it is true, $x \in X_k$ is assumed; otherwise the next pattern is picked up.

The established structure makes us remind why the continuous group approach differs from the traditional pattern recognition technique. The question is how to organize the procedure that makes decisions about an object x belonging to a class X_k. By tradition "the decision space" is subdivided into "class domains" treated, for instance, as admissible variations of the feature vector around the given class pattern x_k. The object x is assumed to belong to the class X_k if its feature vector is close enough to its pattern vector.

Practically it means that the procedure will try all the possible classes in turn until success is obtained or there are no more classes.

So, one can see only one class taking part in the comparison process at any step of the procedure. It may be considered in two ways, either as sequential scanning all the K classes in the same space or as scanning the sequence of K similar spaces with only one class in each.

In general case, this dual interpretation has only technological sense. But it is of fundamental importance for the continuous group approach.

In fact, with this approach the admissible variation domain in the decision space is replaced by the domain of admissible transformation set T_k in the transformation space. The pattern word x_k then will be replaced by the identical transformation t_{0k}. But if we map all the sets T onto a general transformation space, only one pattern (say x_k^*) will be corresponded by the identical transformation. The other $K-1$ patterns will be represented as transformations of x_k^*, which is impossible within the limits of transformation types allowed by Postulate P23.1. Thus, the continuous group approach needs each of the K classes to be provided with its own transformation space of dimension depending on the length of the word x_k.

The word recognition problem has another specific feature in comparison with other problems of the continuous group nature. This feature will be discussed in the next chapter.

Chapter 24
CORRESPONDENCE PROBLEM

24.1 Character correspondence and quasi-correspondence. The transformation t identification non-uniqueness

In order to reconstruct the transformation relating two objects, the continuous group theory uses the so called corresponding points of these objects [49]. In the discussed case we have to consider word characters as object points, and word character positions as coordinates. Therefore, we are going to expand the concept of correspondence to words.

Let us say that characters a' and a'' are *of the same name* if both of them are spaces or are represented by the same alphabetical letter (the notation is: $a' = a''$). Now let us introduce an integer $\Delta r \geq 1$. The character $a_r^{(k)}$ of the word x_k and the character a_s of the word x are called *quasi-corresponding* (QC) characters if

$$\begin{aligned} a_r^{(k)} &= a_s\,, \\ |s-r| &\leq \Delta r\,. \end{aligned} \tag{24.1}$$

They are designated $a_r^{(k)} \leftrightarrow a_s$. Δr is the maximal permitted difference between positions of QC-characters. The quantity $\mu_r = s - r$ is called the *displacement parameter* (or just displacement) of the character a_s of the word x in reference to its QC-character $a_r^{(k)}$ of the word x_k. Characters of one of the words, which have QC-characters in the other word, will be called *supported.* Other characters will be named *unsupported.* Let us illustrate the above definitions and quantities for $x_k =$ "transformation" , $x =$ "trasformaition" , $\Delta r = 1$.

	0	1	2	3	4	5	6	7	8	9	10	11	12	13	14	15
x_k	□	t	r	a	n	s	f	o	r	m	a	t	i	o	n	□
x	□	t	r	a	s	f	o	r	m	a	i	t	i	o	n	□

In reference to x_k, the word x contains 2 errors: an LSE(1) at $s = 4$ and an RSE(1) at $s = 10$ (the total length of the word is preserved). The QC-characters at positions from 0 to 3 are not shifted, i.e. $\mu_r = 0$. The characters $a_4^{(k)} =$ "n" and $a_{10} =$ "i" are unsupported. $\mu_r = -1$ for $a_5^{(k)} \ldots a_9^{(k)}$ and $\mu_r = 0$ for $a_{11}^{(k)} \ldots a_{15}^{(k)}$ again. By the way, the word x is not a natural derivative from x_k because it contains 2 errors in contradiction to Postulate P23.1.

In the above example one can easily and uniquely find the corresponding characters of the words, using their being of the same name. The presence of two "o" (or two "a" or two "t") does not complicate the matter because the permitted (in terms of Postulate P23.1) transformations can not mix them up due to condition Eq. (24.1) sounding here as $|\mu_r| \leq \Delta r = 1$. Therefore, we may speak about the character correspondence instead of the quasi-correspondence.

But here is another example with the same $\Delta r = 1$: $x_k =$ "banana" and $x =$ "bannana".

$$\begin{array}{ccccccccc c} & 0 & 1 & 2 & 3 & 4 & 5 & 6 & 7 & 8 \\ x_k & \square & \text{b} & \text{a} & \text{n} & \text{a} & \text{n} & \text{a} & \square & \\ x & \square & \text{b} & \text{a} & \text{n} & \text{n} & \text{a} & \text{n} & \text{a} & \square \end{array} \tag{24.2}$$

It is easy to see that $a_6^{(k)}$ has two QC-characters in the word x. They are a_5 and a_7. It means that two values of the displacement parameter μ_6 are possible ($\mu' = -1$ and $\mu''' = +1$). Similarly, $a_5^{(k)}$ has two QC-characters, namely a_4 and a_6. Next, a_3 and a_4 are QC-characters in reference to $a_3^{(k)}$ ($\mu'' = 0$ and $\mu''' = +1$ respectively). However, from the semantics it becomes clear that the true correspondence (denoted as $\Leftrightarrow$) is as follows: $a_6^{(k)} \Leftrightarrow a_7$, $a_5^{(k)} \Leftrightarrow a_6$. As for characters a_3 and a_4, any of them can be considered as QC-character in reference to $a_3^{(k)}$. Another one should be treated as erroneous character, causing RSE(1).

Since there is no semantics available at the lexical level, we can use only features Eq. (24.1) to establish corespondences and the situation becomes non-uniquely determined.

What is the reason for this non-uniqueness? The example (24.2) gives a hint: it occurs when in a word there are two (or more) nearby characters of the same name. Let us express this in a formal manner.

Suppose that in one of the words (x or x_k) there are characters a_{v_1} and a_{v_2} $(v_2 > v_1)$, and in the other word there is a character a_w. Let these letters be of the same name, i.e. $a_{v_1} = a_{v_2} = a_w$.

Definition 24.1 *Characters a_{v_1} and a_{v_2} are called* nearby doubling characters *(NDC) of the word they are parts of, if there can be a position of the character a_w that*

$$\begin{cases} w - v_1 & \leq & \Delta r \\ v_2 - w & \leq & \Delta r \,. \end{cases} \tag{24.3}$$

For instance, $a_4^{(k)}$ and $a_6^{(k)}$ in example (24.2) are NDC in x_k and their $a_w = a_5$. Similarly, a_5 and a_7 are NDC in x; $a_w = a_6^k$. Notice that $w - v_1 = v_2 - w = 1$ in both cases.

A special question connected with NDC is whether the starting and finishing spaces can be NDC. An answer to this important question appears as a separate lemma.

Lemma 24.1 *If the class X_k satisfies Postulate P23.1, $\forall x \in X_k$ the starting and finishing spaces of neither x_k nor x can be NDC's with $\Delta r = 1$.*

Proof: In an LSE(1) case x_k must be made up of no less than 2 letters. In fact, if it comprises only one letter, an LSE(1) removes it, which is nonsense. If x_k is a two-lettered word, the space positions are 0 and $R_k + 1 = 3$. After an LSE(1) makes x one-lettered, the starting space remains the same (it always occupies position $s = 0$, see Section 23.1). Consequently, the finishing space will occupy position $S + 1 = 2$.

Let us try all the four obtained spaces as a_w. At first assume $a_w = a_0$; then $a_0^{(k)}$ and $a_3^{(k)}$ should be treated as a_{v_1} and a_{v_2} in Eq. (24.3). Since $w - v_1 = 0 - 0 = 0$ and $v_2 - w = 3 - 0 = 3$, the second condition of the system Eq. (24.3) fails. Furthermore, if $a_w = a_{S+1}$ then $S + 1 = 2$ and $w - v_1 = 2 - 0 = 2$ and $v_2 - w = 3 - 2 = 1$, violating the first condition. Resume: $a_0^{(k)}$ and $a_3^{(k)}$ are not NDC.

Let $a_w = a_0^{(k)}$. Then a_0 and a_2 should be treated as a_{v_1} and a_{v_2} respectively. Having calculated the differences $w - v_1 = 0 - 0 = 0$ and $v_2 - w = 2 - 0 = 2$, we see Eq. (24.3) fail. At last, assuming $a_w = a_3^{(k)}$, we obtain $w - v_1 = 3 - 0 = 3$ and $v_2 - w = 2 - 3 = -1$: it is a failure of Eq. (24.3) again. It means that a_0 and a_2 are not NDC either. Thus, the lemma is true with a two-lettered word and an LSE(1). Evidently, it is even more true with words of length more than 2.

The above reasoning still works with an SE(1) and an RSE(1). It makes sense to consider the case of a TE(1) only with words no shorter than 2 and with this reserve the reasoning works with this type of errors. Thus, the lemma is proved.

The NDC effect intricates the matter, while the problem is being solved by features Eq. (24.1): a letter can correspond to more than one character of the other word thus bringing a *non-uniqueness*. It gives several (say q) possible transformations which are called *derivable from a given quasi-correspondence system*. Only one of them is true (sometimes two are, like with letters "n", a_3 and a_4 in example (24.2)).

Since transformations must be classified in the transformation space (this is the point of the approach), we encounter rather a strange situation, never occurred in the pattern recognition. Namely, an inevitable procedure (a transition to transformations) necessarily converts an originally single object (the word x) into $q \geq 1$ of a priori equal secondary objects (transformations) and those secondary objects are to be classified.

A problem, if it generates a situation like this, may be called a problem with *an input non-uniqueness*. Such problems resemble optical illusions, for instance, a picture of a staircase visible either from its top or from its bottom: a spectator's interpretation depends upon his spontaneous psychological state. The next section will propose some means to solve this sort of problems.

24.2 The word recognition problem heterogeneity and the displacement coordination concept

An input non-uniqueness can be overcome if the word recognition problem is treated as a heterogeneous problem (Section 13.7) though it seems homogeneous at first. It means that the recognition itself is preceded by a pre-recognition stage with its designation determined by a particular case. Here the pre-recognition serves to find the best among the q considered transformations for the word pair x, x_k, thus eliminating the non-uniqueness. Let us make clear what pre-recognition techniques fit the problem.

The "frontal attack" is to write down all the q variants explicitly and test them in turn for the requirements of Postulate P23.1.

This rather stupid technique wants an improvement, i.e. some more efficient regularizing means than an exhaustive search. While staying on the pure lexical level (not touching semantics), we should look for such means in the above introduced word changeability model only. Fortunately, this model is able to regularize the pre-recognition problem due to the displacement coordination concept. Here we are interested in one aspect of this concept, namely, in that given as the following postulate.

Postulate P24.1 *The longer is the chain of characters displaced with the same parameter μ, the higher is the probability of this displacement being truth for each of those characters.*

In other words, if a comparison of words x_k and x determines the displacement of some character non-uniquely, a more probable displacement is that which displaced more successive characters.

The practical use of Postulate P24.1 requires two formal objects to be introduced. Namely, they are:

(a) the list of all possible displacements for each character of the word x_k in comparison with the word x,

(b) the sequence of successive characters permitting the same displacement.

At first we shall write down the set of values μ permitted by a certain Δr. Designated by $\{\mu\}$, this set consists of all the integers from $-\Delta r$ to $+\Delta r$. If $\Delta r = 1$ then $\{\mu\} \equiv \{-1, 0, +1\}$.

Next, each character of the word x_k (for example, $a_r^{(k)}$) is associated with an *s-list* (or simply list). This list is denoted as $\{s\}_r$ and formed in the following way.

An s-list has $2\Delta r + 1$ positions (the number of possible values of μ). Let one of those values be μ'. If the character $a_{r+\mu'}$ of the word x is a QC of the character $a_r^{(k)}$, the number $s = r + \mu'$ is placed at the position of μ' in the s-list $\{s\}_r$. Otherwise, this position remains empty (denoted as $\odot$). For instance, with

$\Delta r = 1$ the s-list has 3 positions: $\mu' = -1$, $\mu'' = 0$, $\mu''' = 1$. For $\forall x_k, x$ the list $\{s\}_0$ looks like $(\odot, 0, \odot)$ because the starting spaces always have the same position (Section 23.1). In example (24.2) $\{s\}_3 = (\odot, 3, 4)$, $\{s\}_6 = (5, \odot, 7)$ and so on. If a character is unsupported, all positions of its s-list are empty.

Let us also introduce the so called *coherent character μ-chain* that will help us to calculate how many characters with the same μ go in succession in their s-lists.

Let $r_1 \leq r_2$; r_1,r_2 be integers no less than zero, $d = r_2 - r_1 + 1$. A *linked numeric chain of length d* is a sequence of all the integers from r_1 to r_2. A sequence of characters is termed a linked character *μ-chain* (or simply μ-chain) of length d if it complies with the following conditions:

1) all the characters of the chain have a property μ,

2) their subscripts form a linked numeric chain of length d,

3) the characters $a^{(k)}_{r_1-1}$ and $a^{(k)}_{r_2+1}$ do not have the property μ.

With a word pair x_k, x, we shall take some $\mu' \in \{\mu\}$. For the property μ we shall consider the property of a character having a non-empty position μ' in its s-list. Let us expose all the μ'-chains and fix their lengths. Then let us do the same for another μ'' and so on until $\{\mu\}$ is exhausted.

Those s-lists and μ-chains can be conveniently represented by means of a special table (a quasi-correspondence table or *q-table*). In the next section we are going to describe the construction of such a table and to give some examples.

24.3 q-tables as a tool of displacement coordination revealing

Table 24.1 illustrates the structure of a q-table. One should fill in a q-table in the following way. The character "n", occupying the 3rd position of x_k, has its QC at the 2nd position of x. That means $\mu_3 = -1$ and we put $s = 2$ in the cross of column 3 and row -1. For $a^{(k)}_2 =$ "o", $\mu_2 = +1$ and $s = 3$ is put in the row $+1$ at position 2, and so on. Thus, the columns of Table 24.1 display the s-lists of the appropriate characters (empty cells denote empty s-list positions), and its rows for all values of μ hold the appropriate μ-chains.

We give examples of q-tables in Tables 24.2–24.6 for the case of $\Delta r = 1$ ($\mu' = -1$, $\mu'' = 0$, $\mu''' = +1$).

Table 24.2 illustrates the case of an LSE(1). Here $\mu' = -1$ has one chain of length $d = 7$, $\mu'' = 0$ has a chain of length 2, and $\mu''' = +1$ has two μ'''-chains of lengths 1. This table also shows that the list $\{s\}_4$ contains two values of s, meaning that the character $a^{(k)}_4$ has two QC-characters: a_3 and a_5 (only one of them is really corresponding). Just the same, 3 and 5 are involved into two s-lists each, meaning that either of a_3 and a_5 has two QC-characters in x_k: $a^{(k)}_2$, $a^{(k)}_4$ and $a^{(k)}_4$, $a^{(k)}_6$ respectively. Only one character of each pair is really corresponding.

Table 24.1

	r, s	0	1	2	3	4	...	R_k	$R_k + 1$	...
	x_k	$\square$	m	o	n	o	...	...	$\square$	
	x	$\square$	m	n	o	p	...	...	...	...
	$-\Delta r$						...			
	$-\Delta r + 1$						...			
	$\vdots$						$\vdots$			
	-1				2	3	...			
μ_r	0	0	1				...			
	$+1$			3			...			
	$\vdots$						$\vdots$			
	$\Delta r - 1$						...			
	Δr						...			

Table 24.2

	r, s	0	1	2	3	4	5	6	7	8	9
	x_k	$\square$	m	o	n	o	p	o	l	y	$\square$
	x	$\square$	m	n	o	p	o	l	y	$\square$	
	-1				2	3	4	5	6	7	8
μ_r	0	0	1								
	$+1$			3		5					

Table 24.3

r, s		0	1	2	3	4	5	6	7	8
x_k		□	b	a	n	a	n	a	□	
x		□	b	a	n	n	a	n	a	□
μ_r	-1						4	5		
	0	0	1	2	3					
	$+1$				4	5	6	7	8	

Table 24.4

r, s		0	1	2	3	4	5	6	7	8	9	10	11
x_k		□	c	o	o	r	d	i	n	a	t	e	□
x		□	c	o	r	o	d	i	n	a	t	e	□
μ_r	-1				2	3							
	0	0	1	2			5	6	7	8	9	10	11
	$+1$				4								

An RSE(1) case of example (24.2) is illustrated by Table 24.3. There is one μ'-chain of length 2, one μ''-chain of length 4 and one μ'''-chain of length 5. Three characters ($a_3^{(k)}$, $a_5^{(k)}$ and $a_6^{(k)}$) have s-lists of two elements, with either of 4 and 5 taking part in two of these lists.

Here is a TE(1) case (Table 24.4). We see one μ'-chain of length 2, two μ''-chains of lengths 3 and 7, and one μ'''-chain of length 1. $s = 2$ can be found in two s-lists, and one s-list (namely, $\{s\}_3$) has two non-empty positions.

And now an SE(1) case (Table 24.5). There is one μ'-chain of length 1, one μ'''-chain of length 1, and two μ''-chains of length 3 and 4. $s = 3$ can be found in two s-lists ($\{s\}_2$ and $\{s\}_4$); besides, these s-lists have two nonempty positions each.

Table 24.5

r, s		0	1	2	3	4	5	6	7
x_k		□	b	a	n	a	n	a	□
x		□	b	a	a	a	n	a	□
μ_r	-1					3			
	0	0	1	2		4	5	6	7
	$+1$			3					

Table 24.6

r, s		0	1	2	3	4	5	6	7	8
x_k		□	c	o	l	l	e	c	t	□
x		□	c	o	l	l	e	c	t	□
μ_r	-1					3				
	0	0	1	2	3	4	5	6	7	8
	$+1$				4					

An errorless example with ambiguous correspondences is given in Table 24.6.

It is apparent that q-tables are constructed redundantly. In particular, nonempty cells could be filled with not values of s but with some general sign (an asterisk, for instance). In fact, s can be easily calculated from r and μ_r: $s = r + \mu_r$. However, the here used filling method is easier to understand and more convenient in discussions. This easiness is of much help with the mentioned "frontal" method of overcoming the non-uniqueness, where all possible variants are tested. With this method, in Table 24.2 both a_3 and a_5 should be regarded as a $a_4^{(k)}$–corresponding character, but in the latter case $s = 3$ will be removed from the s-list $\{s\}_2$ because otherwise a_3 will correspond to $a_2^{(k)}$ and $a_4^{(k)}$ at a time. At the final recognition stage each unique and self-consistent variant is tested for accordance with Postulate P24.1, and it leads to the ultimate solution for the pair x_k, x.

Such an exhaustive search for true correspondences can be avoided if one takes into account the displacement coordination concept expressed by Postulate P24.1. In the next chapter we shall consider this question in a general way. Then we shall expose further simplifications proposed by Postulate P23.1 in addition to Postulate P24.1.

Chapter 25

OVERCOMING THE NON-UNIQUENESS OF CORRESPONDENCES (A GENERAL PROCEDURE)

25.1 Processing of q-tables in view of Postulate P24.1

Now we know that words x_k and x can have more than one QC character. This fact affects their q-table in two ways. Firstly, a character $a_r^{(k)}$ of the word x_k has more than one non-empty position in its column (s-list). Secondly, a character a_s of the word x has identical values in different columns.

In this connection we propose certain regularization rules to represent Postulate P24.1. Rules R25.1 and R25.2 establish non-uniqueness resolution mechanisms for both mentioned manifestations. Rules R25.3 and R25.4 are designed to eliminate a possible indeterminacy after an application of Rules R25.1 and R25.2. It easy to notice that all of these rules are based on the displacement coordination concept.

Rule R25.1 (of different s-lists) *If the same s occurs in more than one s-list, it is preserved in the longest μ-chain.*

Rule R25.2 (of a single s-list) *If an s-list involves more than one nonempty position, then that from the longest μ-chain is preserved.*

Rule R25.3 (of R25.1–R25.2 rules priority) *If some s fits both R25.1 and R25.2 rules, then the rule dealing with the longest μ-chain is applied. If the two rules deal with the same μ-chain, the application order does not affect the result and either rule will do.*

Rule R25.4 (of failure) *If there is an indeterminacy in applying one of the rules R25.1–R25.3 (i.e. if compared μ-chains are equally long), the next rule should be tried. If the indeterminacy remains after all the rules are tried, one should make an exhaustive search of all possible unique correspondences.*

We see that an exhaustion is necessary only if different displacements are identically corresponded. As the non-uniqueness itself is a rare occasion (tables 24.2–24.6 show especially selected cases), an exhaustive search is expected to be performed rather rarely.

Let us give examples of R25.1–R25.4 being applied.

Table 24.2. $s = 3$ fits both R25.1 ($s = 3$ is included in $\{s\}_2$ and $\{s\}_4$ simultaneously) and R25.2 ($\{s\}_4$ has another non-empty position in μ'''). The longest chains of both rules are the same. R25.3 says that any application order of R25.1 and R25.2 will do. Let us agree to start from R25.1 in such cases. Then $s = 3$ in $\{s\}_2$ and $s = 5$ in $\{s\}_4$ are erased. The latter erasing eliminates the need for R25.2 to be applied to the list $\{s\}_4$. The correspondence is now unique. Note that R25.1 emptied the list $\{s\}_2$ and made $a_2^{(k)}$ unsupported which is true due to the LSE(1) in the word x. It is easy to see that the result would be the same if R25.2 were the first: an erasing of $s = 5$ in $\{s\}_4$ would have been followed by R25.1 with $s = 3$ being erased in $\{s\}_2$.

Table 24.3. Just as in the preceding example, $s = 4$ fits both R25.1 and R25.2 and the longest μ-chains are the same: μ''', length 5. R25.1 erases $s = 4$ from the list $\{s\}_5$ and leaves two nonempty positions in $\{s\}_3$. R25.2 preserves $s = 4$ and erases $s = 3$, because the former has a longer μ-chain: μ'''-chain of length 5. At last, R25.1 preserves only one of two fives in $\{s\}_4$ and $\{s\}_6$: it is that of $\{s\}_4$. That is all.

Table 24.4. Thought $s = 2$ fits both R25.1 and R25.2, their μ-chains differ and have different length, unlike the above discussed examples. In fact, R25.1 deals with μ''-chain of length 3, and R25.2 deals with μ'-chain of length 2. Thus R25.1 comes first, erasing $s = 2$ from $\{s\}_3$. Then R25.2 is not necessary. The correspondence becomes unique and indicates an inversion at positions 3 and 4, as it should.

Table 24.5. To deal with $s = 3$ here R25.2 should come first because of its μ''-chain having a length of 3, not 1 as it were with R25.1. As a result $s = 3$ is erased from $\{s\}_2$, putting away R25.1. Then $s = 3$ is erased from $\{s\}_4$ and the correspondence is unique now. The list $\{s\}_3$ is empty, thus the character $a_3^{(k)}$ is unsupported (we know it is due to the SE(1) at position 3 of x).

Table 24.6. The same situation but there are no unsupported characters here. R25.1 (as well as R25.2) erases $s = 4$ from $\{s\}_3$ and $s = 3$ from $\{s\}_4$, making the correspondence unique.

Now it is clear that rules R25.1–R25.4 provide an easy and simple pre-recognition even if words are especially selected to have a lot of non-uniqueness. Nevertheless, it can be even simpler under Postulate P23.1. In the next section we shall prove that this postulate helps to work out the structure of the sets X_k and $\{x\}^{(k)}$. This structure, in its turn, will help to improve the processing of q-tables.

25.2 The structure of the class X_k and of the working area $\{x\}^{(k)}$ in view of Postulate P23.1

Once taken into consideration, Postulate P23.1 often allows testing quasi-correspondences for a whole μ-chain and even a row μ_r of a q-table at once. The matter is that the working area $\{x\}^{(k)}$ of the k-th pattern can be divided into subsets for q-tables of words of any subset to arrange true and false QC's in some determined way.

It means that the search for true correspondences is preceded by the stage that determines what of the mentioned subsets of $\{x\}^{(k)}$ an input word x belongs to (certainly, we suppose $x \in \{x\}^{(k)}$). Thus another pre-recognition stage is necessary.

Postulate P23.1 limits the working area $\{x\}^{(k)}$ so that its subsets are determined by the simplest feature, namely by the length s of subset words. Let us prove that. First of all, we should remark that Postulate P23.1 directly gives $\Delta r = 1$ because no error listed in P23.1 displaces a character to more than one position left or right. If a word x_k is made up of R_k characters (spaces excluded), any word of the class X is made up of no less than $R_k - 1$ and no more than $R_k + 1$ characters. Words of other lengths are naturally removed from the working area $\{x\}^{(k)}$ of the pattern x_k. Thus $\{x\}^{(k)}$ contains words of three lengths: $S_0 = R_k$, $S_{-1} = R_k - 1$, $S_{+1} = R_k + 1$. Let us divide $\{x\}^{(k)}$ into three subsets:

$\{x\}_0^{(k)}$ – the subset of all words of length S_0;
$\{x\}_{+1}^{(k)}$ – the subset of all words of length S_{+1};
$\{x\}_{-1}^{(k)}$ – the subset of all words of length S_{-1}.

The class X_k turns out to be broken into 3 subclasses as well: $X_{k,0} \subset \{x\}_0^{(k)}$, $X_{k,-1} \subset \{x\}_{-1}^{(k)}$ and $X_{k,+1} \subset \{x\}_{+1}^{(k)}$.

Now we can specify the assertion stated at the beginning of the section as follows: instead of a huge, but general true transformation searching procedure we may use three much simpler procedures for the three subsets $\{x\}_0^{(k)}$, $\{x\}_{-1}^{(k)}$, $\{x\}_{+1}^{(k)}$. Such procedures usually do not require analyzing every value of s. Though they demand a proper subset to be pre-recognized, the feature (the word length) is very simple, and this new problem becomes trivial.

The direct way of proving these statements is to develop the mentioned procedures and to test their properties. It is what we shall do, but at first we are going to formulate some important requirements imposed on q-table changing procedures.

25.3 q-table processing requirements and their fulfillment conditions

Any q-table processing must comply with two following demands.

Demand D25.1 *If the relation $t \in T_k$ is true with a word pair (x, x_k) and t is derivable from the original q-table, this t should be derivable from a processed q-table.*

This demand guarantees that the word $x = tx_k$ will be finally recognized as a part of X_k, i.e. there will not be a misrecognition or a missing.

Demand D25.2 *If the relation* $q > 1$ *is true with a word pair* (x, x_k) *and all derivable transformations of the original q-table belong to* $T_{\neg k}$ *then all derivable transformations of a processed q-table should belong to* $T_{\neg k}$.

With this demand complied, the word x will not be placed into the class X_k, i.e. a "false alarm" will not occur.

In order to develop q-table processing procedures properly in terms of D25.1 and D25.2, one should realize how this or another change of the table affects the belonging of a derivable t to T_k or $T_{\neg k}$.

Certainly, it will be cleared up by the final recognition but the point is to understand it before that stage. Thus, we should proceed from some general regularity, disregarding any particular change of the q-table.

When working out such a regularity we find it more convenient to speak about x as a part/not a part of X_k instead of t as a part/not a part of T_k $(x = tx_k)$. Generally, it does not matter due to "one-to-one mapping" $X_k \leftrightarrow T_k$.

We have already noticed that the question of x belonging to the class X_k is generally associated with the notion of *likeness* between x and x_k. For instance, it can be a metric distance in a decision space. Notions of the kind have already been proposed in the word matching branch. Among them there is the so called Levenstein distance [50, 42], which is a nondecreasing function of the number of SE's, LSE's an RSE's in a word.

Such a notion of likeness can work correctly only if the class domains comply with some wellknown conditions (the symmetry, for example). But here we shall be satisfied by a practically always true simple property. This property will be formulated as a postulate.

Postulate P25.1 *If an object* x *and the class* X_k*, with* x_k *as its pattern, relate as* $x \notin X_k$ *then a decrease of likeness (an increase of difference) between* x *and* x_k *does not alter this relation.*

To use this postulate, we should stuff the notion of word likeness so that it is adequate to our interpretation of the problem, where x and x_k are words related by a transformation t. Proceeding from Postulate P24.1, we intuitively come to another assertion. With x_k transformed into x, the more coordinated and less intensive character displacements, the more similar are those words.

This statement must be reformulated to avoid a shade of intuition:

Statement S25.1 *The likeness of words* x_k *and* x *is a* nonincreasing *function of the number of unsupported characters of* x_k *with respect to* x.

In fact, an unsupported character cuts μ-chains short and pulls down the displacement coordination degree.

The last statement and Postulate P25.1 give us the desired general law, revealing how changes of a q-table affect the belonging of derivable transformations to T_k class. Off course, we are interested in erasing of values of s. The desired law is set forth as two statements: S25.2 and S25.3. The first of them is evident and the second follows from the above presented reasoning.

Statement S25.2 *Let t be derivable from a q-table. If $t \in T_k$ and some s in this table determines a false QC, then the relation $t \in T_k$ does not alter after this s is erased from the table.*

Statement S25.3 *If $t \notin T_k$ for any derivable t of a q-table, this relation remains the same after any s is erased from the table, no matter whether this s determines a true or false QC. It means any derivable transformation of a processed table keeps the relation $t \notin T_k$ true.*

Now we may use the restrictions imposed by Postulate P23.1. In the next chapter we shall prove that they will help us to simplify the processing of q-tables and even to recognize a word before the final recognition step itself.

Chapter 26

OVERCOMING THE NON-UNIQUENESS OF CORRESPONDENCES AND FINAL RECOGNITION (A SIMPLIFIED PROCEDURE)

26.1 Basic μ-chains: existence and uniqueness

The processing of a q-table can be simplified if we take into account a certain possibility given by Postulate P23.1. Then with no individual analysis of table cells (i.e. values of s), we can detect μ-chains that give most complete (and, as a rule, uniquely determined) information about the true derivable transformation $t \in T_k$ of the q-table. Those μ-chains are termed *basic* μ-chains. More specifically, a μ-chain is called basic if it starts at position 0 or ends at position R_k+1. Other μ-chains are called *alternative*. For instance, Table 24.2 (Section 24.3) has two basic μ-chains: μ''-chain at positions 0–1 and μ'-chain at positions 3–9. Two μ'''-chains at positions 2 and 4 are alternative.

A basic μ-chain may be either *initial* (if it starts at position 0) or *terminal* (if it ends at position $R_k + 1$). Owing to the left space justification, an initial basic μ-chain is always a μ''-chain in row 0 of a q-table, whereas a terminal chain may occupy any row in the section "μ_r".

This is the first difference between initial and terminal μ-chains. Another difference appears as that the initial μ-chain exists at all times whereas the terminal one may not exist without Postulate P23.1. In fact, with $\Delta r = 1$ and two LSE(1)'s in a word x, we obtain $S = R_k - 2$, and the character at position $R_k + 1$ (i.e. the finishing space) is unsupported. It means that the $(R_k + 1)$-th s-list $\{s\}_{R_k+1}$ is empty, and the terminal μ-chain does not exist by definition.

Now we are going to prove that this will never happen if Postulate P23.1 is taken into account. For the sake of references, we shall formulate it as a lemma.

Lemma 26.1 *A terminal μ-chain exists for* $\forall\, x_k \in X_p$ *and* $\forall\, x \in \{x\}^{(k)}$.

Proof: For a character $a^{(k)}_{R_k+1}$ to become unsupported, $|S - R_k| > 1$ is necessary with $\Delta r = 1$. By the definition of the working area $\{x\}^{(k)}$, $|S - R_k| \le 1$ for $\forall\, x \in \{x\}^{(k)}$ and $a^{(k)}_{R_k+1} = a_{S+1}$ at all times. Consequently, conditions Eq. (24.1) are satisfied and $a^{(k)}_{R_k+1}$ and a_{S+1} turn out to be QC characters. Then μ_{R_k+1}

exists (the s-list $\{s\}_{R_k+1}$ of the q-table is not empty), and the terminal μ-chain exists as well. Q.E.D.

It is time we proved the uniqueness of the initial and terminal μ-chains. It makes sense to formulate it as a separate lemma too.

Lemma 26.2 *For* $\forall\, x_k \in X_p$ *and* $\forall\, x \in \{x\}^{(k)}$ *both initial and terminal basic* μ*-chains are unique in the* q*-table of the words* x, x_k.

Proof: According to Lemma 24.1 (Section 24.1) both initial and terminal spaces do not have NDC if $\Delta r = 1$. It means that the s-list $\{s\}_0$ of the initial space position involves only one value of s (in row $\mu'' = 0$, due to the justification), and the s-list $\{s\}_{R_k+1}$ of the terminal space position $(R_k + 1)$ includes only one value of s in row $\mu = S - R_k$. That is the proof.

The above described basic μ-chains will be the base of the simplified procedure. In this connection we are introducing another piece of notation. Initial and terminal μ-chains are denoted as μ_i-chain and μ_t-chain respectively. The position of the very right character of the μ_i-chain is designated by r_i and the position of the very left character of the μ_t-chain is designated by r_t. The displacement parameter (constant along an entire chain) of the μ_i-chain is denoted as μ_i, whereas that of the μ_t-chain is referred to as μ_t. We have already noticed that $\mu_i = \mu'' \equiv 0$ at all times and $\mu_t = \mu_{R_k+1}$ takes on one of three possible values: $\mu' = -1$, $\mu'' = 0$, $\mu''' = +1$, depending on the type of an error. Let us also designate the length of the μ_i-chain as d_i and the length of the μ_t-chain as d_t. The group of d_i left columns of the q-table is called the *i-zone* and that of d_t right columns is called the *t-zone*.

Having introduced this notation, we are coming down to the discussion about the desired q-table processing procedure.

As Postulate P23.1 clearly establishes the contents of the subclasses $X_{k,-1}$, $X_{k,+1}$, $X_{k,0}$, it is convenient to proceed from them. In fact, any word of X_k is generated by a single error occurred in x_k. As only an LSE(1) cuts a word short by exactly 1 character, $X_{k,-1}$ is made up *only* of words generated by an LSE(1). Similarly, $X_{k,+1}$ comprises *only* words generated by an RSE(1). As for $X_{k,0}$, it covers the results of TE(1)'s and SE(1)'s, and the word x_k itself.

The above observation brings some regularity into movements of characters in a word, and we shall utilize it to construct our simplified procedure. Considering this procedure we shall need formal definitions for all kinds of errors permitted by Postulate P23.1 and for the errorless case. Let us write down such definitions.

26.2 Formal definitions of transformations permitted by Postulate P23.1

Definition 26.1 (of LSE(1)) *Transformation t is a result of an LSE(1) (notation: t=LSE(1)) at position r', if $\exists\, r'$, $0 < r' \le R_k$ such that*

$$\begin{cases} \forall r,\ 0 \le r < r' & : \ \mu_r = 0 \\ \forall r,\ r' < r \le R_k + 1 & : \ \mu_r = -1 \end{cases}$$

Definition 26.2 (of RSE(1)) *Transformation t is a result of an LSE(1) (notation: t=RSE(1)) at position r', if $\exists\, r'$, $0 < r' \le R_k$ such that*

$$\begin{cases} \forall r,\ 0 \le r < r' & : \ \mu_r = 0 \\ \forall r,\ r' \le r \le R_k + 1 & : \ \mu_r = +1 \end{cases}$$

Definition 26.3 (of SE(1)) *Transformation t is a result of an SE(1) (notation: t=SE(1)) at position r', if $\exists\, r'$, $0 < r' \le R_k$ such that*

$$\begin{cases} \forall r,\ 0 \le r < r' & : \ \mu_r = 0 \\ & \quad \mu_{r'} \ne 0 \\ \forall r,\ r' < r \le R_k + 1 & : \ \mu_r = 0 \end{cases}$$

Definition 26.4 (of TE(1)) *Transformation t is a result of a TE(1) (notation: t=TE(1)) at positions r' and $r'+1$, if $\exists\, r'$, $0 < r' \le R_k$ such that*

$$\begin{cases} \forall r,\ 0 \le r < r' & : \ \mu_r = 0 \\ & \quad \mu_{r'} = +1 \\ & \quad \mu_{r'+1} = -1 \\ \forall r,\ r'+1 < r \le R_k + 1 & : \ \mu_r = 0 \end{cases}$$

Definition 26.5 (of errorless case) *Transformation t indicates an errorless case if it is an identity (notation $t = t_0$), i.e. if $\forall\, r$, $0 < r \le R_k + 1$, μ_r exists and $\mu_r = 0$.*

These definitions evidently follow from the essence of the transformations permitted by Postulate P23.1 and need no comments. With the help of these definitions we are going to the simplified q-table processing. Let us start with the subclass $X_{k,-1}$ and the enveloping set $\{x\}^{(k)}_{-1}$.

26.3 The simplified processing of q-tables and the word final recognition with $S = R_k - 1$

Basic μ-chains and their properties allow us to formulate rather simple conditions of a transformation t being a result of an LSE(1). The following theorem expresses such conditions.

Theorem 26.1 *Let* $x = tx_k$. *Then*

$$(S = R_k - 1) \wedge (d_i + d_t \geq R_k + 1) \Rightarrow (t = \text{LSE}(1)) \tag{26.1}$$

Proof: The first thing for us to expose is that $S = R_k - 1$ brings $\mu_t = -1$. In fact, Lemma 26.1 makes $S = R_k - 1$ be followed by μ_{R_k+1} existing and $\mu_{R_k+1} = -1$. Then Lemma 26.2 comes and says that $\mu_t = -1$. Here is the result of the first stage of the proof. As for the μ_i-chain, it was noticed that it existed at all times and $\mu_i = 0$ forever. Keeping this in mind, we are going to another statement that concerns a q-table row with no μ-chains in it. Since this statement will be used in other theorems we shall single it out as a lemma.

Lemma 26.3 *If* $S = R_k - 1$, *the* q*-table row* $\mu''' = +1$ *does not include true correspondences.*

Proof of lemma: $S = R_k - 1$ means that either $x \in X_{k,-1}$ or $x \in \{x\}^{(k)}_{-1} \setminus X_{k,-1}$. If the first relation is true, the transformation is a result of an LSE(1). Suppose it occurs at position r'. From the LSE(1) definition it follows that any character to the left of r' has $\mu_r = 0$ and any character to the right of r' has $\mu_r = -1$. Consequently, each value of s in row $\mu''' = +1$ at any position (except for r') corresponds to a wrong QC and, in accordance with Statement S25.2, it may be erased not violating Demand D25.1. As for position r', it is either unsupported or supported by a false QC originating from an NDC. According to Statement S25.2, the appropriate s may be erased whatever row it is situated in ($\mu''' = +1$ included). Thus, Lemma 26.3 is true with $x \in X_{k,-1}$.

Let us check the second part, i.e. let us suppose $x \in \{x\}^{(k)}_{-1} \setminus X_{k,-1}$. In such a case, either x_k is shortened by several errors or x is just another word of length $R_k - 1$. Let there be q derivable transformations that correspond to x with respect to x_k. Since $x \notin X_{k,-1}$, these transformations do not belong to T_k . Statement S25.3 says that this fact can not be altered by erasing any s from the q-table (and from row $\mu''' = +1$, in particular). Thus row $\mu''' = +1$ does not contain a true correspondence and may be erased with no violation of Demands D25.1 and D25.2. Lemma 26.3 is proved now.

Row $\mu''' = +1$ being erased, we can proceed with the proof of Theorem 26.1. This is how alternative μ-chains can be situated in the other rows, namely in rows $\mu' = -1$ and $\mu'' = 0$. In this connection we are formulating another lemma.

Lemma 26.4 *If* $S = R_k - 1$, *it follows from the inequality* $d_i + d_t \geq R_k + 1$ *that alternative* μ*-chains in row* $\mu' = -1$ *are situated within the* i*-zone of the* q*-table, whereas alternative* μ*-chains in row* $\mu'' = 0$ *lie within the* t*-zone.*

Proof of lemma: Let us consider $d_i + d_t = R_k + 1$ at first. Since the length of x_k (spaces included) is $R_k + 2$ (therefore, the length of a q-table row is $R_k + 2$ too), there is a sole position (say r') not belonging to any basic μ-chain. This position is situated either to the left of a basic μ-chain or to the right of it. As the very left (zero) position belongs to the μ_i-chain and the very right $(R_k + 1)$ position belongs to the μ_t-chain, the r'-th position is situated between r_i and r_t. These two facts mean that $r' = r_i + 1$ and $r_t = r' + 1$, i.e. r_i, r' and r_t are successive. Proceeding from this, we are going to show that the r'-th positions of both $\mu' = -1$ and $\mu'' = 0$ rows of the q-table are empty. In fact, if any of them were occupied by s from an alternative μ-chain, it would make any basic chain in this row longer at least by 1 which would contradict to $d_i + d_t = R_k + 1$. Consequently, alternative μ-chains, if any, in rows $\mu' = -1$ and $\mu'' = 0$ lie within the i-zone and the t-zone of the table.

If $d_i + d_t > R_k + 1$, each position belongs to either of the basic μ-chains and an alternative μ-chain lies in either i-zone or t-zone whatever positions of $\mu' = -1$ and $\mu'' = 0$ rows it is situated at. Lemma 26.4 is proved now.

We are back to the proof of Theorem 26.1. Let us prove that true correspondences in $\mu' = -1$ and $\mu'' = 0$ rows of the q-table are situated in the basic μ-chains. On the one hand, Lemma 26.2 says that alternative μ-chains can include neither zero position nor $R_k + 1$ position. On the other hand, Lemma 26.4 forbids them to exceed the i-zone and t-zones. It means that any alternative μ-chain is shorter than the basic μ-chain, whose zone it lies in. According to Postulate P24.1, the true correspondence is the s belonging to the basic chain (Rule R25.2). Note that here we have another rule of erasing without an individual analysis of characters. Namely, it is as follows: if $S = R_k - 1$ and $d_i + d_t \geq R_k + 1$, one should erase everything except the basic μ-chains, i.e. the entire row $\mu''' = +1$ and all alternative chains of $\mu' = -1$ and $\mu'' = 0$ rows. Any other possible indeterminacy (in particular, identical values of s in different columns) will be eliminated later.

Let us consider the case of $d_i + d_t = R_k + 1$ again. The proof of Lemma 26.4 has shown that the s-list $\{s\}_{r'}$ is then empty, i.e. $a_{r'}^{(k)}$ is an unsupported character. Next, $\mu_r = 0$ for all the positions from zero to $r' - 1$, because all true correspondences (see above) at those positions belong to the μ_i-chain with $\mu_i = \mu'' = 0$. As for the positions from $r' + 1$ to $R_k + 1$, $\mu_r = -1$ for them because all true correspondences here belong to the μ_t-chain with $\mu_t = \mu' = -1$. It is the definition of an LSE(1).

Now we are coming down to the last case of $d_i + d_t > R_k + 1$. Suppose $d_i + d_t = R_k + 2$ first, i.e. the total length of the basic μ-chains is equal to the number of positions in the word (spaces included). It means that there are no

Table 26.1

r, s		0	1	2	3	4	5	6	7	8
x_k		□	c	o	l	l	e	c	t	□
x		□	c	o	l	e	c	t	□	
	-1					3	4	5	6	7
μ_r	0	0	1	2	3					

empty columns in the q-table, i.e. each character of x_k has a QC character of x. Since x comprises one character fewer than x_k (remember $S = R_k - 1$), some character of x (say the s'-th one) serves as an NDC for two characters of x_k (say the r'-th and r''-th ones). Therefore, the same s' occupies columns r' and r''.

What rows does this s' belong to in each of these columns? On the one hand, $\mu_{r'} = s' - r'$, $\mu_{r''} = s' - r''$ and $r' \neq r''$, then $\mu_{r'} \neq \mu_{r''}$ and we find s' in different rows. On the other hand, after the performed erasings all QC's, both true and false, are parts of the basic μ-chains (other μ-chains are erased) and, consequently, lie in two rows: $\mu' = -1$ and $\mu'' = 0$. From this the following facts can be derived:

1. If $r' < r''$, then s' is situated in column r' in row $\mu'' = 0$ and makes a part of the μ_i-chain. As for column r'', s' is situated in row $\mu' = -1$ and makes a part of the μ_t-chain.

2. Since $\mu_{r'} = \mu'' = 0$ and $\mu_{r''} = \mu' = -1$, $\mu_{r'} - \mu_{r''} = 1$, i.e. $a^{(k)}_{r'}$ and $a^{(k)}_{r''}$ are adjacent, $r'' = r' + 1$. What is more, they are of the same name because they correspond to the same character $a_{s'}$.

Now we can say that $d_i + d_t = R_k + 2$ takes place if there is a double letter in x_k and one of the couple has been lost in x. Table 26.1 gives an example. Here $x_k =$ "collect", $x =$ "colect", $s' = 3$, $r' = 3$, $r'' = 4$. It does not matter which of two letters "l" of the word x_k is skipped and which of them the "l" of the word x is associated with. Either of the values $s = 3$ in columns 3 and 4 can be erased. Let it be $r' = 3$. Then $\mu_r = 0$ for all positions from 0 to $r' - 1$, and $\mu_r = -1$ for all positions from $r' + 1$ to $R_k + 1$. It is clear that the result is the same with r'' instead of r'. So, we have obtained the LSE(1) definition again.

At last let us consider $d_i + d_t > R_k + 2$. Suppose $d_i + d_t = R_k + 3$. It takes place only if $r_i = r_t$, i.e. μ_i-chain and μ_t-chain share a position (let us keep it as r_i). For such a position to exist, the character $a^{(k)}_{r_i}$ of the word x_k must be of the same name as two characters of x, namely as $a_{r_i - 1}$ (the value $s = r_i - 1$ occupies the cross of row $\mu' = -1$ and column r_i in the q-table) and a_{r_i} ($s = r_i$ occupies row $\mu'' = 0$ of the same column). But for column $r_i + 1$ to have the value s in row $\mu' = -1$ so that s could make a part of the μ_t-chain, the character

a_{r_i+1} must be of the same name as a_{r_i} and hence as $a^{(k)}_{r_i}$. In the same vein, for column $r_i - 1$ to have the value s in row $\mu'' = 0$ so that s could be a part of the μ_i-chain, the character a_{r_i-1} must be of the same name as a_{r_i-1} and hence as $a^{(k)}_{r_i}$. The total conclusion is that $a^{(k)}_{r_i-1}$, $a^{(k)}_{r_i}$ and $a^{(k)}_{r_i+1}$ are of the same name, i.e. the word x_k includes a triple character. The impossibility of such a situation in most languages[†] makes the case of $d_i + d_t = R_k + 3$ impossible. An evident induction spreads the truth of this conclusion to the cases of $R_k + 4$, $R_k + 5$, etc.

Thus, $d_i + d_t \geq R_k + 1$ admits only two feasible cases. They are $d_i + d_t = R_k + 1$ and $d_i + d_t = R_k + 2$. Both of them lead to the LSE(1) definition, thus proving Theorem 26.1.

26.4 The simplified processing of q-tables and the word final recognition with $S = R_k + 1$

Here we are going to formulate similarly simple conditions for t in $x = tx_k$ to be a result of an RSE(1).

Theorem 26.2 *Let* $x = tx_k$. *Then*

$$(S = R_k + 1) \wedge (d_i + d_t \geq R_k + 2) \Rightarrow (t = \text{RSE}(1)) \tag{26.2}$$

Proof: As it was done in the preceding section, we can easily prove that with the equality $S = R_k + 1$ Lemmata 26.1 and 26.2 give us $\mu_t = +1$ in addition to the existence and uniqueness of the μ_t-chain. As for the μ_i-chain, $\mu_i = 0$ at all times. Thus, row $\mu' = -1$ of the q-table does not contain basic μ-chains if $S = R_k + 1$.

Then the following statement is true:
If $S = R_k + 1$, *then row* $\mu' = -1$ *of the* q*-table does not contain true correspondences.*

The proof looks like the proof of Lemma 26.3 and we skip it. The statement itself allows us to erase row $\mu' = -1$ entirely with no analysis of its contents.

The next fact is that Lemma 26.4 remains true under conditions Eq. (26.2) i.e. with $S = R_k + 1$ and $d_i + d_t \geq R_k + 2$; one should only change $\mu' = -1$ for $\mu''' = +1$ in its statement. No special proof is necessary because even with $d_i + d_t = R_k + 2$ i-zone and t-zone contact each other.

So, just as it was in the previous section, alternative chains are shorter than the basic ones, and can be erased without analyzing their contents. Thus we have to analyze a q-table, considering only its basic μ-chains.

Let us start with the case of $d_i + d_t = R_k + 2$. The total length of the basic μ-chains equals the number of characters in the word x_k (spaces included). It means that there is only one value of s in each s-list (q-table column) and

---

[†] Russian language includes two anecdotic words "длинношеее" and "змееед"

those values belong to the basic μ-chains. Consequently, $r_t = r_i + 1$. Suppose $r' = r_t$. Then all values of s, situated at the positions from r' to $R_k + 1$, belong to the μ_t-chain; for them $\mu_r = +1$. As for the positions to the left of r' (from 0 to $r' - 1$), they have $\mu_r = 0$ and from $r' - 1 = r_t - 1 = r_i$ we obtain the RSE(1) definition.

Let $d_i + d_t > R_k + 2$ now. For the sake of definiteness suppose $d_i + d_t = R_k + 3$. This can happen only if $r_i = r_t$, i.e. the μ_i-chain and the μ_t-chain share a position (let us keep designating it as r_i). For such a position to exist, the character $a^{(k)}_{r_i}$ of the word x_k must be of the same name as two characters of x, namely as a_{r_i} (the value $s = r_i$ occupies then the cross of row $\mu'' = 0$ and column r_i in the q-table) and a_{r_i+1} ($s = r_i + 1$ occupies row $\mu_{r_i} = s - r_i = r_i + 1 - r_i = +1 \equiv \mu'''$ of the same column). Consequently, $a_{r_i} = a_{r_i+1}$, but $a_{r_i+1} \neq a^{(k)}_{r_i+1}$. (Otherwise $s = r_i + 1$ will occur in the cross of row $\mu'' = 0$ and column $r_i + 1$, i.e. position $r_i + 1$ will be a part of the i-zone. This contradicts to our supposition that the i-zone ends at position r_i). At the same time, position $\tilde{r} = r_i + 1$ does not have $s = r_i + 1$ in row $\mu'' = 0$, but contains $s = \tilde{r} + 1 = r_i + 2$ in row $\mu''' = +1$, because this s is a part of the μ_t-chain. Relation $s = r + 1$ keeps true up to position $R_k + 1$, because the t-zone involves only the μ_t-chain. Now we can conclude that the word x differs from x_k by a new character between $a^{(k)}_{r_i}$ and $a^{(k)}_{r_i+1}$ and this character is of the same name as $a^{(k)}_{r_i}$, i.e. there is a special RSE(1), an erroneous duplication of $a^{(k)}_{r_i}$. All the characters to the right of $a^{(k)}_{r_i}$ are displaced with the displacement parameter $\mu = +1$. Essentially, we have an RSE(1) at position $r_i + 1$ and nothing more should be done if we learn that $S = R_k + 1$ and $d_i + d_t = R_k + 3$. In order to make the obtained q-table literally fit the RSE(1) formal definition we should get rid of the rest of indeterminacy by erasing one of two values of s from the s-list $\{s\}_{r_i}$. This can be done in accordance with Rule R25.2, i.e. we erase $s = r_i$ if $d_i < d_t$, or $s = r_i + 1$ if $d_i > d_t$, or any of them if $d_i = d_t$.

In the same manner we can show that $d_i + d_t = R_k + 4$ with $S = R_k + 1$ takes place only if an error adds the third element to a double character of x_k ("correspondence"— "corrrespondence"). Rule R25.2 will give a q-table answering the RSE(1) definition.

As for $d_i + d_t > R_k + 4$ situations, they demand a triple character in x_k. This is impossible in most languages as we noticed in Section 26.2. Thus Theorem 26.2 is completely proved.

26.5 The simplified processing of q-tables and the word final recognition with $S = R_k$

In Section 26.1 we noted that $S = R_k$ was possible in three situations: a correctly spelled word ($t = t_0$), an SE(1) and a TE(1). Let us consider them all.

Theorem 26.3 *Let* $x = tx_k$. *Then*

$$(S = R_k) \wedge (d_i + d_t = R_k + 2) \;\Rightarrow\; (t = t_0)\,, \tag{26.3}$$
$$(S = R_k) \wedge (d_i + d_t = R_k + 1) \;\Rightarrow\; (t = \mathrm{SE}(1))\,, \tag{26.4}$$
$$(S = R_k) \wedge (d_i + d_t = R_k) \;\Rightarrow\; (t = \mathrm{TE}(1))\,. \tag{26.5}$$

Proof: From the presence of $S = R_k$ in Eqs. (26.3) and (26.4) it follows that $\mu_t = \mu_{R_k+1} = 0 = \mu_i$ in both cases, i.e. both basic μ-chains are situated in the same row $\mu'' = 0$ of the q-table. Retracing Lemma 26.3 we can show that here both row $\mu' = -1$ and row $\mu''' = +1$ can be eliminated from consideration with no analysis of their contents. As for row $\mu'' = 0$, its length equals the total length of the basic chains in Eq. (26.3) and is greater by one in Eq. (26.4).

Thus, if the left part of Eq. (26.3) is true, we obtain $r_t = r_b + 1$, i.e. the μ_i-chain and the μ_t-chain merge and cover all the positions of row $\mu'' = 0$. It means that all the characters of the word x_k are supported (i.e. μ_r exists for every value of r) and that the displacement parameter $\mu_r = 0$ for all the characters. Those conclusions form the definition of the identical transformation (ref. to Section 26.2). Thus implication Eq. (26.3) is true.

If Eq. (26.4) is fulfilled, from both basic μ-chains being in row $\mu'' = 0$ and the condition $d_i + d_t = R_k + 1$ it follows that this row has only one empty position (say the r'-th one), i.e. a position with $\mu_{r'} \neq 0$. In fact, the proof of Lemma 26.3 noticed that in such a case we have $r' = r_i + 1$ and $r_t = r' + 1$. It means that position r' contacts both μ_i-chain and μ_t-chain. Therefore, if this position were occupied by a value of s setting $\mu_{r'} = 0$, it would merge the basic chains. Then we would have $d_i + d_t = R_k + 2$, which is in conflict with Eq. (26.4). Hence $\mu_{r'} \neq 0$. As for the other positions, $\mu_r = 0$ for all of them since the basic μ-chains are situated in row $\mu'' = 0$. It fits the SE(1) definition and Eq. (26.4) is now proved.

At last, here is the case of a TE(1). The left condition of Eq. (26.5) means that both μ_i-chain and μ_t-chain lie in row $\mu'' = 0$ of the q-table. The right condition says that there are two empty positions in this row and those positions are adjacent (suppose their numbers are r' and $r' + 1$). In fact, if those empty positions were separated by at least one nonempty position, the total length $d_i + d_t$ could not exceed $R_k - 1$ and we would have a contradiction to the mentioned condition.

Then the conditions $S = R_k$ and $d_i + d_t = R_k$ can be true at a time in two cases only:

1. There is a block substitution (an SE(2) in our notation) at positions r' and $r' + 1$.

2. There is a single inversion TE(1) on those positions.

The first case is impossible under Postulate P23.1. Thus Eq. (26.5) corresponds to a TE(1) only. The theorem is proved now.

We have described the ideas and methods of the final recognition of misspelled words. The next chapter is devoted to the pre-recognition implementations.

Chapter 27

PRE-RECOGNITION OF GARBLED SUBTEXTS IN THE PROCESS OF DICTIONARY RETRIEVAL

27.1 A review of existing methods

After reading the preceding chapters it becomes apparent that the pre-recognition stage plays a leading role in the dictionary retrieval of garbled words. This chapter is entirely devoted to this stage. Let us estimate first how the usual garbled word recognition methods fit the pre-recognition.

As we noticed in Chapter 22, it is conventional to distinguish two problems here: 1) whether a given word contains errors (a spelling check or proofreading); 2) which correct word is the most probable candidate for a given misspelled word (a spelling correction). Methods used to solve these problems should be classified into two groups: dictionary methods and non-dictionary methods in accordance with their use of an NL dictionary. Dictionary-based spelling correction methods are often referred to as dictionary lookup.

Non-dictionary methods calculate an occurrence probability of the input character chain and compare it with a threshold, constant or dependent of the word length. When calculating a chain probability they use this or that probabilistic model (the simplest case is the Markov chain model [53]). The model parameters (such as character-to-character transition probabilities) are evaluated in the course of a preliminary statistical analysis. These methods are not reliable by their very nature and work mainly in spelling checkers. In orientated linguistics these methods run across another obstacle because the address language of each particular NPD may have its own statistics, considerably different from that of the entire language. Thus every new NPD requires a new statistical exploration. The only merit of the non-dictionary methods is that they do not use the external memory and, consequently, their performance is high.

Dictionary methods (most popular) use rather a huge NL dictionary that is usually kept in the external memory. The dictionary volume depends mainly on whether words are represented explicitly or implicitly. In Chapter 18 we preferred the explicit representation, which is followed by a greater dictionary volume. The dictionary methods can be subdivided into two types.

The first type performs a through-dictionary search for an *exact match*. This technique is well studied and exploits classical algorithms, for instance, an indexed dictionary binary search or various hashing algorithms [54]. The idea of hashing was elaborated in [55]. Their spelling check method proposes some special mathematical functions to calculate a few (usually two) numeric values for every input word. Those values are treated as coordinates in the dictionary located in RAM. The dictionary looks like a sparse binary matrix with its 1's corresponding to correct words. The functions are taken lest a garbled word lead to a one of the matrix; a zero result indicates an error in the word. The method works quickly and do not demand any external memory, but no set of functions can guarantee an absolute reliability.

The exact-match methods can be easily and effectively used in spelling checkers but not in spelling correctors. In fact, a search can stop far from the best candidate, no matter whether indexing or hashing is used. Therefore, they often implement an indirect method. Namely, a set of fixed rules generates spellings close to a garbled word. Then they are looked up by means of the above described techniques. The correcting ability of this method is entirely determined by these rules: the method cannot correct a word if it is garbled in an unexpected manner.

Methods of the second type search for a *best-match*. Their base is the following. There is a distance function in the space of character chains over a finite alphabet, established explicitly or via a calculating algorithm [43], [55]–[59]. This metric is used to evaluate the likeness of two arbitrary words. If the distance function is chosen correctly, it guarantees that the proper candidate will be found. However, this technique shows very little promise in the direct recognition of a garbled word, because it has to calculate distances between the input word and all the dictionary words. As the dictionary is usually located in the external memory, the process takes a great amount of time to give a result, no matter how quickly the distance is calculated.

These methods can be considerably accelerated with the use of the pattern recognition problem heterogeneity, if this property has been exposed. As applied to the best-match dictionary retrieval technique, it means minimizing the number of potential candidates. Certainly, this way is justified only if the candidate selection is easier and quicker than the final recognition. A natural boundary comes from the barrier between external and internal memory activities because in most computers the former is two orders slower than the latter. Due to this fact, the pre-recognition calls for procedures doing without a disk dictionary. At the same time, developers should be very careful here because the quality of pre-recognition procedures determines the whole recognition algorithm efficiency (i.e. performance and correctness). The candidate selection methods use different combinations of input word features. Let us review some of these features.

The word length. This feature is very attractive because it is independent of character substitutions or transpositions. As for the other types of errors (insertions and deletions), a length deviation never exceeds the number of errors. In Chapter 25 we proved this feature to be very efficient with

Postulate P23.1 accepted. In general the word length can be helpful because it speeds up the candidate filtration process. Its drawback is that it generates an extremely nonuniform classification. We made an experiment on a Russian dictionary of 100 000 words. The word length varied from 1 to 25 characters, but the length range of 8–10 characters covered 41.3% of the dictionary and that of 7–11 covered 62.3% of it (more specific data are given below, in Section 27.6). Therefore, this feature is often accompanied by stronger ones [43, 57].

Characters at fixed positions. Sometimes selecting procedures make use of characters situated at word positions where an error rarely occurs. The keyboard input commonly employs the first letter of a word, optical character recognizers take advantage of both first and last characters (at least one of them is expected to be correct [55, 59]), the acoustic input may use stressed vowels ([51], Chapter 8). The fundamental drawback of this feature is its poor tolerance for disturbance: if the test character is wrong then the proper candidate will be missed for sure. Another potential drawback derives from the nonuniform distribution of alphabet characters at any position, which gives an irregular dictionary classification again. This effect can be decreased by involving adjacent characters [52], but they are even less reliable for selection procedures.

Numeric values calculated from the set and the sequence of word characters via certain functions. These values are usually used for hashing [55]. A pre-recognition procedure selects candidates with values differing from the input word value by no more than some threshold. This selecting technique is rather fast but does not assure success with various types of errors, as we have already mentioned.

***n*-grams,** i.e. chains of n neighboring characters (in practice one can meet only digrams and trigrams) [60, 61, 41]. They are more tolerant than characters at fixed positions. Nevertheless, even a single substitution in a 6-lettered word damages half of the features (3 of 6 trigrams) and this prevents from developing reliable pre-recognition algorithms. As it was shown in Chapter 22, this disadvantage can not be improved any substantially.

Key characters taken in a word as N characters in ascending order of their occurrence in the given NL [59]. The role of features is played by various combinations of M key characters (N=const, M=const, $M < N$). Those combinations elaborate the idea of n-grams but are more tolerant for errors, particularly for those not touching a key character (rarely used). If there is a key character error, the number of tested candidates goes down with increasing M and N, but the number of features runs up exponentially, provoking an increase of the dictionary index size. (with N=4, M=3 from [59] the index is greater than the dictionary itself!).

The alphabetical makeup, i.e. the set of the characters of a word, their order and recurrence disregarded. Like the word length, it is a good invariant for various spelling errors: any single error alters no more than one element of its alphabetical makeup, and a transposition does not change it at all. In Russian (with its alphabet including 33 letters) a single error alters no more than 6.5% of features and even less if repeated characters are taken into account. Unfortunately, this feature can not be applied directly to the candidate selection: though it is easy to compare alphabetical makeup of two words, the problem is how to classify the whole dictionary in accordance with this feature.

We have compared the wellknown methods of the garbled word pre-recognition. Now we can conclude that the candidate selection at the pre-recognition stage should be founded on the most robust features, i.e. on the word length and the alphabetical makeup. It will allow us to apply q-tables (Chapters 25–26) or distance calculations to the final recognition. The next section proposes a method to classify a dictionary with these two features.

27.2 An error-tolerant dictionary classification method

As we noticed in Chapter 18, the orientated linguistic approach prefers an explicit dictionary that comprises all the wordforms responsible for the identification of subtexts determining a proper reaction. Furthermore, we saw that a dictionary could contain not only words but word-combinations used in the problem domain address language. It makes us consider two kinds of spaces in written NL texts: the first one divides a word-combination into parts (we treat it as an alphabetical character called "blank") and the second one separates words or word-combinations in a text (it is like a punctuation mark and we call it "separator" or just "space").

After this note we are starting a discussion about our dictionary classification method. To start with, we shall introduce a new notation (for this chapter only!). Let $A = \{a_1, a_2, \ldots, a_S\}$ be an alphabet of S characters (the "blank" included); let there be a dictionary

$$D = \{D_i^{(l)}:\ D_i^{(l)} = (d_{1,i}\, d_{2,i}\, \ldots\, d_{l,i}),\ d_{k,i} \in A,\ k \in \overline{1,l},\ i \in \overline{1,N_l},\ l \in \overline{1,L}\,\}$$

comprising $N = \sum_{l=1}^{L} N_l$ words of length no more than L. N_l designates the number of words with the length of l.

The classification is made in two stages.

Stage 1

Let us break the dictionary into L subdictionaries in accordance with the word length feature:

$$D = V_1 \cup V_2 \cup \ldots \cup V_L, \quad V_l = \{D_i^{(l)} : i \in \overline{1, N_l}\}, \quad l \in \overline{1, L}$$

The following operations are similar for all the subdictionaries; thus we fix some value l and re-denote V_l as $W = \{W_1, \ldots, W_n\}$, $n = N_l$, where $W_j = (w_{j,1}\, w_{j,2}\, \ldots\, w_{j,l})$, $w_{j,k} \in A$ is a wordform (or a word-combination).

Definition 27.1 *The characteristic vector (CV) of the word* $W_j \in W$ *is a vector* $\boldsymbol{R}(W_j) = (r_1, r_2, \ldots, r_S)$ *such that*

$$r_p = \begin{cases} 0: & \forall u \in \overline{1,l} \quad w_{j,u} \neq a_p \\ 1: & \exists u \in \overline{1,l} \quad w_{j,u} = a_p \end{cases}, \quad p \in \overline{1, S}$$

In other words, the CV dimension equals the alphabet size and a CV component is 1 if the word contains the corresponding letter of the alphabet. The rest of components are zero-valued. If the alphabetical order is fixed, the CV uniquely determines the word alphabetical makeup. Nevertheless, it cannot determine the word itself (for instance, the words "dictionary" and "indicatory" have identical CV's).

Using the alphabetical makeup, we shall estimate the likeness of two words W' and W'' as the Hamming distance between their CV's:

$$\mathcal{H}(\boldsymbol{R}(W'), \boldsymbol{R}(W'')) = |\boldsymbol{R}(W') \oplus \boldsymbol{R}(W'')| \tag{27.1}$$

The symbol $\oplus$ stands for a component-wise modulo 2 summation, $|\ldots|$ means a Hamming module calculation, i.e. how many components are equal to 1.

Suppose that W' is a correct word and W'' is a misspelled variation with m_1 characters substituted, m_2 characters deleted and m_3 characters inserted. As for transpositions, the features in use are tolerant for them. It is obvious that

$$\mathcal{H}(\boldsymbol{R}(W'), \boldsymbol{R}(W'')) \leq 2m_1 + m_2 + m_3 , \tag{27.2}$$

and, consequently,

$$\mathcal{H}(\boldsymbol{R}(W'), \boldsymbol{R}(W'')) \leq 2m , \tag{27.3}$$

where m is the total of errors in the word W''. Now we may go down to the second stage of the process.

Stage 2

The second stage should break W into subsets called clusters. Inside a cluster, words must be close in terms of the distance given by Eq. (27.1). At the same time, words from different clusters must be as far from each other as possible. Evidently, one can do this in many ways if there are no additional restrictions on the number of clusters or on their size. The heterogeneity of the problem imposes a simple restriction removing this non-uniqueness.

Actually, with a set of cluster features fixed, the pre-recognition process labor consumption (for definiteness sake, estimated as computation time) is given by a function $\varphi(M)$ depending only on the number M of partition clusters. The final recognition labor consumption, resulted from loading a cluster into RAM and testing all the words, is given by a function $\psi(q)$ depending only on the cluster size, i.e. on the number q of its words. The functions φ and ψ are specifically determined by a specific implementation, but practice allows us to think them linear (as the first approximation):

$$\begin{cases} \varphi(M) & = & K_1 \cdot M \\ \psi(q) & = & K_2 + K_3 \cdot q \\ K_1, K_2, K_3 = const > 0 \end{cases} \tag{27.4}$$

Now say we have built a uniform classification (this situation is the most attractive one), i.e. $q = n/M$. Then the recognizing algorithm labor consumption is

$$\theta(q) = \varphi\left(\frac{n}{q}\right) + \psi(q) \tag{27.5}$$

Substituting Eq. (27.4) into Eq. (27.5) and differentiating by q we obtain an extremum condition as follows:

$$\frac{d\theta}{dq} = K_3 - \frac{K_1 \cdot n}{q^2} = 0 \tag{27.6}$$

It gives the final value q^* minimizing the total labor consumption Eq. (27.5):

$$q^* = \sqrt{\frac{K_1 \cdot n}{K_3}} \tag{27.7}$$

It is interesting that $\varphi(q^*)$ equals $\psi(q^*)$, except for an additive constant K_2, i.e. the final recognition and the pre-recognition share the labor consumption equally in the optimum case.[†]

The obtained value q^* of the average number of words in a cluster is a reference-point for the classifying procedure. As we can not do without it, let us assume that

$$q \leq \kappa \cdot q^* , \tag{27.8}$$

where $\kappa > 1$ is a reserve coefficient absorbing a classification nonuniformity. Using Eq. (27.8) we shall construct a deterministic algorithm $\mathcal{D}$ to break a subdictionary into clusters

$$\begin{cases} W = C_1 \cup C_2 \cup \ldots \cup C_M \\ \forall i \neq j \quad C_i \cap C_j = \emptyset \end{cases} \tag{27.9}$$

[†]We are thankful to M.A.Kronrod who drew our attention to this fact.

Algorithm $\mathcal{D}$

Step 1. Assume $C_0 = W$ (all the words are placed in one cluster).

Step 2. Take the next cluster C_i that does not meet condition Eq. (27.8). If no such a cluster, the desired classification Eq. (27.9) is ready (the only thing to do is to renumber the built clusters).

Step 3. Take an alphabetical character $a_s \in A$ that complies with two conditions:

$$\begin{cases} \exists\, W' = (w'_1 w'_2 \ldots w'_l) \in W, & \exists\, k' \in \overline{1,l}: \quad w'_{k'} = a_s \quad (27.10) \\ \exists\, W'' = (w''_1 w''_2 \ldots w''_l) \in W, & \forall\, k'' \in \overline{1,l}: \quad w''_{k''} \neq a_s \quad (27.11) \end{cases}$$

In other words, we take a character occurring in some words of the cluster but not in all of them. The best choice method must be discussed separately. Let us prefer the character splitting the set into as equally powered subsets as possible. This will result in a more balanced tree.

Step 4. Break C_i cluster into two clusters C'_i and C''_i: C'_i contains all the words under Eq. (27.10) and C''_i—under Eq. (27.11). Then go to step 2.

The algorithm $\mathcal{D}$ is finite because every step 4 breaks a cluster down into two nonempty clusters (the case of W including more than $\kappa \cdot q^*$ words with identical alphabetical makeups never occurs in practice). The obtained clusters can not intersect and any word from W belongs to some cluster, thus we get an Eq. (27.9)-like cluster system. In the following section we shall explore some properties of this classification.

27.3 Properties of clusters. The theorem on the errorless search uniqueness

Let us try to generalize word features for the whole of a cluster. Without this done, we shall never ever pre-recognize an appropriate cluster. This concerns only the alphabetical makeup, because the first stage of the classification fills each cluster with words of the same length; this length is a key feature of the whole cluster.

Definition 27.2 *The vector* $\boldsymbol{R}_{AND}(C) = \boldsymbol{R}(W_1) \wedge \ldots \wedge \boldsymbol{R}(W_q)$ *is termed* AND-vector *of a cluster* $C = \{W_1, \ldots, W_q\} \subseteq W$ *and the vector* $\boldsymbol{R}_{OR}(C) = \boldsymbol{R}(W_1) \vee \ldots \vee \boldsymbol{R}(W_q)$ *is referred to as* OR-vector *of this cluster ($\wedge$ and $\vee$ are component-wise disjunction and conjunction respectively).*

In other words, ones of the AND-vector correspond to characters met in all the words of the cluster and zeros of the OR-vector correspond to characters not occurring in these words. Intuition suggests that these vectors and algorithm $\mathcal{D}$ are correlated. We shall reveal this correlation later. Now we are going to prove an assertion that will support the following discussion.

Lemma 27.1 *An Eq. (27.9)-like cluster set built by the algorithm $\mathcal{D}$ cannot have a pair of clusters with identical AND-vectors.*

Proof: Step 4 of the algorithm $\mathcal{D}$ breaks the next cluster $\widetilde{C}$ not under Eq. (27.8) condition into two clusters C' and C''. Their AND-vectors differ at least in the s-th component; a_s is the alphabetical character chosen at step 3. Succeeding operations on those clusters will not touch the s-th component of the AND-vectors, because the character a_s will never meet the selecting conditions of step 3 again. Thus, no cluster derived from C' can possess the same AND-vector as a cluster derived from C''. As for clusters derived from C' (or from C'') in the subsequent process, the same reasoning can be applied. The starting cluster C_0 can be taken for $\widetilde{C}$ as well, meaning that the assertion of the lemma is proved.

Corollary 27.1 *A cluster set produced by the algorithm $\mathcal{D}$ includes no more than one cluster with a zero AND-vector.*

AND/OR-vectors will be used as pre-recognition features. For this purpose we should define the distance between an arbitrary word W_0 and a cluster C as follows:

$$\rho(W_0, C) = (S - |\boldsymbol{R}_{AND}(C) \Rightarrow \boldsymbol{R}(W_0)|) + (S - |\boldsymbol{R}(W_0) \Rightarrow \boldsymbol{R}_{OR}(C)|), \quad (27.12)$$

with $\Rightarrow$ denoting a component-wise implication.

The physical meaning of Eq. (27.12) is that the distance between W_0 and C is a sum of two terms. The first one is the number of characters present in each word of C but absent in W_0. The second term is how many characters of W_0 do not occur in the words of C at all.

Now let us consider an arbitrary word $W_j \in C$. The Hamming distance between its characteristic vector and that of the word W_0 is the number of their mismatching components by definition. In detail, this distance can be considered as a sum of two items. The first one is the number of alphabet characters that are present in W_j and absent in W_0. This item is no less than the first term to the right of Eq. (27.12) because only a part of those characters will nullify the implication result (namely, the characters of W_j that are marked by 1 in $\boldsymbol{R}_{AND}(C)$). The second item is the number of characters that are present in W_0 and absent in W_j. It is evidently greater than or equal to the second term of Eq. (27.12), since the vector $\boldsymbol{R}_{OR}(C)$ has no more zeros than $\boldsymbol{R}(W_j)$. Thus,

$$\forall W_j \in C \quad \rho(W_0, C) \le \mathcal{H}(\boldsymbol{R}(W_0), \boldsymbol{R}(W_j)) \quad (27.13)$$

where the equality case corresponds to all the words of the cluster C having the same alphabetical makeup.

Note that Eq. (27.13) is true for any word W_0, including garbled ones. Though function Eq. (27.12) is not a "distance" in the strict mathematical sense, its value (the minimum of distances from W_0 to all the words of a cluster) appears to be useful for rejecting clusters without a proper candidate for W_0. To judge the efficiency of this rejection (at least in errorless cases), we are proving the theorem on the errorless search uniqueness.

Theorem 27.1 *Let there be a word* $W_0 \in W$ *and an Eq. (27.9)-like cluster set produced by the algorithm* $\mathcal{D}$. *Then there exists one and only one cluster* $C^* \in \{C_1, \ldots, C_M\}$ *with* $\rho(W_0, C^*) = 0$.

Proof: The existence of such a cluster is evident: it is the cluster containing W_0. In fact, the OR-vector is defined so that all its components responding to the characters of W_0 are equal to 1 thus nullifying the second term to the right of Eq. (27.12). At the same time, a one-valued component of the AND-vector must respond to a character (characters) of W_0, i.e. the first term is 0 too. As a result, $\rho(W_0, C^*) = 0$.

For the uniqueness to be proved, let us assume the opposite: $\exists\, C', C'' \subset W$ that $\rho(W_0, C') = \rho(W_0, C'') = 0$. New symbols:

$\vec{0}$ is an S-dimensional vector with all its components being 0;

$\vec{1}$ is an S-dimensional vector with all its components being 1;

δ_k is an S-dimensional vector with its k-th component being 1 and the rest being 0.

It follows from the assumption that W_0 contains all the alphabetical characters responding to 1's in the AND-vectors of both clusters, and vise versa, all the characters of W_0 respond to 1's in the OR-vectors of both clusters, i.e.

$$\begin{cases} (\boldsymbol{R}_{AND}(C') \Rightarrow \boldsymbol{R}(W_0)) \ \wedge \ (\boldsymbol{R}_{AND}(C'') \Rightarrow \boldsymbol{R}(W_0)) = \vec{1} & (27.14) \\ (\boldsymbol{R}(W_0) \Rightarrow \boldsymbol{R}_{OR}(C')) \ \wedge \ (\boldsymbol{R}(W_0) \Rightarrow \boldsymbol{R}_{OR}(C'')) = \vec{1} & (27.15) \end{cases}$$

Let us consider an arbitrary character a_k of W_0. It means that the word CV has the appropriate component $r_k = 1$. There are three possibilities:

(A) a_k belongs to the AND-vectors of both clusters;

(B) a_k belongs to none of the AND-vectors;

(C) a_k belongs to only one of these AND-vectors.

We shall discuss them in succession.

(A) $\boldsymbol{R}_{AND}(C') \wedge \delta_k = \boldsymbol{R}_{AND}(C'') \wedge \delta_k = \delta_k$.

Let us take another $a_k \in W_0$. It must exist. Otherwise, $\boldsymbol{R}_{AND}(C') = \boldsymbol{R}_{AND}(C'')$ because all their components responding to the characters of W_0 are 1's and the rest are 0's to preserve Eq. (27.14). But Lemma 27.1 says that the AND-vectors can not be equal. It means that there are a_k leading to another possibility.

(B) $\boldsymbol{R}_{AND}(C') \wedge \delta_k = \boldsymbol{R}_{AND}(C'') \wedge \delta_k = \vec{0}$.
Here we do the same, taking another a_k. If all the characters a_k are within this possibility, i.e.

$$\forall k : (r_k = 1) \Rightarrow (\boldsymbol{R}_{AND}(C') \wedge \delta_k = \boldsymbol{R}_{AND}(C'') \wedge \delta_k = \vec{0}),$$

then $\boldsymbol{R}_{AND}(C') = \boldsymbol{R}_{AND}(C'') = \vec{0}$. In fact, if both AND-vectors were nonzero vectors, their one-valued components would break Eq. (27.14): they respond to zeros in the CV of W_0. At the same time, the corollary of Lemma 27.1 asserts that the algorithm $\mathcal{D}$ can construct no more than one cluster with the zero AND-vector.

Note that these two possibilities together cannot cover all the characters of the word W_0 either. In fact, for the distance Eq. (27.12) to be 0, the AND-vectors of both clusters must have zero components responding to characters absent in W_0. As for the rest of components, both vectors have them respectively equal. It means that the AND-vectors are identical, and this fact runs counter to the proved lemma.

(C) The discussion above makes us conclude that the word W_0 never fails to contain a character a_k that belongs to the AND-vector of only one cluster. For definiteness sake we shall assume

$$\begin{cases} \boldsymbol{R}_{AND}(C') \wedge \delta_k = \vec{1} \\ \boldsymbol{R}_{AND}(C'') \wedge \delta_k = \vec{0} \end{cases} \tag{27.16}$$

with

$$\boldsymbol{R}_{OR}(C') \wedge \delta_k = \boldsymbol{R}_{OR}(C'') \wedge \delta_k = \vec{1}. \tag{27.17}$$

The latter means that C'' includes a word with a_k in.

Let us take a look at where C' and C'' clusters are situated in the binary tree representing the algorithm $\mathcal{D}$ (Fig. 27.1). Each node of the tree breaks a current subset of the initial dictionary W into two subsets of words containing and missing respectively some alphabetical character a_s. Either of these subsets is represented by two subtrees situated below the node (let us agree the left subtree to carry words with a_s and the right one to carry words missing a_s). If a subtree meets condition Eq. (27.8), it forms one of the desired clusters as the figure shows.

Suppose G to be the node where the routes to C' and C'' diverge (it may be the root of the tree). If we admit the dichotomy by a_k to take place in the point G, C'' can not include a word with this character and we shall obtain a contradiction. If another point F does the same and this point is situated above G (closer to the root), then the words of both clusters must either include or miss a_k. This contradicts to Eq. (27.16) or to Eq. (27.17). If the character a_k splits the subtree in a point P below G or if it has not been used as a splitter on the route to C' (i.e. it is a part of the AND-vector of C' accidentally), then words

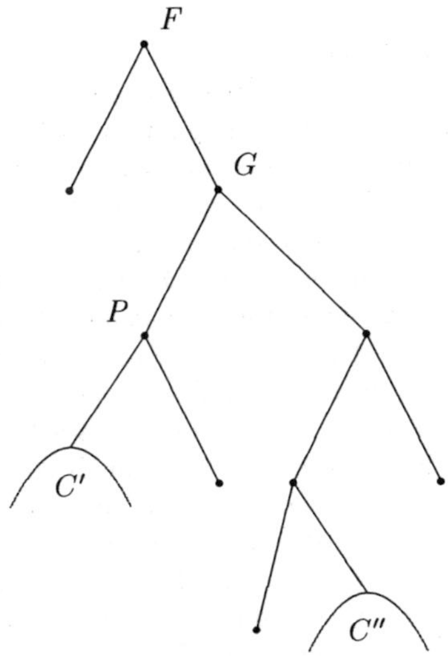

Figure 27.1

with a_k can seem to be found in C''. However, $\rho(W_0, C') = \rho(W_0, C'') = 0$ and any nonzero component of $\boldsymbol{R}_{AND}(C')$ responds to a nonzero component of either $\boldsymbol{R}_{AND}(C'')$ or $\boldsymbol{R}_{OR}(C'')$, including the component responding to the character that breaks the tree in point G. This conclusion runs counter to the algorithm $\mathcal{D}$ construction because the dichotomy by some character in the point G guarantees that no word of C'' contains this character and the appropriate components of both vectors are 0. Thus, we obtain a contradiction, Q.E.D.

This theorem is very important in practice. The described dictionary classifying procedure provides a diskless spelling check facility: if there are two or more clusters corresponding to the input word length and nullifying the distance Eq. (27.12), then the input word is misspelled (or absent in the dictionary). Furthermore, the cluster of the correct word is defined uniquely, i.e. this word can be taken in a single disk operation. The following two chapters show how the pre-recognizer cooperates with the final recognizer.

27.4 A candidate pre-recognition algorithm under conditions of Postulate P23.1

The described dictionary classifying procedure allows constructing a disk dictionary with a *dictionary index* stored in memory. The index has two designations: to pre-recognize clusters with possible candidates and to locate these clusters in the external memory (to make them loadable and processable for the final recognition procedure).

Like the dictionary itself, the index is made up of records, each having feature and description components. However, a record corresponds to a cluster not a word. For the first mentioned designation to be met, a dictionary index record includes all the cluster features in use: a length of cluster words, the cluster AND-vector and the cluster OR-vector (most languages take only 12 bytes to store this information). As for second designation, a record keeps the cluster offset from the beginning of the dictionary file (usually, 4 bytes are enough). As a result, a cluster takes only 16 bytes of RAM but includes dozens of even hundreds of words. Anyone can afford that. Therefore, a record can carry some additional features peculiar to its cluster only as well as a page table entry and an activity counter necessary to arrange the disk dictionary as a virtual storage.

Let us discuss this storage technique in detail. The RAM region for dictionary clusters loading from the disk is divided into blocks (pages) of a size calculated by Eq. (27.8) for a cluster to fit a page. If a cluster is in the RAM and occupies a page, a special activity counter keeps track of calls. If such-and-such cluster is required to perform the candidate final recognition, its page table entry is checked up to know if the cluster is already in the RAM. If so, the system does not load it but just makes an increment of the appropriate counter. Otherwise, the cluster will be loaded into one of free pages and its counter will be initialized. If there is not any free page, then the system cleans the page with the smallest counter value (another strategy is also acceptable, for example, the page of the longest idle period is released). If the number of pages is great enough, the RAM will evidently collect the most necessary clusters and the average number of disk events will decrease.

As for additional features, one can use them to limit the final recognition search area. Sometimes all the words of some cluster obey a certain simple criterion; for instance, they may have the same first letter, or any of two fixed letters, etc. (In [52] we put forward several techniques of this kind). Since such features are secondary, they can not be generalized but if one manages to expose any, he should use them to make his search procedure more purposeful.

Now let us describe how the recognition procedure uses the dictionary and its index. At first, let us consider the simplest case of Postulate P23.1 admitted. This postulate asserts that an input word contains no more than one error. This error can be either an insertion, or a deletion, or a substitution (transpositions do not affect our pre-recognition algorithm, as we have already noticed). Under these conditions, a possibly garbled word W_0 of length l is looked up in the dictionary as follows:

Step 1. Make a cluster queue, initially empty. Using the dictionary index in the memory and Eq. (27.12), calculate the distance $\rho(W_0, C_j)$ for all clusters C_j with the length feature of l. There are 3 subcases:

(a) Only one cluster with $\rho(W_0, C_j) = 0$ is found. Then load this cluster in the RAM and process it by any final recognition procedure (for instance, with the use of q-tables — see Chapter 26). If the word W_0 is found, stop the search; otherwise, put j at the beginning of the queue and go to step 2.

(b) If there are several clusters with $\rho(W_0, C_j) = 0$ then put their numbers into the queue and go to step 2, because the proved theorem says that the word W_0 can not be errorless.

(c) If no cluster with $\rho(W_0, C_j) = 0$ then go to step 2.

Step 2. At the end of the queue put the numbers of clusters with $\rho(W_0, C_j) = 1$ and then with $\rho(W_0, C_j) = 2$. Eqs. (27.13) and (27.3) advise to reject other clusters with words of the length l.

Step 3. Load the clusters into the RAM one by one in accordance with the queue. Search them for candidates with a single error. (To optimize the function of the virtual memory, one should start the search procedure from already loaded clusters). If no candidates, go to step 4. If a candidate with a single error is found, stop the algorithm or go to step 4 in dependence of whether the first candidate is enough or a post-search choice will be made among all candidates.

Step 4. Using the dictionary index, calculate distances Eq. (27.12) from the input word to all clusters with the length feature of $l+1$ (assuming here that a character is more likely to be deleted than inserted). The final recognition operates clusters C_j with $\rho(W_0, C_j) \leq 1$ because a candidate must match the input word completely, except for the deleted character. All those clusters are placed into the queue.

Step 5. All the clusters selected at the previous step are searched for candidates with a single error, just like it was done at step 3. Next, the work is stopped or continued at step 6.

Step 6. Similar to step 4, but the length feature equals $l-1$, i.e. the input word is supposed to contain an extra character. Clusters with $\rho(W_0, C_j) \leq 1$ are transferred to the final recognition procedure by putting them into the queue.

Step 7. Similar to step 5. After this step, make the final selection among the candidates. If no candidates found, the input word is absent in the dictionary or Postulate P23.1 is violated.

Here go some comments on the above described procedure. Naturally, first comes an attempt to find a word as a correct one, because the Theorem 27.1 proposes the fastest way to do that. However, if the errorless search is not successful at the final recognition stage, the procedure makes the final recognition in the already loaded clusters instead of the pre-recognition with a weakened admissible distance from the input word. This trick is done to avoid repeated loadings.

Thus, the described procedure performs the pre-recognition (steps 1(b), 1(c), 2, 4, 6) and the final recognition (steps 1(a), 3, 5, 7) alternately. The same is peculiar to the general case discussed in the next section.

27.5 A pre-recognition algorithm in the general case

The more errors in a word, the more difficult to find its correct candidate in the dictionary; it is common knowledge. A greater dictionary complicates the problem. People overcome this trouble, analyzing the context and the object domain information. Today our system does not use any context, but the object domain is taken into account when the address language dictionary is being compiled. Nevertheless, practice suggest limiting the number of admissible errors per word by some λ (usually $\lambda = 1$ or $\lambda = 2$).

We propose the following algorithm $\mathcal{R}$ to pre-recognize candidates for a word W_0 of length l. This algorithm generalizes the procedure of the previous section.

Algorithm $\mathcal{R}$

Step 1. Calculate the distance $\rho(W_0, C_j)$ for all clusters C_j with the length feature of l and arrange the cluster queue in ascending order of this distance but no more than 2λ (use Eq. (27.3)).

Step 2. Pick up clusters from the queue, make the final recognition in them and arrange the found candidates in ascending order of the number of errors (no more than λ). If there is a candidate with 0 errors, stop the work. If there is a candidate with 1 error, the work is terminated or continued depending on if the task is to find all suitable variants with a single error.

Step 3. Calculate the distance Eq. (27.12) for all clusters with the length feature of $l + 1$ and arrange the queue of clusters with distances no more than $2\lambda - 1$ (due to Eq. (27.2) and one deletion in W_0 pre-supposed).

Step 4. Similar to step 2. The only difference is that an errorless candidate cannot be found here since the number of errors is no less than 1.

Step 5. Similar to step 3 but for clusters with the length feature of $l - 1$, supposing one insertion in the word W_0.

Step 6. The same as step 4 and so on.

The following steps of algorithm $\mathcal{R}$ reproduce steps 3–6, increasing a length deviation:

$$l + 2, l - 2, \ldots, l + \lambda, l - \lambda .$$

When analyzing words of $l \pm t$, the queue is formed of clusters with the distance Eq. (27.12) no more than $2\lambda - t$. As we have already said, the algorithm can be terminated as soon as an acceptable candidate is found or as the search time limit is over.

One could see that the general case demanded much more clusters to be loaded for the final recognition stage. In particular, a greater λ results in a greater value of t, calling for more clusters at step 2 and similar steps. That is why the importance of the mentioned additional features is difficult to overestimate. The only problem is that one cannot reveal those features before clusters are constructed. So, we do not propose any enhancement in order that the algorithm

Table 27.1

l	N_l	l	N_l	l	N_l	l	N_l	l	N_l
1	11	6	6281	11	10101	16	1391	21	58
2	85	7	9318	12	7672	17	824	22	21
3	541	8	12477	13	5409	18	470	23	6
4	1762	9	13235	14	3739	19	256	24	10
5	3953	10	12449	15	2227	20	118	25	1

$\mathcal{D}$ (Section 27.2) could generate additional features automatically when building an Eq. (27.9)-like cluster set. Of course, it does not prevent from using special algorithms to reveal special features for a ready cluster. Such features could be as far sophisticated as easy to test. As a result, we can conclude that developing a smart feature system is for the most part a sort of art, especially in the general case.

27.6 An experimental test of the method

In the case of garbled words we have not obtained any theoretical estimates looking like the Theorem 27.1. For this reason we had to make an experiment to test the described pre-recognition method before integrating it into our system.

We used a Russian dictionary of $N = 92\,415$ separate words, taking only main wordforms (Nouns: nominative case, singular; Verbs: the infinitive; etc.). The lengths of the alphabet and of the longest word were $S = 32$ and $L = 25$ respectively. The word length distribution is shown in Table 27.1.

We tried two versions of clusterization. They differed by the appearance of condition Eq. (27.8) used in the algorithm $\mathcal{D}$.

The condition of the first version established an upper limit on the number of words per cluster: $q \leq 2\sqrt{N_l}$. The algorithm built 836 clusters (Table 27.2). The first column gives lengths of subdictionary words, the second one gives the number of clusters built by the algorithm $\mathcal{D}$ over each subdictionary. (Data on lengths 1, 2, 21–25 are taken away from the table because each of those subdictionaries produced a sole cluster). The words were distributed in clusters as shown in columns 3–7 giving respectively the minimum, the lower quartile, the median, the upper quartile and the maximum of words per cluster. The right side of the table illustrates the behavior of the AND-vectors. It demonstrates how many of the built clusters had this or that value of $|\boldsymbol{R}_{AND}(C_j)|$ from the range on the top of the table.

In the second version the disk room per cluster was limited by 1 Kbyte, i.e. $q \leq 1024/l$, with l as a cluster word length (since the experiment was just a test, dictionary records did not include any additional information). The algorithm $\mathcal{D}$ built 1313 clusters. Table 27.3 gives all the information on them in the manner similar to that of Table 27.2.

Each cluster index record took 16 bytes with 9 of them representing the features. The total size of the dictionary index was 13 Kbytes in the first version and 21 Kbytes in the second one.

The above proposed algorithm $\mathcal{R}$ used to be run on a personal computer. For the experiment we had prepared a testing set of 4 word groups, 2500 words each (100 words of each possible length, taken from the dictionary randomly). The words of each group were defected by a single error of the same type: either a substitution, or a transposition, or an insertion, or a deletion. In this way the experiment simulated all kinds of errors as equiprobable which is rather a rough approximation.

As a base of comparison we used the number of clusters selected for the final recognition, i.e. the number of disk events. This removed the computer performance from our consideration. The algorithm $\mathcal{R}$ work results are given in Fig. 27.6 and 27.6. Both versions are illustrated by an average number of disk events and a median of these events. The percentage of words recognized in a single step (in its dependence of the word length) is given in Fig. 27.6. This figure shows that 50–60% of one-error words are usually recognized as quickly as errorless words. Since an error is an accident rather than a rule, one disk operation is enough to recognize most words.

This chapter brings to a close the description of our research in the field of computer NL understanding. The obtained results prove the possibility to develop practical systems with appropriate characteristics. What is more, some systems of the kind have already been brought into service. Thus the understanding problem gives way to the problem of entering texts to be understood. In our opinion, a text entering facility must be as natural as possible, meaning a speaker independent continuous speech input. At the same time, this worthful purpose should not obscure the question of high reliability. The last chapter of the book makes a "bridge" to this new problem.

Table 27.2

l	M_l	Words per cluster					Clusters with $\boldsymbol{R}_{AND}$ value of								
		ξ_0	$\xi_{\frac{1}{4}}$	$\xi_{\frac{1}{2}}$	$\xi_{\frac{3}{4}}$	ξ_1	0	1	2	3	4	5	6	7	8
3	25	10	12	14	23	47	1	6	18	0	0	0	0	0	0
4	36	12	29	48	73	84	1	6	20	9	0	0	0	0	0
5	54	23	46	70	102	126	1	7	18	26	2	0	0	0	0
6	63	38	73	95	123	158	1	6	16	28	12	0	0	0	0
7	68	47	105	145	163	192	1	6	17	23	17	4	0	0	0
8	80	48	127	158	189	221	1	6	16	25	19	11	2	0	0
9	83	85	124	160	196	229	1	7	17	24	20	13	1	0	0
10	73	83	132	178	200	220	1	6	14	22	16	11	3	0	0
11	68	76	130	151	170	194	1	6	15	20	12	12	2	0	0
12	66	61	101	116	129	167	1	6	13	22	16	5	3	0	0
13	58	57	83	90	96	144	1	4	10	20	14	8	1	0	0
14	41	47	76	94	105	122	1	4	10	11	6	7	2	0	0
15	32	38	59	71	79	91	1	5	8	10	6	2	0	0	0
16	25	33	45	52	67	75	1	2	9	6	2	4	1	0	0
17	20	20	35	42	50	53	1	1	7	6	4	1	0	0	0
18	17	17	24	26	29	38	0	2	4	3	3	4	1	0	0
19	12	14	16	20	24	30	1	1	0	3	3	2	1	0	1
20	8	11	12	14	15	19	0	1	1	4	0	1	0	0	1

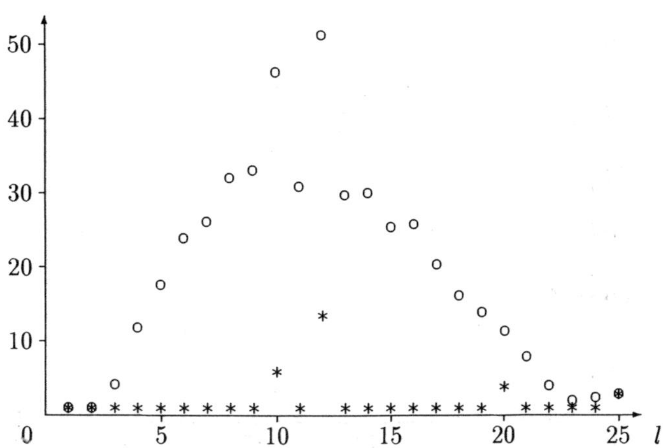

Figure 27.2: Number of clusters to load (version 1)
o average * median

Table 27.3

l	M_l	Words per cluster ξ_0	$\xi_{\frac{1}{4}}$	$\xi_{\frac{1}{2}}$	$\xi_{\frac{3}{4}}$	ξ_1	Clusters with $\boldsymbol{R}_{AND}$ value of 0	1	2	3	4	5	6	7	8
3	3	123		136		282	1	2	0	0	0	0	0	0	0
4	12	73	84	106	194	213	1	4	7	0	0	0	0	0	0
5	33	49	75	113	156	203	1	5	14	13	0	0	0	0	0
6	59	38	80	106	132	170	1	6	15	26	11	0	0	0	0
7	101	33	68	143	110	145	1	6	22	31	28	13	0	0	0
8	148	31	69	85	100	127	1	7	22	40	37	30	11	0	0
9	168	30	63	79	97	113	1	8	23	44	33	15	1	0	0
10	174	23	55	72	88	102	1	7	22	40	44	34	21	5	0
11	155	24	54	67	77	91	1	7	19	40	36	28	16	6	2
12	133	28	48	59	66	82	0	8	16	34	37	23	13	2	0
13	111	31	41	47	53	78	1	5	13	22	32	24	11	3	0
14	78	22	41	49	55	73	1	3	11	24	15	13	9	2	0
15	51	24	36	41	50	68	1	3	10	12	14	7	3	1	0
16	34	25	34	39	46	57	1	2	7	5	12	6	1	0	0
17	20	20	35	42	50	53	1	1	7	6	4	1	0	0	0
18	13	24	27	32	38	51	0	2	4	3	3	1	0	0	0
19	8	24	27	30	36	39	1	1	0	4	2	0	0	0	0
20	4	25	25	25	34	34	0	2	2	0	0	0	0	0	0
21	2	29	29	29	29	29	1	1	0	0	0	0	0	0	0

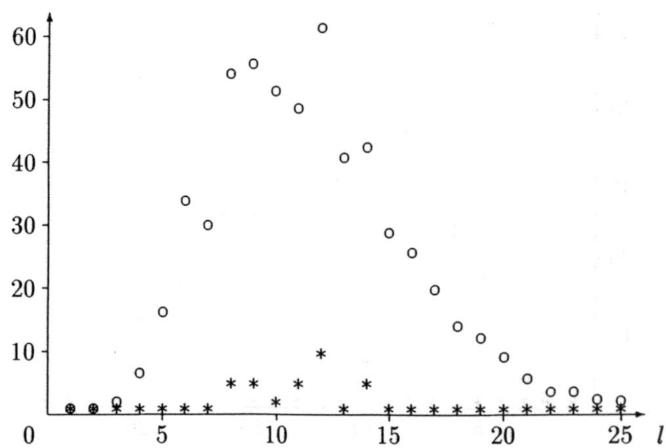

Figure 27.3: Number of clusters to load (version 2)
o average * median

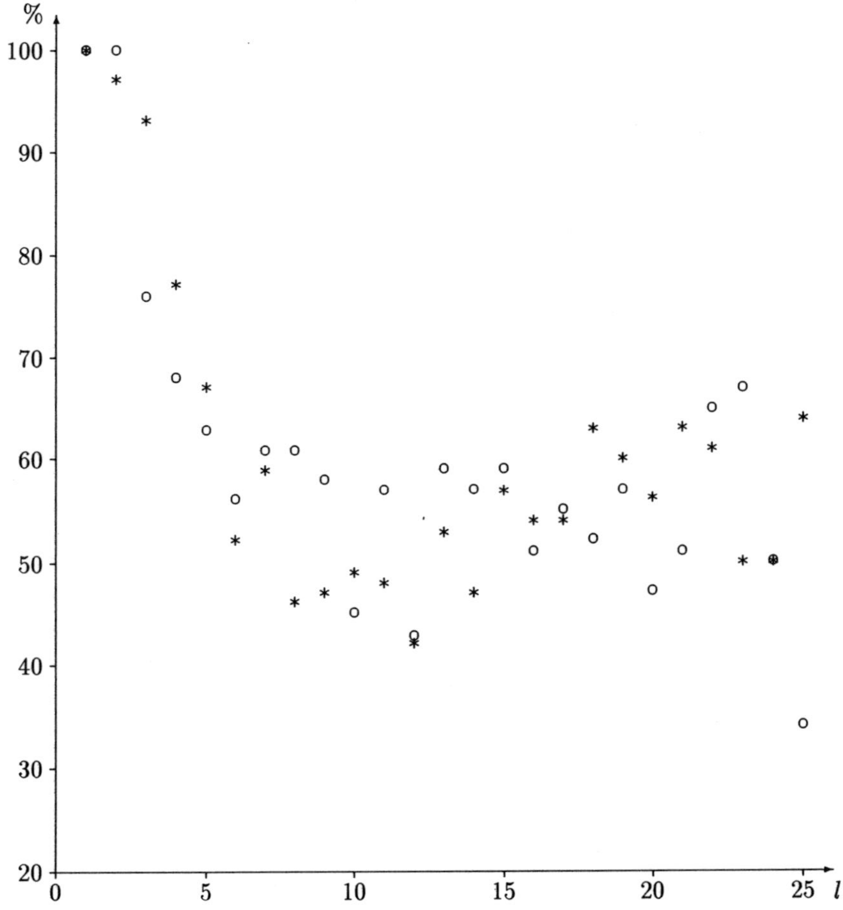

Figure 27.4: Percentage of words recognized in a single loading
o version 1 * version 2

Chapter 28
ORIENTATED LINGUISTICS AND ORAL SPEECH

28.1 Semantics as a tool for combating misunderstandings

With the book almost read, one can summarize it to answer the question: why can orientated linguistics ignore errors and provide a high reliability of text understanding? A brief answer is as follows: orientated linguistics leans upon a finite deterministic model of activity.

Let us give more details. NL misunderstandings stem from the ambiguity (non-uniexpressiveness) inherent in all NL texts. This ambiguity can be removed only by means of exhaustive *semantic* knowledge including pragmatics, a world model, etc. Studying the "entire language", conventional linguistics does not possess such knowledge for fundamental reasons. In fact, the "entire language" semantics reflects the entire world; thus it is as immense and unformalizable as the entire world itself.

This is where the main trait of orientated linguistics exposes itself. Due to the concepts of K-stationarity and NPD this linguistics is able to construct exhaustive semantic knowledge. What is more, desired knowledge already exists there: the developed *model of activity* is no other than a formal representation of the wanted exhaustive semantics.

It is this vigorous factor that enables orientated linguistic systems to have an extremely high understanding reliability and to be much less sensitive to errors than conventional linguistic systems. This fact used to be mentioned above, and we shall comment on it.

However, "much less sensitive to errors" does not mean "insensitive to errors". We cannot help remembering this circumstance when going to the next (or, may be, already current) stage. This problem is communication with the computer by means of *normal continuous speech* instead of the keyboard.

One could catch a glimpse of the grounds for this statement in the preceding stuff. Specifically speaking, an oral word is much more prone to dispersion than a written one. Ratio between radical and aesthetical errors in an oral speech symbolic (phonemic, for instance) representation is much worse than in written speech. All present-day investigations into the oral speech recognition attempt to overcome the mentioned dispersion. Nevertheless, their recognition reliability cannot actually exceed some "physical" threshold which is not too high.

This issue will be discussed in the next section.

In this connection a very amazing fact about orientated linguistics can be observed. This linguistics seemingly concerns the highest (i.e. semantic) level of NL understanding. Nevertheless, it unexpectedly proposes a source of increasing recognition reliability for the acoustic speech recognition, i.e. for a low level. This source is so generative that the said physical threshold can be overwhelmed.

The nature and operation of the orientated linguistic source of improvements will be considered in Section 28.3. As for the next section, it is devoted to the "physical" threshold. More specifically, we are going to discuss the limits that prevent conventional linguistic systems from having the 100% acoustic recognition capability.

28.2 Absolutely errorless computer understanding of free oral speech as a physically insoluble problem

In Introduction it was said that changing to a free acoustic speech input was a prerequisite for man-to-computer communication to become really natural. Here "free acoustic speech" means the speech type used in normal man-to-man communication: no artificial restrictions on the lexicon, intonations or speaking manner are permitted; words are said continuously; the speaker-independence is supposed. In this way we are coming to a self-contained problem which many scientists work at. This is the acoustic speech computer recognition problem.

For a better start, we shall review the up-to-date results obtained in the worldwide practice. Two characteristics are usually considered: the speech *freedom* and the recognition *reliability*. As a rule, the higher the former, the lower the latter. Both characteristics are compound. The speech freedom includes the degrees of lexical and phraseological freedoms, the speech continuity, the speaker-independence and some other factors. This characteristic is usually measured as a dictionary volume, because the other items are either binary (continuous - discontinuous, for instance) or difficult to evaluate. Just the same, the recognition reliability is a combination of several values: the correct recognition probability, the misrecognition probability, the missing probability, the "false alarm" probability. For this characteristic to become one-dimensional, the correct recognition probability is taken as the basic item called the correct recognition reliability almost everywhere, including this consideration. The misrecognition probability, as well as the missing or "false alarm" probabilities, is then regarded as the opposite event probability. Results of investigations are mostly reported in terms of these characteristics.

There are three common statements of the acoustic speech recognition problem: separate words or commands, connected texts said word by word, connected texts said continuously. Since only the third statement is really natural, we shall dwell on it. Each of these statements strongly depends on the system dictionary volume. Systems designed to be used in practice need a large dictionary, i.e. 20–30 thousand words. Another characteristic is the system speaker-dependence: whether the system functions with only one speaker, or can be adjusted to many speakers, or readily works with many speakers. Our concern is the third option, as it gives the highest speech freedom.

Systems of such capabilities were developed over many years. A lot of really interesting discoveries were made. Unfortunately, we have no room for even a brief review of these works. Therefore, we are presenting here only the main implication of such a review: the initially rapid increase in the correct recognition reliability was slowing down from year to year [63] and probably stopped at all by the current moment. In other words, enhancing recognition algorithms and input devices has brought the recognition reliability progress to a horizontal asymptote. The obvious conclusion is grievous: this asymptote is not 100% but *no more than 97%* (see [63, 64], for instance). It is unlikely that any further technological improvement will change the matter.

In Section 22.4 we observed the same phenomenon in written speech. Let us briefly remind its roots, paying more attention to oral speech.

First of all, a large dictionary never fails to contain a pair of identically spelled words with different meanings (polysemy, homonymy): band, pawn, etc. Oral speech complicates the case because there are acoustically identical words such as "scent", "cent", "sent". This group also includes acoustically similar words: a noise can objectively prevent them from being distinguished. Another problem comes as successive words merging to form a new word, which fact gives another objective reason for a system failure.

Obviously, even the most sophisticated technology will not completely recognize such words because they are *physically* indistinguishable from each other. The presence of these words in the system dictionary limits the acoustic recognition reliability to approximately 97%. This limit can be called the "physical" threshold. Let it be denoted as P_{sup}.

In the preceding section we mentioned that orientated linguistics nevertheless proposed tools for surmounting this threshold. The completely formalized semantic level provides a large dictionary decomposition into a group of much smaller subdictionaries, whose properties are much better in terms of our concern. We shall explain and prove this statement in the next section.

28.3 The dictionary decomposition theorem and the increase in the acoustic speech recognition reliability

In order to make a single consideration for both written and oral inputs we shall assume system input data to be a *chain of characters.* Those characters are letters when fed by the scanner or keyboard, or acoustic speech components (phonemes, for instance) when the microphone is used as an input device. Such chains are agreed to represent words of NL addresses.

Any business system dictionary comprises words of NL addresses occurred during the system training period. Let V stand for a set of words (wordforms) involved in the dictionary of a business system designed for routine activity. This set includes all the words used by the word source (S_G) in his addresses to the system. From the system K-stationarity it follows that S_G will always use the same words. The total number of these words is denoted as $N_t(V)$.

If S_G is a sane person, he likes to use a word for its meaning but not for its appearance. There is no determined correlation between the meaning of a word and its symbolic representation, to leave aside very fine poetic effects like the alliteration or the assonance. That is why we have to admit that the dictionary V includes $N_t(V)$ character chains selected from the set of all possible chains in a *random* manner. The latter set will be indicated by W; its cardinality is designated $N(W)$. A word length is denoted as n, the total number of alphabetical characters is represented by m. If a given language allows its words to vary in their lengths from 1 to n_{max}, then

$$N(W) = \sum_{n=1}^{n_{max}} 2^{n \log_2 m} . \tag{28.1}$$

The source transmits character chains via an information transmission channel (oral or written). As in any real channel, there is some noise: 1) individual pronunciation peculiarities (oral) or misspellings (written); 2) acoustic or printing imperfection. The noise garbles a chain so that it differs from the word pattern stored in the dictionary V. Let W' stand for this garbled chain. Apparently, this chain can also result from transmitting some other words similar to that meant by the source. The number of all dictionary words that can be transformed into W' by the channel noise will be denoted as $N_t(W|W')$.

As known, the triad $N_t(V)$, $N_t(W|W')$ and $N(W)$ (or the corresponding triad: the source entropy, the channel entropy and the set of chains entropy) form a complete premises system to pose the problem on the average probability of recognizing words going through the channel by the maximum likelihood rule. And it is this problem that we are interested in. In case of oral speech with the microphone input this problem is especially important.

Luckily, we do not have to invent an approach to solve this problem. In fact, the aforementioned problem fits the discrete noisy channel information transmission problem which is well studied in the information theory. It was C. Shannon who proposed the smartest solution to this problem [65].

Let us remind some concepts and notions connected with Shannon theorem on a discrete noisy channel.

There is an information source picking up messages from a set A of all possible messages. The cardinality of A is $N_t(A)$. A message from A is *randomly* encoded as a chain of n characters taken from an alphabet of m characters. Shannon considers chains ("code words") of the same length, i.e. a uniform code. In this case the set of all possible chains is denoted as B, and $N(B)$ stands for a cardinality of this set. Apparently,

$$N(B) = 2^{n \log_2 m} . \tag{28.2}$$

The value n is taken great enough to provide $N_t(A) < N(B)$. This allows selecting chain to encode messages from A. If chains are picked randomly, a sufficiently high n results in the fact that some chains are highly probable ("typical") in comparison with the others. The encoding set is therefore sure to include mostly high-probability chains, thus having rather a great code distance. By the way, it is the random choice of encoding chains that makes the speech recognition problem fit Shannon's problem. Though the former problem deals with a variable (within some range!) chain length and the latter considers a fixed one, this difference does not affect the essence of the issue. After this remark we are coming back to the classical problem.

Our way to describe the channel noise by means of the quantity $N_t(W|W')$ is, of course, borrowed from the classical problem where the same quantity would be denoted as $N_t(B|B')$.

Following Shannon, the introduced $N_t(A)$, $N_t(B|B')$ and $N(B)$ allow us to calculate the lower boundary of the average correct recognition probability for messages transmitted through the channel. Let us denote this probability as $\bar{P}_{cor}$. The method of calculating $\bar{P}_{cor}$ can be found in [65, 66], for example. For instance, $\bar{P}_{cor}$ is calculated as follows:

$$\bar{P}_{cor} > 1 - \frac{N_t(B|B')N_t(A)}{N(B)} \tag{28.3}$$

(after I.Lipkin, Eq.(7.32) in [66]).

Note that up to this moment the speech recognition problem has not been differing any essentially from the general problem considered in the information theory.

Fundamental differences appear as soon as we put forward the *main* problem: *how* to raise the lower boundary of the correct recognition probability $\bar{P}_{cor}$. The difference can be seen not only between the classical problem and the speech recognition problem. What is particularly important, the possibilities for solving this main problem turn out to be different in conventional and orientated linguistics. Therefore, we shall consider three cases:

1. The classical problem on the noisy discrete channel and its solution by Shannon;

2. The speech recognition problem in conventional linguistics;

3. The speech recognition problem in orientated linguistics.

These cases differ in which of the quantities in Eq. (28.3) can be controlled. Let us consider the cases one by one.

Case 1. The channel properties represented in Eq. (28.3) by $N_t(B|B')$ are considered as given and constant. By the way, the same situation takes place in the other cases. $N_t(A)$ is thought to be preset as well. Consequently, the only changeable quantity is $N(B)$. From Eq. (28.2) it follows that $N(B)$ depends on both n and m, but the dependence of n is stronger. And Shannon's wonderful result is that a sufficiently high n makes the lower boundary of $\bar{P}_{cor}$ as close to 1 as desired without the information transmission rate tending to 0.

Case 2. The value $N_t(W|W')$ is preset as above. In conventional linguistic developments the volume $N_t(V)$ of the ensemble V (the system dictionary) is also established; at least it cannot be reduced. And what is fatal for the case, $N(W)$ cannot be changed either, as we see from Eq. (28.1). Unlike case 1, existing words of the language cannot be lengthened to comply with our requirements. Just the same, the number m of phonemes (letters) is given and cannot be changed either.

Consequently, conventional linguistics has no means to raise the lower boundary of the average correct recognition probability $\bar{P}_{cor}$ in case of a "large" dictionary V.

Case 3. $N_t(W|W')$ and $N(W)$ are prescribed as in case 2. However, orientated linguistics allows *varying* the quantity $N_t(V)$. Let us discuss this statement.

The orientated linguistic model of activity is shaped as a polytrapezium (Chapter 3). If a problem is associated with the upper OPT, the subject's going down to the lowest elements (executable operations, Section 3.2) explicates a *decomposition* of the problem into subproblems. Let us look at subproblems involving an NL dialogue. In Chapter 11 it is said that S_G's addresses are nothing but a data complex concerning $t_{(b..)}$, t_k, t_{am}, t_w (i.e. NPD, the algorithm name, the algorithm arguments). This complex can be completed with t_{NIL} subtexts representing the man-to-man communication inertia. Any subproblem has an individual data complex, thus requiring an individual *subdictionary* of words from only this subproblem. No subproblem involves the whole dictionary V. (NB: Training sets indicate that t_{NIL} subtexts are somehow distributed among subproblems as well. Namely, a subproblem involves just a small part of the set t_{NIL} that is a part of the dictionary V in conventional linguistic systems.)

The aforesaid means that the polytrapezium decomposition of a problem is followed by the *decomposition of the system dictionary.* Thus, any subproblem dialogue never exceeds the subdictionary of the subproblem. As for actual subdictionary volumes, we can mention our latest system that was designed to reconstruct a criminal's face from an eyewitness's talking and pointing at the computer screen (we refer to this type of communication as the "conversation-demonstration" or "tell-and-show"). When developing a model of activity for this system, we found out that the average subdictionary volume equals 7.06 words with 1 word as the minimum and 19 words as the maximum. At the same time, the total dictionary volume ($N_t(V)$) is above 5000 words.

Let us work out why the dictionary decomposition is so advantageous. First of all, we should formally define this operation.

Definition 28.1 *The* decomposition *of a set (dictionary) V is a bounded set $\{V^*\}_I$ of its subsets:*

$$\{V^*\}_I \equiv \{V_1^*, \ldots, V_i^*, \ldots, V_I^*\}; \quad \forall i: \; V_i^* \neq \emptyset, \quad \bigcup_{i=1}^{I} V_i^* \subseteq V.$$

A subset V_i^* is spoken of as subdictionary with its cardinality denoted as $N_t(V_i^*)$.

A decomposition $\{V^*\}_I$ is termed *contractive* if the relation $V_i^* \subset V$ is a strict inclusion for $\forall i \in \overline{1, I}$.

Ratio between the cardinalities of the dictionary V and the subdictionary V_i^* is designated by k_i:

$$N_t(V) = k_i \, N_t(V_i^*) \,. \tag{28.4}$$

Evidently, a contractive decomposition gives

$$\forall i \; : \; k_i > 1 \,. \tag{28.5}$$

The OPT recursion theorem (Theorem 2.1) and, in particular its part on object domains nonintersecting readily suggest the conclusion that a polytrapezium always determines a *contractive decomposition.*

Now we are going to discuss the advantages of such a decomposition. Let us rewrite Eq. (28.3) to adjust it to the speech recognition problem. As before, we should change A, B and B' for V, W and W' respectively. Besides, we would like to remind that the upper boundary of $\bar{P}_{cor}$ in the speech recognition is less than 1 as opposed to the classical case of the information theory Eq. (28.3). Namely, the empirical upper boundary is established by the mentioned "physical" limit P_{sup} at the level of $P_{sup} \approx 0.97$. With this taken into account, the speech case changes Eq. (28.3) for the following:

$$P_{sup} \geq \bar{P}_{cor} > 1 - \frac{N_t(W|W') \, N_t(V)}{N(W)} \,. \tag{28.6}$$

For brevity sake we shall denote the fraction

$$\frac{N_t(W|W') \, N_t(V)}{N(W)}$$

as F. The whole expression in the right-hand part of the Eq. (28.6), i.e. the difference $1 - F$, will be designated by

$$P_{inf} \equiv 1 - F \,. \tag{28.7}$$

Then Eq. (28.6) can be rewritten for the dictionary V as follows:

$$P_{sup} \geq \bar{P}_{cor} > P_{inf} \,. \tag{28.8}$$

Let us go down to the subdictionary V_i^*. The average correct recognition probability for V_i^* is denoted as $\bar{P}_{i,cor}^*$. Obviously, the lower boundary of $\bar{P}_{i,cor}^*$ can be obtained by substituting $N_t(V)$ by $N_t(V_i^*)$ in the expression for F. Along with Eq. (28.4) it gives

$$\bar{P}_{i,cor}^* > 1 - \frac{1}{k_i} F \,. \tag{28.9}$$

The right-hand part of this inequality can be denoted as $P_{i,inf}^*$. Let us consider the following question: is it possible to make $P_{i,inf}^*$ equal or even greater than P_{sup} by varying k_i?

For this question to be answered, set $P_{i,inf}^*$ equal to P_{sup} and derive the necessary value of k_i from the resulting equation:

$$P_{sup} = 1 - \frac{1}{k_i} F \,,$$

or

$$k_i = \frac{F}{1 - P_{sup}} \,. \tag{28.10}$$

The value of F in Eq. (28.10) can be estimated by considering the worst case. For the dictionary V it is when $\bar{P}_{cor}$ in Eq. (28.8) is close to the lower boundary: $\bar{P}_{cor} \approx P_{inf}$, in other words. According to Eq. (28.7),

$$k_i = \frac{1 - P_{inf}}{1 - P_{sup}} \,.$$

This means that if

$$k_i \geq \frac{1 - P_{inf}}{1 - P_{sup}} \,, \tag{28.11}$$

then

$$\bar{P}_{i,cor}^* \geq P_{sup} \,, \tag{28.12}$$

Q.E.D.

For instance, with $P_{sup} = 0.97$ as before and $P_{inf} = 0.7$ we see that Eq. (28.12) is obtained with even $k_i \geq 10$. The practical example has the average k_i of about $5000/7.06 \approx 710$, convincing that a dictionary decomposition is sure to give $k_i > 10$. It means that orientated linguistics, unlike conventional one, can exceed the speech recognition reliability of the very speech recognizer with the dictionary V and, in particular *the "physical" limit* $P_{sup} \approx 0.97$.

This result is another simple application of the classical conclusions drawn by Shannon. Nevertheless, it is extremely important. That is why we dare state it as a theorem:

Theorem 28.1 *Let $\{V^*\}_I$ be a contractive decomposition of a dictionary V. If the volume of the subdictionary $V_i^* \in \{V^*\}_I$ is k_i times smaller then the volume of V then the lower boundary for $\bar{P}^*_{i,cor}$ goes up according to the Eq. (28.9). In particular, if k_i complies with Eq. (28.11), the lower boundary of $\bar{P}^*_{i,cor}$ equals or exceeds the "physical" limit.*

The above presented reasoning is a proof draft of this theorem. A complete proof is included in our next book devoted to the construction technology for real models of activity as well as to the development technology for orientated linguistic systems with the NL dialogue supported. This book is now in progress.

28.4 Additional comments

We see NL distributing similar words among different NPD's thus providing a very high probability of correct understanding (remember Table 22.1). This fact seems to be a miracle done by the one who created the language. Now we know what this miracle is and where it comes from. A random choice leads to quite non-random results; this fact never fails to amaze people who come in contact with probabilistic categories.

However, this increase in reliability is not gratis. In comparison with conventional linguistic systems, an orientated linguistic system demands at least two more development stages. Firstly, any particular situation should be provided with a model of activity. Secondly, this model should be thoroughly studied to clarify the training set structure. Then a training set should be accumulated and processed. Furthermore, any subdictionary should be preprocessed because it usually contains a subset of the set t_{NIL}. Words from "useful" subtexts (i.e. $t_{(b..)}$, t_k, t_{am}, t_w) and t_{NIL} subtexts should be compared in pairs to obtain necessary information for two operations:

1. A subdictionary can be cleared of t_{NIL} words differing from useful words so that they never result in errors.

2. The other words of the subdictionary can define the appropriate recognizing procedure structure and complexity. As a rule, the greater is the difference between objects to be recognized, the simpler is the procedure. It can be profitable to have different recognizing procedures for different subdictionaries and even for different words of a subdictionary. This is another tool for increasing the system efficiency, impossible in conventional linguistics. In orientated linguistics it becomes possible due to the reversed dictionary retrieval method. In fact, orientated linguistic techniques scan a text for a dictionary word, as opposed to conventional linguistics. It allows a dictionary entry of each subdictionary word to include an identifier or number of the appropriate recognizing procedure.

Certainly, these operations are possible and profitable owing to a small number of words in every subdictionary.

Orientated linguistic systems have some other peculiarities that are less clear but no less useful. Unfortunately, we have no room here to consider them. This will be done in our next book mentioned above.

Nevertheless, even the presented information gives an opportunity of appreciating the capabilities of orientated linguistics in both theoretical and practical aspects.

Conclusion: What Is Ahead?

Hopefully, the reader have got rather a comprehensive idea of orientated linguistics, its capabilities and methods. Now he may legitimately ask: "What is ahead?". Is it true that the theoretical research is accomplished and only practical systems remain to be developed?

Unfortunately (or fortunately), the answer is "No". Of course, orientated linguistics clarified a number of urgent questions. But like any other theory, it nevertheless looks forward, thus raising new, sometimes unexpected issues. We specify some of them to encourage our readers who would like to continue with orientated linguistics.

First comes the problem of making man-to-computer communication more and more natural. In fact, free NL communication with computers is not the top limit of this progress. The NL dialogue involves the hearing only and leaves aside the eyesight, though the latter is another basic information transmission channel. When communicating naturally, people usually exploit both conversation and demonstration (of things, photos, drawings, pictures, etc.). Abandoning demonstrations will lead to unnatural communication in many cases. Thus, a user is often supposed to point at the objects he is talking about. The modern computer display is a powerful visualizing tool, providing every facility for effective demonstrations - from cursors to touch-sensitive screens. The only thing to invent is a technique of such integrated communication.

In this way we are coming to the absolutely new problem of developing a theory and practice of the mentioned "conversation-demonstration". There are several basic challenges. Firstly, an object can be demonstrated in many ways: a user may point at the object, or enclose it in a circle, or show the direction where the object lies. A demonstration is always fuzzy, and the computer should interpret it to obtain precise data. Secondly, the man distributes information non-uniformly between the conversation and the demonstration. After the computer extracts data from both sources, it will find two results complexly correlating, corroborating or even contradicting to each other. One of our currently developed systems implements the "tell-and-show" idea. In the process of its development we formulated a few theoretical concepts, but there is still a great room for further investigations. By the way, the mentioned system is designed to help the police in reconstruction of a criminal's image from a witness's words. The below given examples are taken from the training set of this "police" system.

Another challenge is that orientated linguistics is effective only if every NPD involved is thoroughly studied for its activity structures, dialogue constructions, etc. It is a huge and challenging piece of work. The question is if a general approach can be proposed to process an NPD automatically, extracting necessary data right from a description of this NPD.

The same question arises when one is constructing a model of the subject's problem solving activity in an NPD. The NPD polytrapezium usually offers many routes to a goal operation; we mentioned this fact in Part I of the book. That is why the decision scheme shapes as a tree or even a more general graph, if nodes of the same name are glued. As the subject (user) may choose any route in the tree, account should be taken of all the branches of a node. This must be done on the base of a training set accumulated from the subject's activity in the node. Here we see another interesting piece of work, which puts forward the discussed question: is it possible to invent a technique to derive the best branching scheme from a node description? When developing the aforementioned orientated system, we gained some experience in construction of such trees. Now we dare suppose that the number of standard branching schemes is not too great and allows an exhaustive list of them to be made.

Many complicated and interesting questions are connected with the subject's behavior in a dialogue. For the above considered trees to be simpler, the computer should always guide the man in the dialogue, i.e. the latter only answers the computer's questions. This is quite possible due to the property of K-stationarity. Nevertheless, sometimes the man wants to be the leader in the dialogue, and the computer must provide such an opportunity. For instance, the computer's suggestion "Let us do the mouth" can be answered "No, I like we do the nose". In such a case the dialogue can go many ways: the computer either persists in doing the suggested thing but discomforts the man, or follows the principle "Right is the client" but takes an ineffective branch, or explains its suggestion and repeats it. What strategy is the best? This is another problem to be solved.

In the aforesaid situation the man makes his choice among operations of the same type and the same level in the tree. There also exists another case. The man can "jump" in the tree, either confirming or objecting the computer's suggestion. Then the suggested operation must be changed for an operation of another type and level. For instance, the suggestion "Let us do the mouth" can be confirmed as "OK, the lips should be thicker" or objected as "No, first make the nose longer". Both cases involve jumping some levels and/or types of operations. An activity model should be ready for such a jump.

Other problems concern the theoretical foundations for the decomposition of OD into a system of NPD's, the extraction and description of NPD reacting algorithms, etc. We can not dwell on these problems here, because the book is finishing.

Any of the outlined questions calls for a great amount of research work, both theoretical and experimental. It will invoke mathematics, the algorithm theory, the pattern recognition theory, psychology, linguistics and many other scientific branches. All this work lies ahead.

However, fundamental research should not obscure the important and interesting aspect that deals with practice. We shall keep accumulating and processing training sets, populating and adjusting subdictionaries, developing and improving recognizers and so on. Being regular, this work is sure to become simpler and simpler, better and better organized.

Thus, this book has presented only the heart of orientated linguistics. The further development still lies ahead.

Bibliography

1. L.K. Yanshina, An Object-Oriented Approach to Software Development Not Demanding Programming Knowledge, in: *Proceedings 33rd International Scientific Colloquy, Ilmenau (Germany)*, (1988), p.143–147.
2. В.С. Файн, Ориентированная Лингвистика, *Известия Академии Наук. Техническая кибернетика,* N 1, (1994) с.214–223.
   [V.S. Fain, Orientated Linguistics, *Izvestiya Akademii Nauk. Technical Cybernetics,* No.1, (1994) p.214–223].
3. N. Nilsson, *Problem Solving Methods in Artificial Intelligence,* (McGrow-Hill, New York, 1971) p.270.
4. J.A. Robinson, New Directions in Mechanical Theorem Proving, *Information Processing'68* **1** (North-Holland, Amsterdam, 1969) p.63–67.
5. J.-L. Lauriere, A Language and a Program for Stating and Solving Combinatorial Problems, *Artif. Intell.* **10** (1978) p.29–127.
6. Л.И. Микулич и А.Я. Червоненкис, Специализированная диалоговая система, в кн.: *Вопросы разработки прикладных систем,* (ВЦ СО АН СССР, Новосибирск, 1979) с.111–129.
   [L.I. Mikulich and A.Y. Chervonenkis, Specialized Conversational System, in: *On Applied Systems Development,* (VC SO AN SSSR, Novosibirsk, 1979) p.111–129].
7. Э.В. Попов, *Общение с ЭВМ на естественном языке,* (Наука, Москва, 1982).
   [E.V. Popov, *Communication with a Computer in Natural Language,* (Nauka, Moscow, 1982)].
8. R.C. Schank, *Conceptual Information Processing,* (North-Holland, New York, 1975).
9. А.Н. Тихонов, О решении некорректно поставленных задач и методе регуляризации, *ДАН СССР* **181**, N 3 (1963).
   [A.N. Tihonov, On Ill-Posed Problem Solution and Regularization Method, *DAN SSSR* **181**, No.3 (1963)].
10. А.Н. Тихонов и В.Я. Арсенин, *Методы решения некорректных задач,* (Наука, Москва, 1974).
    [A.N.Tihonov and V.Y.Arsenin, *Incorrect Problem Solving Methods,* (Nauka, Moscow, 1974)].

11. О.С. Кулагина, *Исследования по машинному переводу,* (Наука, Москва, 1979).
[O.S. Kulagina, *Investigations on Machine Translation,* (Nauka, Moscow, 1979)].

12. C.J. Filmore, The Case for Case, in: *Universals in Linguistics Theory,* E. Bach and R. Harms, Eds. (Holt, Rinehart and Winston, New York, 1968).

13. Н.Н. Леонтьева, База знаний и автоматический перевод (проект многоязычной информационно-справочной системы), в кн.: *Международный семинар по машинному переводу "ЭВМ и перевод 89" (Тбилиси): Тезисы докладов,* (Москва, 1989) с.178–182.
[N.N. Leontyeva, Knowledge Base and Automatical Translation, in: *Proceedings International Seminar "Computer and Translation 89", Tbilisi (Georgia)* (Moscow, 1989) p.178–182].

14. Н.Н. Леонтьева, Построение базы текстовых фактов, *Научно-техническая информация,* **2**, N 7 (Москва, 1990) с.2–11.
[N.N. Leontyeva, Textual Fact Base Design, *Scientific-Technical Information,* **2**, No.7 (Moscow, 1990) p.2–11].

15. Н.Н. Леонтьева и З.М. Шаляпина, Современное состояние машинного перевода, в кн.: *Искусственный интеллект. Справочник. Под ред. Э.В. Попова,* (Радио и связь, Москва, 1990) 464 с.
[N.N. Leontyeva and Z.M. Shalyapina, Current State of Machine Translation, in: E.V. Popov, ed. *Artificial Intelligence: Reference,* (Radio i Svyaz, Moscow, 1990) p.464].

16. In Depth: Natural Language Processing, *Byte* **12**, No.14 (1987) p.224–276.

17. А.А. Харкевич, Опознавание образов, *Радиотехника* **14**, N 5 (1959) с.17–24.
[A.A. Kharkevich, Pattern Recognition, *Radiotechnika* **14**, No.5 (1959) p.17–24].

18. В.Н. Вапник и А.Я. Червоненкис, *Теория распознавания образов: статистические проблемы обучения,* (Наука, Москва, 1974) 416 с.
[V.N. Vapnik and A.Y. Chervonenkis, *Pattern Recognition Theory: Statistical Problems of Learning,* (Nauka, Moscow, 1974) p.416].

19. A. Novikoff, On Convergence Proofs for Perceptrons, in: *Proceedings of Symposium on Mathematical Theory of Automata* **XII** (Polytechnic Institute of Brooklin, 1963).

20. L.A. Zadeh, *The Concept of a Linguistic Variable and its Application to Approximate Reasoning,* (American Elsevier, New York, 1973)

21. С.О. Варосян и Д.А. Поспелов, Неметрическая пространственная логика, *Известия Академии Наук. Техническая кибернетика,* N 5, (1982) с.86–99.
[S.O. Varosyan and D.A. Pospelov, Nonmetric Spatial Logic, *Izvestiya Akademii Nauk. Technical Cybernetics,* No.5, (1982) p.86–99].

22. Р.М. Грановская, *Элементы практической психологии,* (ЛГУ, Ленинград, 1984).
[R.M. Granovskaya, *Elements of Practical Psychology,* (Leningrad State University, Leningrad, 1984)].

23. Ю.И. Журавлев и В.В.Никифоров, Алгоритмы распознавания, основанные на вычислении оценок, *Кибернетика* N 3 (1971) с.1–11.
[Y.I. Zhuravlev and V.V. Nikiforov, Recognizing Algorithms Based on Estimation, *Cybernetics* No.3 (1971) p.1–11].

24. В.С. Файн, Новые аспекты машинного понимания сообщений, *Известия Академии Наук. Техническая кибернетика,* N 5, (1982) с.100–112.
[V.S. Fain, New Aspects of Machine Understanding of Information, *Izvestiya Akademii Nauk. Technical Cybernetics,* No.5, (1982) p.100–112].

25. *Автоматизация ввода письменных знаков в ЦВМ,* (Каунас, 1973).
[*Automation of Character Input into Computer,* (Kaunas, Lithuania, 1973)].

26. *Автоматизация ввода письменных знаков в ЦВМ,* (Каунас, 1977).
[*Automation of Character Input into Computer,* (Kaunas, Lithuania, 1977)].

27. B.I. Grosz, The Representation and Use of Focus in a System for Understanding Dialog, in: *Proceedings 5th International Joint Conference on Artificial Intelligence,* (MIT, Boston, 1977).

28. В.С. Файн, Модально-целевая структура предложения в задаче машинного понимания естественно-языковых сообщений, в кн.: *Proceedings 2nd International Conference on Artificial Intelligence and Information-Control Systems of Robots,* (ITK SAV, Bratislava (Slovakia), 1982) с.69–72.
[V.S. Fain, A Modal-Goal Oriented Structure of a Sentence in a Computer Understanding of Natural Language Messages, *Proceedings 2nd International Conference on Artificial Intelligence and Information-Control Systems of Robots,* (ITK SAV, Bratislava (Slovakia), 1982) p.69–72].

29. А.К. Жолковский и др., К построению действующей модели языка "смысл — текст", в кн.: *Машинный перевод и прикладная лингвистика,* **14**, с.114–135.
[A.K. Zholkovsky et al., On Development Acting Language Model "Meaning — Text", in: *Machine Translation and Applied Linguistics,* **14**, p.114–135].

30. В.С. Медовый, К проблеме перенастройки лингвистических процессоров, *Известия Академии Наук. Техническая кибернетика,* N 5, (1982) с.113.
[V.S. Medovy, On Linguistic Processor Readjustment Problem, *Izvestiya Akademii Nauk. Technical Cybernetics,* No.5, (1982) p.113–120].

31. В.Ф. Хорошевский, ATNL — язык представления лингвистических знаний в естественно-языковых системах, *Вопросы кибернетики* **55** (Москва, 1979) с.158–167.
[V.F. Khoroshevsky, Linguistic Knowledge Representation Language ATNL for Natural Language Systems, *Voprosy Kibernetiki* **55** (Moscow, 1979) p.158–167].

32. В.Ф. Хорошевский, ATNL-машина — вопросы программной и аппаратной реализации, в кн.: *Труды международного симпозиума по искусственному интеллекту,* (Ленинград, 1983) с.1–18.
[V.F. Khoroshevsky, ATNL-Machine: on Software and Hardware Development, in: *Proceedings International Symposium on Artificial Intelligence,* (Leningrad, 1983) p.1–18].

33. W.A. Woods, Transition Network Grammars for Natural Language Analysis, *Comm. ACM* **13**, No.10, (1970) p.591–606.

34. W.A. Woods, The Generalizations of ATN Grammars, in: *Research in Natural Language Understanding, Report No.3963,* (Bolt Beranek and Newman, 1978) p.21–77.

35. W.A. Woods, Cascaded ATN Grammars, *Amer. J. Comput. Linguist.* **6**, No.1 (1980) p.5–73.

36. *Reading in Human-Computer Interaction: A Multidisciplinary Approach,* (Morgan and Kaufman, San Mateo, Calif., 1989).

37. *IBM Personal Computer Software: Disk Operating System Technical Reference,* (IBM, Boca Raton, Florida, 1985).

38. V.S. Fain, L.I. Rubanov, L. Tovarek and M. Bukovcan, Multilingual Multiproblem Natural Language Preprocessor Based on ATNR Nets, in: *Proceedings 5th International Conference on Artificial Intelligence and Information-Control Systems of Robots,* (North-Holland, Amsterdam, 1989).

39. T. Winograd and F. Flores, *Understanding Computers and Cognition,* (Addison-Wesley, Reading, Mass., 1987).

40. А.М. Довгялло, В.И. Брановицкий, К.П. Вершинин и др., *Диалоговые системы. Современное состояние и перспективы развития,* (Наукова думка, Киев, 1987) 246 с.
[A.M. Dovgyallo, V.I. Branovitsky, K.P. Vershinin et al., *Dialogue systems. Current state and prospects,* (Naukova dumka, Kiev, 1987) p.246.

41. Ö. Ekeberg, Robust Dictionary Lookup Using Associative Networks, *Intern. J. Man-Machine Stud.* **22**, No.1 (1988) p.29–43.

42. E. Reuhkala, Pattern Recognition for Strings of Discrete Symbols, in: *Proceedings VI International Joint Conference on Pattern Recognition,* **1** (London, 1982) p.969.

43. T. Okuda, E. Tanaka and T. Kasai, A Method for the Correction of Garbled Words Based on the Levenstein Metric, *IEEE Trans. Comput.* **25** (1976) p.172–177.

44. L.R. Bahl and F. Jelinek, Decoding for Channels with Insertions, Deletions and Substitutions with Applications to Speech Recognition, *IEEE Trans. Inform. Theory* **21**, No.4 (1975) p.404-411.

45. И.М. Бояринов, А.А. Давыдов, Э.М. Мамедли и Ю.Б. Смеркис, Использование помехоустойчивого кодирования для защиты информации от ошибок оператора, *Автоматика и телемеханика* N 2 (1983) с.5–49.
[I.M. Boyarinov, A.A. Davydov, E.M. Mamedli and Y.B. Smerkis, Use of Noise-Immune Coding for Information Protection from Operator's Errors, *Automatics and Telemechanics* No.2 (1983) p.5–49].

46. J.J. Stiffler, *Theory of Synchronous Communications,* (Prentice Hall, Englewood Cliffs, New Jersey, 1971).

47. В.С. Файн, Принцип изменчивости и его применение в задачах распознавания образов и формообразования, *Диссертация на соискание ученой степени доктора технических наук,* (ИППИ АН СССР, Москва, 1987) 306 с.
[V.S. Fain, Changeability Principle as Applied to Pattern Recognition and Shape Formation Problems, *Dr.Sci. Thesis,* (IPPI AN SSSR, Moscow, 1987) p.306].

48. U. Frith, *Cognitive Process in Spelling,* (Academic Press, New York, 1980).

49. В.С. Файн, *Опознавание изображений,* (Наука, Москва, 1970). [V.S. Fain, *Image Recognition,* (Nauka, Moscow, 1970)].

50. Л.С. Левенштейн, К определению расстояния в пространствах символьных последовательностей, *ДАН СССР* **263**, N 4 (1965) с.845–848.
[L.S. Levenstein, On Distance Definition in Spaces of Character Sequences, *DAN SSSR* **263**, No.4 (1965) p.845–848].

51. В.С. Файн, *Распознавание образов и машинное понимание естественного языка,* (Наука, Москва, 1987) 176 с.
[V.S. Fain, *Pattern Recognition and Computer Understanding of Natural Language,* (Nauka, Moscow, 1987) p.176].

52. В.С. Файн и Л.И. Рубанов, *Машинное понимание текстов с ошибками,* (Наука, Москва, 1991) 151 с.
[V.S. Fain and L.I. Rubanov, *Computer Understanding of Texts with Errors,* (Nauka, Moscow, 1991) p.151].

53. J. Raviv, Decision Making in Markov Chains Applied to the Problem of Pattern Recognition, *IEEE Trans. Inf. Theory* **13**, No.4 (1967).

54. D.E. Knuth, *The Art of Computer Programming, Vol.3: Searching and Sorting,* (Addison-Wesley, Reading, Mass., 1973).

55. W.S. Rosenbaum and J.J. Hillard, Multifont OCR Postprocessing System, *IBM J. Research and Development* **19**, No.4 (1975) p.398–421.

56. A.J. Szanser, *Automatic Error-Correction in Natural Language,* (Pergamon Press, London, 1970).

57. J.L. Peterson, Computer Programs for Detecting and Correcting Spelling Errors, *Comm. ACM* **23**, No.12 (1980) p.676–687.

58. P.M. Hahn, A Best Match File Search Procedure for Postal Dictionaries, in: *Proceedings International Conference on Cybernetics and Society* (Washington, 1972).

59. H. Takahashi, N. Itoh, T. Amano and A. Yamashita, A Spelling Correction Method and its Application to an OCR System, *Pattern Recogn.* **23**, No.3/4 (1990).

60. E.M. Riseman and R.W. Ehrich, Contextual Word Recognition Using Binary Digrams, *IEEE Trans. Comput.* **20**, No.4 (1971) p.397–403.

61. E.M. Riseman and A.R. Hanson, A Contextual Postprocessing System for Error Correction Using Binary n-grams, *IEEE Trans. Comput.* **23**, No.5 (1974) p.480–493.

62. J.L. Flanagan, *Speech Analysis, Synthesis and Perception,* (Springer Verlag, New York, 1965).

63. X.D. Huang, K.F. Lee, On Speaker-Independent, Speaker-Dependent, and Speaker-Adaptive Speech Recognition, in: *Proceedings ICASSP,* (Carnegie Mellon University, Toronto, 1991)

64. W. Ward, Understanding Spontaneous Speech: the Phoenix System, in: *Proceedings ICASSP,* (Carnegie Mellon University, Toronto, 1991).

65. C.E. Shannon and W. Weaver, *The Mathematical Theory of Communication,* (University Illinois Press, 1949) p.3–89.

66. И.А. Липкин, *Основы статистической радиотехники, теории информации и кодирования,* (Советское радио, Москва, 1978) 238 с.
[I.A. Lipkin, *Fundamentals of Statistical Radiotechnics and Information and Coding Theory,* (Sovetskoe Radio, Moscow, 1978) p.238].

Appendix

This appendix outlines a complete description of the augmented transition network with returns (ATNR) for the orientated algorithm (Variant 2) considered in Chapter 20. The algorithm analyzes users' NL addresses in the NPD Ω (see the same chapter). The description exploits the notation introduced in Section 20.3. First, we would like to make edge attributed conditions easier to understand. For this reason we enlist all the hyperdictionary lexical categories. Their identifiers can be extracted from the hyperdictionary by the operator `CAT`:

`"A"` = supplier's name,

`"B"` = consumer's name,

`"C"` = oil-product name,

`"D"` = total data indicator,

`"E"` = generic supplier indicator,

`"F"` = generic consumer indicator,

`"G"` = supplier/consumer's name,

`"H"` = word order indicator,

`"I"` = dispatch-FROM indicator,

`"J"` = dispatch-TO indicator,

`"K"` = preposition,

`"L"` = conjunction,

`"M"` = punctuation mark.

As we mentioned in Chapter 20, text objects may have an ambiguous role. This ambiguity can be overwhelmed with the use of the feature "case". Some records of the hyperdictionary keep information on the appropriate wordform case. The operator `CASE` returns a string of 6 characters. Each of them is responsible for one of the Russian cases. If a word is registered in a case form, its returned string has a character at the position of this case. Otherwise, the position is empty. The involved characters are as follows:

"1" = nominative case,

"2" = genitive case,

"3" = dative case,

"4" = accusative case,

"5" = instrumental case,

"6" = locative case.

When applied to a record, the operator `KEY` returns the role information of the record, i.e. a search key to the database D_Ω. The operator `WORD` returns a wordform as it is stored in the current record.

With all these remarks made, we can present the description.

```
/* THE ATNR REGISTERS:
          A   = KEYS OF SUPPLIERS
          B   = KEYS OF CONSUMERS
          P   = KEYS OF OIL-PRODUCTS
          U   = KEYS OF OBJECTS WHOSE ROLE IS NOT DETERMINED YET
          X   = KEYS OF OBJECTS WHOSE ROLE IS AMBIGUOUS
          D   = SHIPPING DIRECTION ("F"=FROM, "T"=TO)
          C   = POSSIBLE CASES (AS IN A DICTIONARY)
          C1  = LIKE C, AN AUXILIARY REGISTER
          A1  = GENERIC SUPPLIER FLAG
          B1  = GENERIC CONSUMER FLAG
          Q   = TOTAL DATA FLAG
          NS  = THE NUMBER OF SUPPLIERS INVOLVED
          NT  = THE NUMBER OF CONSUMERS INVOLVED
          NST= THE NUMBER OF INVOLVED OBJECTS THAT CAN BE
                    A SUPPLIER AND A CONSUMER AT A TIME
          NDF= THE NUMBER OF DISPATCH-FROM INDICATORS
          NDT= THE NUMBER OF DISPATCH-TO INDICATORS
          ND  = THE TOTAL NUMBER OF DISPATCH INDICATORS
          M   = AN AUXILIARY REGISTER
```

```
          N  = REACTING ALGORITHM IDENTIFICATION NUMBER */

FROM S    DO A="",B="",P="",U="",X="",D="",D1="",C="",C1="",M=0,
             A1=0,B1=0,Q=0,NS=0,NT=0,NST=0,NDF=0,NDT=0,ND=0 TO Q1

FROM Q1   IF EOT DO BACK TO Q2
          IF CAT="D" DO Q=1, EXCL, NEXT TO Q1
          IF CAT="E" DO A1=1, EXCL, NEXT TO Q1
          IF CAT="F" DO B1=1, EXCL, NEXT TO Q1
          IF CAT="A" DO NS=NS+1, NEXT TO Q1
          IF CAT="B" DO NT=NT+1, NEXT TO Q1
          IF CAT="G" DO NST=NST+1, NEXT TO Q1
          IF CAT="I" DO NDF=NDF+1, NEXT TO Q1
          IF CAT="J" DO NDT=NDT+1, NEXT TO Q1
          IF ¬EOT DO NEXT TO Q1

FROM Q2   IF NST=0 TO Q3
          IF NST>0 ∧ NDF=0 ∧ NDT=0 TO Q5
          IF NST>0 ∧ NDF=0 ∧ NDT>0 DO D="T" TO Q5
          IF NST>0 ∧ NDF>0 ∧ NDT=0 DO D="F" TO Q5
          IF NST>0 ∧ NDF>0 ∧ NDT>0 DO M=0, U="",
                    ND=NDF+NDT, NST=NST+NS+NT TO Q26

FROM Q3   IF EOT TO Q4
          IF CAT="C" DO P=P||KEY, NEXT TO Q3
          IF CAT="A" ∨ CAT="G" DO A=A||KEY, NEXT TO Q3
          IF CAT="B" ∨ CAT="G" DO B=B||KEY, NEXT TO Q3
          IF ¬EOT DO NEXT TO Q3

FROM Q4   IF A≠"" ∧ B≠"" ∧ P≠"" DO N=1 POP
          IF A≠"" ∧ B≠"" ∧ P="" DO N=2 POP
          IF A≠"" ∧ B="" ∧ P≠"" ∧ Q=0 DO N=3 POP
          IF A≠"" ∧ B="" ∧ P≠"" ∧ Q=1 DO N=4 POP
          IF A="" ∧ B≠"" ∧ P≠"" ∧ Q=0 DO N=5 POP
          IF A="" ∧ B≠"" ∧ P≠"" ∧ Q=1 DO N=6 POP
          IF A≠"" ∧ B="" ∧ P="" ∧ Q=0 DO N=7 POP
          IF A≠"" ∧ B="" ∧ P="" ∧ Q=1 DO N=8 POP
          IF A="" ∧ B≠"" ∧ P="" ∧ Q=0 DO N=9 POP
          IF A="" ∧ B≠"" ∧ P="" ∧ Q=1 DO N=10 POP
          IF A="" ∧ B="" ∧ P≠"" ∧ (Q=0 ∨ A1=0 ∧ B1=0) DO N=11 POP
          IF A="" ∧ B="" ∧ P≠"" ∧ Q=1 ∧ A1=0 ∧ B1=1 DO N=12 POP
          IF A="" ∧ B="" ∧ P≠"" ∧ Q=1 ∧ A1=1 ∧ B1=0 DO N=13 POP
          IF A="" ∧ B="" ∧ P≠"" ∧ Q=1 ∧ A1=B1 DO N=14 POP
```

```
FROM Q5   IF EOT DO BACK TO Q6
          IF CAT="C" DO P=P||KEY, EXCL, NEXT TO Q5
          IF ¬EOT DO NEXT TO Q5

FROM Q6   IF EOT TO Q25
          DO C="" PUSH POST, TO Q7
          DO C="" PUSH POTR, TO Q12
          DO U="" TO Q17
          IF ¬EOT DO NEXT TO Q6

FROM Q7   IF EOT TO Q25
          IF WORD="C" DO C1=C, C="", EXCL, NEXT PUSH POST TO Q8
          IF WORD="," ∨ CAT="L" DO C1=C, C="", EXCL, NEXT
                  PUSH POST TO Q9
          IF WORD="C" DO EXCL, NEXT TO Q10
          IF WORD="," ∨ CAT="L" DO EXCL, NEXT TO Q11
          IF ¬EOT TO Q6

FROM Q8   IF STR(C,5,1)="5" DO C=C1∧C TO Q7

FROM Q9   IF C1∧C≠" " DO C=C1∧C TO Q7

FROM Q10  IF CAT="G" ∧ STR(CASE,5,1)="5" DO A=A||KEY,
                  C=C∧STR(CASE,5,1), EXCL, NEXT TO Q7

FROM Q11  IF CAT="G" ∧ (C∧CASE)≠" " DO A=A||KEY,
                  C=C∧CASE, EXCL, NEXT TO Q7
          IF CAT="K" DO EXCL, NEXT TO Q11

FROM Q12  IF EOT TO Q25
          IF WORD="C" DO C1=C, C="", EXCL, NEXT PUSH POTR TO Q13
          IF WORD="," ∨ CAT="L" DO C1=C, C="", EXCL, NEXT
                  PUSH POTR TO Q14
          IF WORD="C" DO EXCL, NEXT TO Q15
          IF WORD="," ∨ CAT="L" DO C1=C, C="", EXCL, NEXT TO Q16
          IF ¬EOT TO Q6

FROM Q13  IF STR(C,5,1)="5" DO C=C1∧C TO Q12

FROM Q14  IF C1∧C≠" " DO C=C1∧C TO Q12

FROM Q15  IF CAT="G" ∧ STR(CASE,5,1)="5" ∧ STR(CASE,2,1)=" "
                  DO B=B||KEY, C=C∧CASE, EXCL, NEXT TO Q12
```

```
FROM Q16  IF CAT="G" ∧ (C∧CASE)≠" " DO B=B||KEY, C=C∧CASE,
                  EXCL, NEXT TO Q12
          IF CAT="K" DO EXCL, NEXT TO Q16

FROM Q17  IF EOT TO Q25
          IF CAT="G" DO U=U||KEY, C=C∧CASE, EXCL, NEXT TO Q18
          IF CAT="K" DO EXCL, NEXT TO Q17

FROM Q18  IF EOT DO X=X||U, U="" TO Q25
          IF WORD="C" DO C1=C, C="", EXCL, NEXT PUSH POST TO Q19
          IF WORD="," ∨ CAT="L" DO C1=C, C="", EXCL, NEXT
                  PUSH POST TO Q20
          IF WORD="C" DO C1=C, C="", EXCL, NEXT PUSH POTR TO Q21
          IF WORD="," ∨ CAT="L" DO C1=C, C="", EXCL, NEXT
                  PUSH POTR TO Q22
          IF WORD="C" DO EXCL, NEXT TO Q23
          IF WORD="," ∨ CAT="L" DO EXCL, NEXT TO Q24
          IF ¬EOT DO X=X||U, U="" TO Q6

FROM Q19  IF STR(C,5,1)="5" DO C=C1∧C, A=A||U, U="" TO Q7

FROM Q20  IF C1∧C≠" " DO C=C1∧C, A=A||U, U="" TO Q7

FROM Q21  IF STR(C,5,1)="5" DO C=C1∧C, B=B||U, U="" TO Q12

FROM Q22  IF C1∧C≠" " DO C=C1∧C, B=B||U, U="" TO Q12

FROM Q23  IF CAT="G" ∧ STR(CASE,5,1)="5" DO U=U||KEY, C=C∧CASE,
                  EXCL, NEXT TO Q18

FROM Q24  IF CAT="G" ∧ (C∧CASE)≠" " DO U=U||KEY, C=C∧CASE,
                  EXCL, NEXT TO Q18
          IF CAT="K" DO EXCL, NEXT TO Q24

FROM Q25  IF X="" TO Q4
          IF X≠"" ∧ A="" ∧ B≠"" DO A=X TO Q4
          IF X≠"" ∧ A≠"" ∧ B="" DO B=X TO Q4
          IF X≠"" ∧ A1=0 ∧ B1=1 DO A=A||X TO Q4
          IF X≠"" ∧ A1=1 ∧ B1=0 DO B=B||X TO Q4
          IF X≠"" ∧ A="" ∧ B="" ∧ A1=B1 DO B=X TO Q4
          IF X≠"" ∧ A≠"" ∧ B≠"" TO Q4

FROM Q26  IF EOT TO Q25
```

```
          IF CAT="I" DO D="F", D1="", ND=ND-1, EXCL, NEXT TO Q27
          IF CAT="J" DO D="T", D1="", ND=ND-1, EXCL, NEXT TO Q27
          IF M=0 DO NST=NST-1, D1="F" PUSH POST, TO Q32
          IF M=0 DO NST=NST-1, D1="T" PUSH POTR, TO Q32
          IF CAT="G" DO U=U||KEY, C=CASE, M=0, D1="", NST=NST-1,
                    EXCL, NEXT TO Q32
          IF CAT="K" DO M=0, EXCL, NEXT TO Q26
          IF CAT="C" DO P=P||KEY, M=0, EXCL, NEXT TO Q26
          IF ¬EOT DO M=0, NEXT TO Q26

FROM Q27  IF M=0 DO NST=NST-1, D1="F" PUSH POST, TO Q28
          IF M=0 DO NST=NST-1, D1="T" PUSH POTR, TO Q28
          IF CAT="G" DO U=U||KEY, C=CASE, M=0, NST=NST-1,
                    EXCL, NEXT TO Q28
          IF CAT="C" DO P=P||KEY, M=1, EXCL, NEXT TO Q27
          IF CAT="K" DO M=1, EXCL, NEXT TO Q27
          IF ¬EOT ∧ CAT≠"A" ∧ CAT≠"B" ∧ CAT≠"G" ∧
                    CAT≠"I" ∧ CAT≠"J" ∧ CAT≠"K" ∧ CAT≠"L"
             DO EXCL, NEXT TO Q27

FROM Q28  IF EOT TO Q25
          IF WORD="C" ∧ NST>ND DO C1="    5 ", EXCL, NEXT TO Q29
          IF WORD="," ∨ CAT="L" ∧ NST>ND DO C1=C,
                    EXCL, NEXT TO Q29
          IF ¬EOT DO D="", M=0, NEXT TO Q26

FROM Q29  IF D1="F" ∧ M=0 DO A=A||U, U="", NST=NST-1
                    PUSH POST TO Q30
          IF D1="T" ∧ M=0 DO B=B||U, U="", NST=NST-1
                    PUSH POTR TO Q30
          IF D1="F" ∧ M=0 DO X=X||U, U="", NST=NST-1, D="", D1="T"
                    PUSH POTR TO Q32
          IF D1="T" ∧ M=0 DO X=X||U, U="", NST=NST-1, D="", D1="F"
                    PUSH POST TO Q32
          IF CAT="G" DO U=U||KEY, M=0, C=CASE, NST=NST-1,
                    EXCL, NEXT TO Q30
          IF CAT="K" DO M=1, EXCL, NEXT TO Q29
          IF CAT="C" DO P=P||KEY, M=1, EXCL, NEXT TO Q29

FROM Q30 DO C=C1∧C TO Q31

FROM Q31  IF C≠" " ∧ NST>0 TO Q28
          IF NST=0 TO Q25
```

```
FROM Q32  IF EOT TO Q25
          IF WORD≠"C" ∧ M=0 DO C1="    5 ", EXCL, NEXT TO Q33
          IF WORD="," ∨ CAT="L" ∧ M=0 DO C1=C, EXCL, NEXT TO Q33
          IF (CAT="I" ∧ D1="F") ∨ (CAT="J" ∧ D1="T")
                    DO X=X||U, U="", M=0, D="", EXCL, NEXT TO Q26
          IF CAT="I" ∧ D1="" DO A=A||U, U="", M=0, D="",
                    EXCL, NEXT TO Q26
          IF CAT="J" ∧ D1="" DO B=B||U, U="", M=0, D="",
                    EXCL, NEXT TO Q26
          IF CAT="C" DO P=P||KEY, M=1, EXCL, NEXT TO Q32
          IF ¬EOT DO M=1, NEXT TO Q32

FROM Q33  IF D1="F" ∧ M=0 DO NST=NST-1 PUSH POST TO Q34
          IF D1="B" ∧ M=0 DO NST=NST-1 PUSH POTR TO Q34
          IF D1="" ∧ M=0 ∧ U≠"" DO A=A||U, U="", NST=NST-1,
                    D1="F" PUSH POST TO Q34
          IF D1="" ∧ M=0 ∧ U≠"" DO B=B||U, U="", NST=NST-1,
                    D1="T" PUSH POTR TO Q34
          IF CAT="G" ∧ D1="F" DO NST=NST-1, M=0, C=CASE,
                    A=A||KEY, EXCL, NEXT TO Q34
          IF CAT="G" ∧ D1="T" DO NST=NST-1, M=0, C=CASE,
                    B=B||KEY, EXCL, NEXT TO Q34
          IF CAT="G" ∧ D1="" DO NST=NST-1, M=0, C=CASE,
                    U=U||KEY, EXCL, NEXT TO Q34
          IF (CAT="I" ∧ D1="F") ∨ (CAT="J" ∧ D1="T") DO M=0,
                    D="", X=X||U, U="", EXCL, NEXT TO Q26
          IF CAT="I" ∧ D1="" DO M=0, D="", A=A||U, U="",
                    EXCL, NEXT TO Q26
          IF CAT="J" ∧ D1="" DO M=0, D="", B=B||U, U="",
                    EXCL, NEXT TO Q26
          IF CAT="K" DO M=1, EXCL, NEXT TO Q33
          IF CAT="C" DO P=P||KEY, M=1, EXCL, NEXT TO Q33

FROM Q34 DO C=C1∧C TO Q35

FROM Q35  IF C≠"       " ∧ NST>0 TO Q32
          IF NST=0 TO Q25

FROM POST IF CAT="K" DO EXCL, NEXT TO PS1
          TO PS1
          IF D="F" ∧ CAT="G" ∧ STR(CASE,3,1)=" " DO A=A||KEY,
                    C=CASE, EXCL, NEXT POP
          IF WORD="ИЗ" ∨ WORD="ОТ" ∨ WORD="У" ∨
```

```
                 (WORD="C" ∧ D="F") DO EXCL, NEXT TO PS2
          IF WORD="B" ∨ (WORD="HA" ∧ D="F") DO EXCL, NEXT TO PS3

FROM PS1  IF ¬EOT ∧ CAT="A" DO C=CASE, A=A||KEY, EXCL, NEXT POP

FROM PS2  IF ¬EOT ∧ CAT="G" ∧ STR(CASE,2,1)="2" DO C=CASE,
                 A=A||KEY, EXCL, NEXT POP

FROM PS3  IF ¬EOT ∧ CAT="G" ∧ STR(CASE,6,1)="6" ∧
                 STR(CASE,4,1)=" " DO C=CASE, A=A||KEY,
                 EXCL, NEXT POP

FROM POTR IF CAT="K" DO EXCL, NEXT TO PT1
          TO PT1
          IF D="T" ∧ CAT="G" DO C=CASE, B=B||KEY, EXCL, NEXT POP
          IF CAT="G" ∧ STR(CASE,3,1)="3" ∧ STR(CASE,2,1)=" " ∧
                 STR(CASE,5,1)=" " DO B=B||KEY, C=CASE,
                 EXCL, NEXT POP
          IF WORD="K" ∨ (WORD="ПО" ∧ D="T") DO EXCL, NEXT TO PT2
          IF WORD="ДЛЯ" ∨ WORD="ДО" DO EXCL, NEXT TO PT3
          IF WORD="B" ∨ WORD="HA" DO EXCL, NEXT TO PT4

FROM PT1  IF ¬EOT ∧ CAT="B" DO C=CASE, B=B||KEY, EXCL, NEXT POP

FROM PT2  IF ¬EOT ∧ CAT="G" ∧ STR(CASE,3,1)="3" DO C=CASE,
                 B=B||KEY, EXCL, NEXT POP

FROM PT3  IF ¬EOT ∧ CAT="G" ∧ STR(CASE,2,1)="2" DO C=CASE,
                 B=B||KEY, EXCL, NEXT POP

FROM PT4  IF ¬EOT ∧ CAT="G" ∧ STR(CASE,4,1)="4" ∧
                 STR(CASE,6,1)=" " DO C=CASE, B=B||KEY,
                 EXCL, NEXT POP
          IF ¬EOT ∧ CAT="G" ∧ D="T" ∧ STR(CASE,6,1)="6"
                 DO C=CASE, B=B||KEY, EXCL, NEXT POP
```

Index